AF763237

Health Data Privacy under the GDPR

The growth of data-collecting goods and services, such as ehealth and mhealth apps, smart watches, mobile fitness and dieting apps, electronic skin and ingestible tech, combined with recent technological developments such as increased capacity of data storage, artificial intelligence and smart algorithms, has spawned a big data revolution that has reshaped how we understand and approach health data. Recently, the COVID-19 pandemic has foregrounded a variety of data privacy issues. The collection, storage, sharing and analysis of health- related data raises major legal and ethical questions relating to privacy, data protection, profiling, discrimination, surveillance, personal autonomy and dignity.

This book examines health privacy questions in light of the General Data Protection Regulation (GDPR) and the general data privacy legal framework of the European Union (EU). The GDPR is a complex and evolving body of law that aims to deal with several technological and societal health data privacy problems, while safeguarding public health interests and addressing its internal gaps and uncertainties. The book answers a diverse range of questions including: What role can the GDPR play in regulating health surveillance and big (health) data analytics? Can it catch up with Internet-age developments? Are the solutions to the challenges posed by big health data to be found in the law? Does the GDPR provide adequate tools and mechanisms to ensure public health objectives and the effective protection of privacy? How does the GDPR deal with data that concern children's health and academic research?

By analysing a number of diverse questions concerning big health data under the GDPR from various perspectives, this book will appeal to those interested in privacy, data protection, big data, health sciences, information technology, the GDPR, EU and human rights law.

Dr. Maria Tzanou is Senior Lecturer in Law at Keele University, United Kingdom.

Routledge Research in the Law of Emerging Technologies

Biometrics, Surveillance and the Law
Societies of Restricted Access, Discipline and Control
Sara M. Smyth

Artificial Intelligence, Healthcare, and the Law
Regulating Automation in Personal Care
Eduard Fosch-Villaronga

Health Data Privacy under the GDPR
Big Data Challenges and Regulatory Responses
Edited by Maria Tzanou

For more information about this series, please visit: www.routledge.com/Routledge-Research-in-the-Law-of-Emerging-Technologies/book-series/LAWTECHNOLOGY

Health Data Privacy under the GDPR

Big Data Challenges and Regulatory Responses

Edited by Maria Tzanou

Routledge
Taylor & Francis Group
LONDON AND NEW YORK

First published 2021
by Routledge
2 Park Square, Milton Park, Abingdon, Oxon, OX14 4RN

and by Routledge
52 Vanderbilt Avenue, New York, NY 10017

Routledge is an imprint of the Taylor & Francis Group, an informa business

© 2021 Taylor & Francis

The right of Maria Tzanou to be identified as the author of the editorial material, and of the authors for their individual chapters, has been asserted in accordance with sections 77 and 78 of the Copyright, Designs and Patents Act 1988.

All rights reserved. No part of this book may be reprinted or reproduced or utilised in any form or by any electronic, mechanical, or other means, now known or hereafter invented, including photocopying and recording, or in any information storage or retrieval system, without permission in writing from the publishers.

Trademark notice: Product or corporate names may be trademarks or registered trademarks, and are used only for identification and explanation without intent to infringe.

Library of Congress Cataloging-in-Publication Data
A catalog record for this book has been requested

ISBN: 978-0-367-07714-3 (hbk)
ISBN: 978-0-429-02224-1 (ebk)

Typeset in Bembo
by Apex CoVantage, LLC

To Alexis, Daphne and Raul

Contents

Preface ix
Acknowledgements xvi

SECTION 1
Health data privacy under the GDPR 1

1 **The GDPR and (big) health data: assessing the EU legislator's choices** 3
MARIA TZANOU

2 **Attribution of responsibility under the GDPR in the context of health data processing** 23
YORDANKA IVANOVA

3 **Healthcare data about children in social media: the challenges raised under the GDPR** 37
ROSEMARY JAY

4 **European-wide big health data analytics under the GDPR** 56
JOS DUMORTIER AND MAHAULT PIÉCHAUD BOURA

5 **Privacy issues in eHealth and mHealth apps** 71
BEATRIZ SAINZ-DE-ABAJO, ISABEL DE LA TORRE-DÍEZ, SUSEL GÓNGORA-ALONSO AND MIGUEL LÓPEZ-CORONADO

SECTION 2
A critical assessment of the GDPR's regulatory solutions 83

6 **Regulating non-personal data in the age of Big Data** 85
BART VAN DER SLOOT

7 Addressing big data and AI challenges: a taxonomy and why the GDPR cannot provide a one-size-fits-all solution 106
MARIA TZANOU

8 The GDPR, AI and the NHS Code of Conduct for Data-Driven Health and Care Technology 133
JOSEPH SAVIRIMUTHU

List of contributors 157
Index 159

Preface

The big data revolution has brought forward a tectonic shift in the ways we understand and approach data. Big data is both about the ability to gather and store huge amounts of data and to analyse these to discover unknown patterns and correlations. Such patterns are ultimately expected to lead to 'better and more informed decisions'[1] in healthcare, medical and scientific research, advertising, policing, surveillance and a whole range of businesses and organisations that develop products and services based on the crunching of data.

The recent COVID-19 pandemic is not only an unprecedented global health emergency; it has also foregrounded a variety of data privacy issues. Billions of people are required to comply with social distancing rules and endure mass digital surveillance of their location, communications and movements. Governments around the globe implement programmes for mobile data tracking, confidential health data are shared with private companies to produce pandemic models,[2] apps are developed to record and trace individuals' personal contact with others,[3] CCTV networks are equipped with facial recognition to monitor individuals' movements, permission regimes are deployed to authorise individuals to go outside and drones are used to enforce social isolation rules.[4]

Over the years, while big data has promised to 'improve preventive medicine' and 'keep us away from hospitals',[5] we are more and more often faced with media stories about sex toys that 'talk data';[6] spying vibrators;[7] a women's fertility app funded by anti-abortion campaigners;[8] the harvesting of 50 million Facebook profiles of US voters by Cambridge Analytica 'to build a powerful software program to predict and influence choices at the ballot box'[9] and so on.

How can the law protect us from such egregious data misuses? What are the appropriate legal solutions to address health data surveillance? Are laws regulating 'personal data' appropriate and fit-for-purpose to regulate big health data as well? These are pertinent questions that legislators worldwide are pondering.

To stay ahead of the technological developments curve, European Union (EU) institutions negotiated and adopted Regulation (EU) 2016/679 of the European Parliament and of the Council of 27 April 2016 on the protection of natural persons with regard to the processing of personal data and on the free movement of such data (the 'General Data Protection Regulation' or 'GDPR').[10] The GDPR entered into force in all EU Member States (MS) on

25 May 2018 with the aim to modernise data protection rules to 'catch up with the digital age'[11] and ensure that 'the EU remains the global gold standard in the protection of personal data'.[12] Indeed, the EU data protection legislative framework is considered as 'a cornerstone of the European human-centric approach to innovation'.[13]

The GDPR has successfully[14] completed its first years of life, but questions arise about its capabilities, functionalities and potential. What role can it play in regulating health surveillance and big (health) data analytics? Can it catch up with Internet-age developments? Can it effectively deal with the 'digital breadcrumbs'[15] that our everyday activities and our own bodies drop online every second?

In ancient Greek mythology, Sisyphos, the king of Ephyra, was condemned by the gods as a punishment for his self-aggrandizing craftiness, to roll for eternity an immense boulder up a hill, only for it to roll down when it neared the top. Reflecting about the GDPR in light of this beautiful myth, we are faced with the following question: Is regulating health data privacy a similar Sisyphean task, doomed to fail under the big data tsunami or indeed under the complexities and the futility of legal regulation itself? To answer this, we need to examine two issues. First, a consideration of the appropriateness of data protection legal methodologies in the face of technological developments, and the new forms of health surveillance that these impose, is required. Second, the ways in which the EU legislator chose to 'catch up' with health data privacy issues must also be explored.

There are several reasons why this investigation matters. First, it can provide valuable insights about regulatory approaches to health data privacy and new technologies. For instance, does it make sense to divide data in categories (personal / non-personal, normal data / sensitive-health data, content data / metadata) and protect according to what the legislator deems as more important, or is this a meaningless exercise in the age of big data? Second, the way the law is shaped may have tremendously practical consequences for the use of new technologies. Even seemingly mundane choices of the legislator, such as the household exemption that makes the GDPR inapplicable to 'personal or household' activities[16] including social networking, may have pervasive implications for children's health data shared on social media by their parents. While the GDPR adopts a clear stance in favour of protecting children's data privacy, it is unclear what its position is in this regard.[17] Finally, important lessons about the GDPR's omnipotent ambition to regulate everything from personal data processed manually to algorithmic decision making and Artificial Intelligence (AI) can be learnt.

This book engages with these questions from a variety of perspectives and disciplinary lenses. The GDPR is a complex and evolving body of law that aims to deal with several technological and societal health data privacy problems, while safeguarding 'public health' interests and addressing its internal gaps and uncertainties. This very idea connects the chapters in this book.

The contributions that follow engage to this open dialogue, by offering new theoretical considerations and a taxonomy of health and big data-related problems as well as solutions, proposals and models. The book is divided into two sections that encounter some of the most pressing and important debates concerning health data privacy and its regulation in the EU.

Section One focuses on the GDPR's approach regarding a variety of health data problems.

Chapter 1 explores the GDPR's provisions relating to health by focusing on two main issues: i) the definitional uncertainties surrounding health data and ii) the legislative choices regarding the balance between the competing interests to data privacy on the one hand, and the interests of 'public health' on the other hand. The chapter finds that the GDPR contains a broad definition of data concerning health and recognises augmented protection to these as sensitive data. This illustrates that the EU legislator considers health data privacy as an important interest often at risk that merits additional protection. At the same time, the GDPR includes several exemptions and restrictions to health data privacy interests. The chapter concludes that while the GDPR's provisions balancing data privacy with public health interests appear flexible and context dependent, its binary definitional distinctions (sensitive (health) / non-sensitive (non-health) data is problematic and may result in rendering the GDPR's rules both overinclusive and underinclusive.

Chapter 2 analyses the GDPR's legal definitions of (joint) controller and processor and their differing interpretation by competent Data Protection Authorities and the Court of Justice of the European Union (CJEU) within the context of three health-related case studies. In particular, the chapter examines how responsibility for compliance with the GDPR is attributed among the actors involved in the case of i) clinical trials, ii) health data processing within the global platforms, and iii) wearables at the workplace. Yordanka Ivanova concludes that there is a need for greater legal certainty in defining the capacity of the data processing actors and calls for a change in the Court's approach in defining the scope of joint controllership from 'single phase' to 'value chain'.

Chapter 3 considers the protections available to children under the GDPR and in United Kingdom (UK) law in respect to the oversharing of personal health information by parents on social media ('sharenting'). According to Rosemary Jay, the GDPR applies some limited safeguards to the processing of personal data about children, particularly in the area of online activity. Nevertheless, the borders of these safeguards are unclear. In particular, those with parental responsibility can post, share or otherwise make public, personal information about children as long as the parent can assert that they are carrying out a 'purely personal or household activity'. The case of 'sharenting' that may result, with potential detrimental effects on children, demonstrates the uncertainties and complexities that surround the scope of the GDPR.

Chapter 4 investigates the rules and conditions under which health data can be brought together on a European-wide platform for the purpose of big data analytics. To understand how the GDPR regulates the processing of health data for research purposes, Jos Dumortier and Mahault Piéchaud Boura make a distinction between research as a primary purpose of processing and research as a secondary purpose. The chapter concludes that the GDPR has not created a harmonised regulatory framework for researchers who wish to perform research based on health data to be collected in multiple European countries. The authors argue that the complexity and fragmentation of the regulatory landscape is not in the first place a consequence of the GDPR having failed to reach its ambitions. Rules and procedures to be respected by researchers planning to use health data for research purposes are not exclusively imposed by data protection law but they are more often related to data ownership. This means that in practice, researchers are requested to meet the conditions set by the health data owners – healthcare institutions and private or public health data repositories. To overcome the complexity of the regulatory framework with which researchers are confronted, initiatives such as the European Commission's creation of European-wide repositories of health images or digital pathology slides are to be welcomed. If successful, the authors consider that such initiatives can shift the burden of bringing health data from different countries together from the researcher to the repository owners.

Chapter 5 examines issues of security and confidentiality concerning eHealth and mHealth applications. A number of technological solutions have been developed over the years to prevent security breaches and make user data information as secure as possible. These techniques include, among others, data modification, cryptographic methods and protocols for data sharing and query auditing methods. The authors argue that as years go by, privacy will continue to gain prominence in eHealth and mHealth and more investment will be made in this respect.

Section Two adopts a more critical approach to examine the GDPR's regulatory solutions on different questions that touch on health personal data.

In Chapter 6, Bart van der Sloot explains that the current data privacy legal regime distinguishes between different types and categories of data. In general, the more personal, private and sensitive data are, the higher the level of protection provided. Among others, the legal regime differentiates between non-personal data and personal data, between metadata and content data and between non-sensitive and sensitive personal data. The chapter goes on to provide three reasons why these legal categories may become redundant in the age of big data. First, it suggests that categorising data only works when the status of the data is relatively stable, while in the current and future technological environment their nature will be highly volatile. Second, it suggests that categorising data only works when it is possible to determine with relative certainty into which category data fall, while this will be ever more difficult because the sensitivity of the data is less and less a quality of the data and more and more a result of the efforts invested by parties having access to the data. Third, it suggests that the underlying rationale for laying down different regimes of protection for different categories of data may become redundant, because metadata can be just as or even more revealing than content communication data, personal data may reveal more sensitive aspects of people's lives than sensitive personal data and aggregated data may be used in ways that have a bigger impact on people than the use of identifying data. The chapter argues that the status of data is not the right starting point for future legal regulation and suggests that as long as the status of data is taken as starting point for regulation, a strong regime should govern the processing of non-personal, non-sensitive and aggregated data in order to protect the interests of citizens.

Chapter 7 challenges the assumption that data privacy frameworks in general and the GDPR in particular can provide an appropriate regulatory solution for big data. It argues that in order to be able to properly reflect on regulatory approaches that wrestle with big data challenges, closer attention should be paid to these particular challenges. Searching for appropriate regulatory solutions requires a focus on the problems that need to be addressed. The chapter makes three distinct contributions to the debate regarding regulatory approaches to big data: First, it develops a taxonomy of big data challenges that allows a comprehensive overview of the issues at stake. Second, it examines the capabilities and limitations of the GDPR to address the risks identified in the proposed taxonomy. Third, it offers some suggestions on the pathways that regulators should be considering when approaching big data and AI.

Chapter 8 engages with two specific problems regarding the role and significance of the UK National Health Service (NHS) Code of Conduct's principles-based approach as critical to the UK government's vision for modernising healthcare. First, it questions the implication that data protection law, unlike the Code of Conduct, is a monolithic centralised framework of rigid rules which constrain the ability of relevant parties to tailor regulations to the novel use of technologies and data-driven processes in discharging their responsibilities towards patients. Second, a close examination of the Code of Conduct suggests that the GDPR already provides a legal infrastructure aimed at promoting a bottom-up approach of spontaneous 'regulatory conversations' with a view to speeding up access to personal information and minimise obstacles to collection, pave the way towards harnessing insights from the use of big data analytical systems and provide assurances of data quality and trustworthiness. Joseph Savirimuthu argues that many of the principles in the Code of Conduct that are perceived as being responsive to the challenges clinicians face in dynamic settings originate in the law's reflexive and flexible framework that is polycentric and provides mechanisms for steering actors processing health data at multiple levels, with the aim of ensuring that collective understandings of norms and practices being developed and operationalised are consistent with the GDPR.

Overall, the book aims to provide readers with new perspectives on health data privacy problems and regulatory solutions from a variety of different backgrounds and disciplines. It is certainly a peculiar time to be reflecting about health data privacy in the COVID-19 era of imposed social isolation and quarantines. Data privacy scholarship needs to be agile and ready to react to the challenges that emerge and that will continue to appear ahead of this unprecedented health emergency. Public health interests should be seriously taken into consideration while ensuring that these extraordinary circumstances and the measures they require do not become the new ordinary as far as our fundamental rights and freedoms are concerned.

Keeping these thoughts in mind, I hope that the following pages, with their broad coverage of a diverse range of health data protection problems and perspectives, will provide the reader with interesting and thought-provoking discussions.

Maria Tzanou
Keele, April 2020

Notes

1 EDPS, Opinion 7/2015 *Meeting the Challenges of Big Data: A Call for Transparency, User Control, Data Protection by Design and Accountability*, 7.

2 Paul Lewis, David Conn and David Pegg, 'UK Government Using Confidential Patient Data in Coronavirus Response', *The Guardian*, 12 April 2020 <www.theguardian.com/world/2020/apr/12/uk-government-using-confidential-patient-data-in-coronavirus-response>.

3 Jack Nicas and Daisuke Wakabayashi, 'Apple and Google Team Up to "Contact Trace" the Coronavirus', *The New York Times*, 10 April 2020 <www.nytimes.com/2020/04/10/technology/apple-google-coronavirus-contact-tracing.html>.

4 Andrew Roth et al., 'Growth in Surveillance May be Hard to Scale Back after Pandemic, Experts Say', *The Guardian*, 14 April 2020 <www.theguardian.com/world/2020/apr/14/growth-in-surveillance-may-be-hard-to-scale-back-after-coronavirus-pandemic-experts-say >.

5 Anita Allen, 'Protecting One's Own Privacy in a Big Data Economy' (2016) 130 *Harv. L. Rev. F.*, 71, 78.

6 Janet Burns, 'The "Spying Vibrator" Suit Is Over, But Sex Toys Are Still Talking Data', *Forbes*, 14 December 2016 <www.forbes.com/sites/janetwburns/2016/12/14/the-spying-vibrator-suit-is-over-but-sex-toys-are-still-talking-data/#692879384417>.

7 Janet Burns, 'We-Vibe Settles For $3.7M In "Spying Vibrator" Data Suit', *Forbes*, 15 March 2017 <www.forbes.com/sites/janetwburns/2017/03/15/we-vibe-settles-for-3-7m-in-spying-vibrator-data-lawsuit/#3ee371316021>.

8 Jessica Glenza, 'Revealed: Women's Fertility App is Funded by Anti-Abortion Campaigners', *The Guardian*, 30 May 2019 <www.theguardian.com/world/2019/may/30/revealed-womens-fertility-app-is-funded-by-anti-abortion-campaigners>.

9 Carole Cadwalladr and Emma Graham-Harrison, 'Revealed: 50 Million Facebook Profiles Harvested for Cambridge Analytica in Major Data Breach', *The Guardian*, 17 March 2018 <www.theguardian.com/news/2018/mar/17/cambridge-analytica-facebook-influence-us-election>.

10 Regulation (EU) 2016/679 of the European Parliament and of the Council of 27 April 2016 on the protection of natural persons with regard to the processing of personal data and on the free movement of such data, and repealing Directive 95/46/EC (General Data Protection Regulation), Official Journal of the European Union, L 119/1, 4 May 2016.

11 European Commission – Statement, Vice-President Ansip and Commissioner Jourová: Concluding the EU Data Protection Reform is Essential for the Digital Single Market, Brussels, 28 January 2015 <https://europa.eu/rapid/press-release_STATEMENT-15-3801_en.htm>.

12 Ibid.

13 European Commission, Communication from the Commission to the European Parliament and the Council, Data Protection Rules as a Trust-Enabler in the EU and Beyond – Taking Stock, Brussels, 24.7.2019, COM(2019) 374 final, 2.

14 Ibid, 2. According to the Commission, '[o]ne key objective of the Regulation was to do away with a fragmented landscape of 28 different national laws that existed under the previous Data Protection Directive and to provide legal certainty for individuals and businesses throughout the EU. That objective has been largely met.'

15 EDPS Opinion 4/2015 *Towards a New Digital Ethics: Data, Dignity and Technology*, 11 September 2015, 12.

16 Article 2 (2) (c) GDPR. See also Recital 18.

17 See Chapter 3 in this book.

Acknowledgements

I would like to acknowledge the help of all the people involved in this project and, more specifically, to the authors and reviewers who took part in the review process.

This edited book has its origins in a workshop titled *Big Health Data and Social Media: Legal and Ethical Challenges*, which took place at Keele University School of Law in December 2017. I am deeply grateful to the Society of Legal Scholars (SLS) for funding this workshop. Without this generous support, this book would not have become a reality.

Finally, special thanks go to my family for their patience and understanding while completing this project.

Maria Tzanou
Keele University, UK

Section 1

Health data privacy under the GDPR

1 The GDPR and (big) health data

Assessing the EU legislator's choices

Maria Tzanou

1. Introduction

The COVID-19 pandemic has not only created an unprecedented health emergency in modern times across the globe; it has also brought forward a variety of data privacy issues. Imposed lockdowns, quarantines and 'self-isolation' measures are examples of what Anita Allen has coined as 'unpopular privacy'.[1] 'Unpopular privacy' refers to coercive mandates that 'impose unpopular privacies on intended targets and beneficiaries' like the COVID-19-related social distancing rules.[2] Schools and workplaces are closed; public events are cancelled; the use of public transport is limited;[3] people are even forbidden to do normal everyday activities,[4] such as sunbathing.[5] At the same time and in order to combat this pandemic, whole populations are required to endure increased surveillance of their location, their movements and their contacts[6] via the invasive monitoring of mobile phone data.[7]

Widespread health data surveillance is not a new phenomenon. Health data and the capture of their enormous potential through big data analytics have been at the forefront of recent debates, before the emergence of a global health pandemic. Data privacy regulatory responses to health data surveillance vary around the world, but the EU's General Data Protection Regulation (GDPR),[8] with its strengthened data privacy rules and principles, remains a point of reference. This chapter critically examines the GDPR's provisions relating to health by focusing on two main issues: i) the definitional uncertainties surrounding health data and ii) the legislative choices regarding the balance between the competing interests to data privacy on the one hand – seen mainly within the context of the enhanced protection that personal health data enjoy – and the interests of 'public health' on the other hand.

The analysis proceeds as follows: The following section assesses the definitional uncertainties that big health data raise. It takes a closer look at big data analytics and the sources of big health data and examines definitional questions within the GDPR's context. Section 3 discusses the GDPR's legislative choices regarding health data by focusing on their enhanced protection as 'special categories of data' and the exemptions and restrictions imposed on these for public health purposes. Section 4 offers brief conclusions.

2. On definitional issues: what are big health data?

2.1 Big data analytics

We are living in a big data world. Every minute, 510,000 comments are posted on Facebook, 293,000 statuses are updated, and 136,000 photos are uploaded. Every day, 3.5 billion Google searches are made; 6,000 tweets are sent per second; and more than 95 million photos and videos are uploaded on Instagram per day. There are 3.3 billion smartphone users worldwide, and the average smartphone user has between 60 and 90 apps on their device[9] collecting some kind of personal data (i.e., name, email address, location).[10] Outside the online world, the Internet of Things (IoT) 'merges physical and virtual worlds'[11] through a range of interconnected devices[12] that communicate data, such as smart thermostats, meters, doorbells, smoke alarms, cameras, digital assistants, TVs and refrigerators.[13] According to the European Commission, the value of European citizens' personal data has the potential to grow to nearly €1 trillion annually.

There is no commonly agreed-upon definition of 'big data'.[14] In broad terms, big data refers to the aggregation of huge volumes of diversely sourced information and their analysis, using sophisticated algorithms to inform decisions.[15] Big data is made possible due to the increasing capabilities of technology to support the collection and storage of large amounts of data, as well as 'its ability to analyse, understand and take advantage of the full value of data (in particular using analytics applications)'.[16] Big data is often described using the five Vs: Volume, Variety, Velocity, Veracity and Value.[17] Volume refers to the expanding amounts of data generated and the large-scale datasets; Variety relates to the different types of data and data sources; Velocity describes both the increasing speed at which data is produced and the increasing demand to analyse the data in near real time to get insights; Veracity[18] refers to the correctness and accuracy of the data; and Value denotes the opportunities of big data to lead to measurable improvements of our lives.[19]

Perhaps the most important characteristic of big data refers to the ways this is analysed. The full potential of big data can be realised using artificial intelligence (AI).[20] AI is needed to 'mine, parse, sort and configure the data into useful packages',[21] build models and draw inferences that are then used 'to predict and anticipate possible future events'.[22] This is often done through machine learning, namely 'algorithms that change in response to their own output, or "computer programs that automatically improve with experience"'.[23] Machine learning means that the system is able to train itself to learn continuously and modify its behaviour during operation, thus acquiring a level of autonomy.[24] Big data, AI and machine learning are closely related concepts and sometimes are referred to interchangeably. However, there are differences between the two. As the UK Government Office for Science astutely puts it: 'If data is the fuel, artificial intelligence is the engine of the digital revolution'.[25] As it might be more accurate in terms of terminology to use the umbrella concept 'big data analytics' to describe all three of them.[26] That being said, this chapter and this book understand 'big data' as 'big data analytics' and the two terms are used interchangeably.

2.2 Big health data

Health data are at the centre of the big data revolution. Over 250,000 health and fitness apps are currently available on the market. The sale of wearables, such as smart watches, fitness trackers, eye gears, smart clothing, smart jewellery and implantables is on the rise, with more than 170 million wearables being purchased in 2018.[27] There are 'vagina fitbits',[28] smart vibrators, smart diapers,[29] and smart baby socks that measure babies' 'temperature, heart rate, oxygen saturation and movement'[30] available on the market. Our bodies emit streams of data: everything from physical activity, calorie intake, sleep and posture to sexual intercourse, menstrual cycles, fertility and breathing patterns can be (self)-tracked, measured, logged and (self)-analysed in order to achieve 'self-knowledge through numbers'.[31] The observation of our bodies through technologies is ingrained in our everyday lives, and global trends such as the Quantified-Self are constantly growing.[32] Platforms like PatientsLikeMe enable the exchange of information about illnesses, creating 'a community of people who are helping each other live their best every day'.[33] According to PatientsLikeMe, over '650,000 people living with 2,900 conditions have generated more than 43 million data points, creating an unprecedented source of real-world evidence and opportunities for continuous learning.'[34]

Big health data analytics promise a number of benefits. Indeed, the convergence between technology and healthcare is expected to i) increase quality of life and contribute to disease prevention,[35] and therefore reduce healthcare expenditure;[36] ii) allow 'better healthcare at a lower cost'; iii) foster 'patient empowerment (i.e. improved control over own healthcare)'; iv) enable 'easier and more immediate access to medical care and information online';[37] and v) develop 'more efficient and sustainable healthcare'.[38] Algorithmic analysis of huge datasets will develop 'personalised medicine' based on more accurate diagnostic predictions and treatment suggestions.[39] Such improvements are not an issue of the future; they are happening right now. Deep learning AI is already 'on a par with human experts'[40] when it comes to making medical diagnoses of diseases from cancers to eye conditions[41] based on images, and it might soon outperform humans. Big data analysis allows the discovery of previously unknown trends, correlations and patterns and, therefore, offers new valuable insights for medical research.[42]

2.3 On definitional uncertainties: what are 'big health data'?

Big health data are generated en masse and offer significant promises to improve our well-being and healthcare. If, therefore, we are to study carefully the challenges that the immense datafication of our bodies is posing and the ways the law can approach these challenges, we need first to define what 'health data' and 'big health data' means.

Unlike its predecessor (the Data Protection Directive[43]), the GDPR contains a definition of 'data concerning health'. This can serve as a starting point for the present analysis. According to the GDPR, 'data concerning health' refers to 'personal data related to the physical or mental health of a natural person, including the provision of health care services, which reveal information about his or her health status'.[44] Recital 35 further explains that

> personal data concerning health should include all data pertaining to the health status of a data subject which reveal information relating to the past, current or future physical or mental health status of the data subject. This includes information about the natural person collected in the course of the registration for, or the provision of, health care services as referred to in Directive 2011/24/EU.[45] . . . to that natural person; a number, symbol or particular assigned to a natural person to uniquely identify the natural person for health purposes; information derived from the testing or examination of a body part or bodily substance, including from genetic data and biological samples; and any information on, for example, a disease, disability, disease risk, medical history, clinical treatment or the physiological or biomedical state of the data subject independent of its source, for example from a physician or other health professional, a hospital, a medical device or an in vitro diagnostic test.

'Genetic data' as defined in the GDPR is also relevant to health data. The GDPR defines 'genetic data' as

> personal data relating to the inherited or acquired genetic characteristics of a natural person which give unique information about the physiology or the *health* of that natural person and which result, in particular, from an analysis of a biological sample from the natural person in question.[46]

The definition of 'health data' is not without problems. First, it appears tautological; it is not clear what is personal data related to the 'physical or mental health' or data that reveals information about a person's 'health status'. The GDPR does not define what constitutes 'health', although the term appears several times in this legislative instrument in different combinations: 'health status', 'public health', 'health purposes', 'health insurance', 'health security'. Nevertheless, it should be acknowledged that the definition of 'data concerning health' in the GDPR is quite broad. It includes healthcare data referring to medical history, diseases and disability, but also information about the past, current and future health status of the data subject, including disease risk.

The big data context complicates things even further. What about data generated outside the health care setting – for instance, fitness and well-being data captured through wearables and fitness apps? Are these considered 'health data'?

Completely trivial and innocuous data, such as supermarket shopping lists, may also reveal information about a person's dietary habits and, consequently, their health status. Indeed, it has been argued that a supermarket shopping database can be used to determine a 'person's current and future health status with a degree of accuracy comparable to that of a medical examination' with the ability to 'detect individuals' propensity to develop diseases such as diabetes, women's cancers, smoking-related cancers, cardiovascular disease, depression, etc.'[47] Furthermore, what constitutes health information can be context dependent; a piece of information might not possess the 'intrinsic nature'[48] of health data but, analysed by algorithms, it might reveal the health status of a person. The case, often cited by privacy scholars, of the department store Target sending a teenage girl ads about pregnancy products – before her family knew of her pregnancy – on the basis of her purchasing certain goods such as lotions and vitamin supplements,[49] demonstrates the potential of big data analytics. Definitional difficulties are exacerbated in the big data environment because data are not static, but dynamic; at one time point, they might be irrelevant to health or even not personal data at all (for instance, the levels of environmental pollution, weather data[50]), and at the next moment, combined and analysed with other datasets (i.e., lifestyle habits), they might reveal sensitive information.

It is not only that the meaning of 'health data' is blurred. Uncertainties also arise as to what constitutes 'big (health) data'. First, the term 'big' can be misleading in different ways.[51] The data is not always 'big'; it's their aggregation and analysis that matters. As Zuboff observes,

> 'big data' are constituted by capturing small data from individuals' computer-mediated actions and utterances in their pursuit of effective life. Nothing is too trivial or ephemeral for this harvesting: Facebook 'likes', Google searches, emails, texts, photos, songs, and videos, location, communication patterns, networks, purchases, movements, every click, misspelled word, page view, and more. Such data are acquired, datafied, abstracted, aggregated, analysed, packaged, sold, further analysed and sold again.[52]

It's not only that 'big data' is made by bits of 'small data'. It is also 'not always easy (or indeed useful) to say whether a particular instance of processing is or is not big data analytics.'[53] As technologies and algorithmic tools are increasingly ingrained in our lives, big data analytics are becoming the new normal, a part 'of business as usual'.[54]

Overall, the definitional boundaries of 'big health data' are not clear cut. What is 'big' data / what is 'small' data; what is 'health' data / what is not health data; what is personal data / what is non-personal data; what is 'big data analytics' and what is business as usual may differ from time to time and from context to context. The implications of these definitional uncertainties matter for this book. The GDPR considers 'data concerning health' as special categories of data (normally referred to as sensitive data) that merit enhanced protection.[55] Yet, the definitional difficulties discussed here cannot be resolved by merely construing 'health data' broadly as proposed by the European Data Protection Supervisor (EDPS).[56] They demand a shift in thinking that can approach the problem in a novel, dynamic way that addresses the big data context.

That being said, this book adopts in general the not so accurate terminology of 'big health data' or 'big health data analytics' as an umbrella concept that covers broadly data generated from a variety of different sources and from which information about a person's health can be inferred. Some chapters focus on what can be seen as 'small' data instances of processing (such as sharenting), not losing sight of the fact that any information, however small, can be potentially rendered big data.[57]

2.4 Sources of big health data

Big health data can be captured in a variety of ways: i) it can be volunteered or surrendered by individuals when they share information about themselves (e.g., patient data shared with healthcare professionals) or third parties (e.g., their children); ii) monitored by tracking their activities (e.g., Google searches, loyalty schemes in gyms that record attendance, supermarkets that record purchasing history); and, finally, it can be 'inferred', based on the analysis or the 'profiling'[58] of volunteered, monitored and other data (e.g., health insurance premiums).[59] According to a report from the Organisation for Economic Co-operation and Development (OECD), the big data 'lifecycle' often follows the following sequence of steps: i) collection/access; ii) storage and aggregation; iii) analysis and distribution; and iv) usage.[60] Each step could potentially involve different stakeholders[61] and data could have several lifecycles entailing further aggregation and analysis.

There is a plethora of sources through which health information can be captured. Outside the traditional medical/healthcare sector, *mHealth* is an important source of big health data. Mobile Health ('mHealth') broadly refers to mobile devices and applications ('apps') that deliver health, well-being and lifestyle services and information.[62] These include wearables – data collection devices worn on the body, such as fitness trackers and smart watches – and health and fitness apps. mHealth solutions can be used to deliver a wide range of services,[63] including measuring and quantifying basic bodily functions (such as breathing rate, sleep, heart rate, blood pressure and blood glucose level) and habits (exercise patterns); offering medication reminders, fitness recommendations and nutritional advice; booking medical appointments; and assisting users with health-related questions. mHealth apps and devices routinely share users' data with third parties[64] such as advertisers. Apps can also be integrated with social media platforms in order to enhance users' experience by showcasing personal statistics and performances. Furthermore, wearables and apps can be used to facilitate 'gamification', understood as the 'use of game-like incentives'[65] (targets, competition) to encourage users to change their behaviour concerning physical activities[66] (i.e., walking) and even intimate relationships.[67]

mHealth devices and apps illustrate the potential of 'surveillance capitalism'.[68] As Lupton has noted,

> These devices could . . . be regarded as disciplinary, working to tame the . . . body by rendering it amenable to monitoring, tracking, and detailed analysis of the data thus generated. . . . These technologies configure a certain type of approach to understanding and experiencing one's body, an algorithmic subjectivity, in which the body and its health states, functions and activities are portrayed and understood predominantly via quantified calculations, predictions and comparisons.[69]

mHealth technologies are often connected to social media – for instance, a Fitbit can share the user's data on Facebook in order to showcase their performance. Social media platforms themselves contain important troves of health-related information. Facebook, Twitter, Instagram and PatientsLikeMe provide significant opportunities to form online communities – among others – around health issues, but they have also increased opportunities for health data surveillance.[70] For instance, PatientsLikeMe state that they share personal data, including information 'you provide about yourself to share with others like the condition you're living with and treatments you're trying' with the Patients-LikeMe community, as well as with partners that include universities, pharmaceutical companies, hospital systems, insurance companies, regulatory bodies and 'members of the Digital Life Alliance – like-minded digital health, science, and technology companies who work closely with PatientsLikeMe to improve health and healthcare around the globe'.[71]

3. On legislative choices: GDPR and health

3.1 The GDPR: an overview

The GDPR constitutes the centrepiece of EU data privacy law. It is a long and complex legislative document. It contains 173 (non-binding) Recitals and 99 provisions laying down 'rules relating to the protection of natural persons with regard to the processing[72] of personal data[73] and rules relating to the free movement of personal data'.[74] The GDPR does not apply to the processing of personal data that falls outside the scope of EU law; concerns national security policy; processing by a natural person in the course 'of a purely personal or household activity'; or processing for the purposes of the prevention, investigation, detection or prosecution of criminal offences or the execution of criminal penalties, including the safeguarding against and the prevention of threats to public security.[75]

In its substance, the GDPR is an omnibus regulation covering processing of personal data by both private and public bodies and addressing 'an immense landscape of potential informational problems'.[76] The provisions of the GDPR are structured around two main actors: the 'data subjects' and the 'controllers'. Data subjects are the natural persons whose personal data are processed. Controllers are the natural or legal persons, public authorities, or other bodies which, 'alone or jointly with others, determine the purposes and means of the processing of personal data'.[77] National Data Protection Authorities (DPAs) oversee the application of the GDPR.[78]

The GDPR is a 'principles-based regulation'.[79] It includes six principles on the basis of which personal data must be processed: 'lawfulness, fairness and transparency'[80]; 'purpose limitation'[81]; 'data minimisation'[82]; 'accuracy'[83]; 'storage limitation'[84]; and 'integrity and confidentiality'.[85] An additional 'accountability' principle makes controllers responsible for complying with these data processing principles.[86]

Data subjects are granted a number of rights under the GDPR: a right of information,[87] access to,[88] rectification[89] and erasure[90] of personal data; a right to data portability;[91] a right to restrict[92] and object to certain types of processing;[93] and a right not to be subjected to fully automated decisions based on profiling.[94] Data breaches must be communicated by controllers to data subjects when they are likely to result in a high risk to the rights and freedoms of natural persons.[95]

The GDPR introduces a risk-based approach to data protection. Recital 75 explains that risks 'of varying likelihood and severity may result from personal data processing' and could lead to 'physical, material or non-material damage' and provides examples of such risk.[96] Controllers are obliged to undertake *ex ante* data protection impact assessments (DPIAs)[97] 'where a type of processing in particular using new technologies, . . . is likely to result in a high risk to the rights and freedoms of natural persons',[98] and notify *ex post* data breaches to supervisory authorities and the data subject[99] when they are 'likely to result in a high risk to the rights and freedoms of natural persons'.[100]

3.2 Health data under the GDPR

The GDPR contains a number of provisions on health data and health. Besides the definitional issues described previously, these concern on the one hand, the enhanced protection of health data as 'special categories of personal data',[101] and on the other hand, the exemptions and restrictions to data protection rules and principles for health reasons.

Health data enjoy increased levels of protection under the GDPR.[102] First, as a basic rule, the GDPR prohibits the processing of data concerning health.[103] There are several exceptions to this prohibition that will be discussed in the next section.

Second, the GDPR considers the processing of health data – and sensitive data in general – as one that might pose a 'risk' to the rights and freedoms of natural persons.[104] More fundamentally, there are cases where the GDPR views personal health data processing as 'high-risk'. For instance, the GDPR recognises that a high risk to the rights and freedoms of natural persons might arise when health data are processed 'on a large scale'[105] and obliges controllers to carry out a DPIA in this context.[106] This would include the case of a large hospital processing patients' genetic and health data,[107] although the GDPR is careful to point out that the processing of personal data of patients by an individual physician or other health care professional would not be considered as 'large-scale'.[108]

Third, the GDPR prohibits automated decision-making including profiling,[109] which produces legal effects concerning a person or significantly affects her to be undertaken based on health data, unless the data subject has given her explicit consent or processing is necessary for reasons of substantial public interest and suitable measures to safeguard the data subject's rights, freedoms and legitimate interests are in place.[110] The GDPR grants data subjects the right not to be subject to fully automated decisions that analyse or predict aspects concerning their health[111] and obliges controllers to undertake a DPIA if they engage in such a systematic and extensive evaluation of natural persons based on automated processing, including profiling.[112]

Fourth, the GDPR specifically mentions the data subject's rights of information and access in relation to their health data. These include the right for data subjects to have 'access to data concerning their health, for example the data in their medical records containing information such as diagnoses, examination results, assessments by treating physicians and any treatment or interventions provided'.[113]

Fifth, additional responsibilities are imposed on controllers processing health data: these must keep records of processing activities even if the organisation employs fewer than 250 persons;[114] they must designate a Data Protection Officer (DPO) if the core activities of the controller or the processor consist of processing health data on a large scale;[115] and controllers and processors not established in the EU must designate in writing a representative in the Union if they process health data on a large scale.[116]

3.3 Exemptions allowing health data processing

The GDPR contains a number of exceptions to the (in principle) prohibition of processing of health data.[117] First, the processing of health data is allowed if the data subject has given her 'explicit consent'.[118] It should be recalled that the GDPR has significantly raised the substantive and procedural requirements on 'consent' for the processing of personal data in general;[119] the bar is even higher when special categories of data, and therefore, health data, are at issue. The GDPR even allows Member States or the EU under certain instances to remove the consent exception altogether.[120]

Health data can also be processed when this is necessary to protect the 'vital interests' of the data subject or of another person when they are physically or legally incapable of giving their consent[121] (e.g., the data subject is unconscious after an accident, and the hospital needs to know her medical history, whether she has any allergies or uses any medication). Health data processing is further allowed where this has been 'manifestly made public by the data subject'.[122] This provision creates a number of uncertainties because, as mentioned earlier, mHealth apps and devices (such as Fitbits) often share users' information on social media and individuals frequently post health-related information on social media platforms both generic (Facebook, Twitter, etc.) and specific (PatientsLikeMe). The GDPR seems to permit the processing of health data in this respect,[123] but I submit that the mere posting of health data on social media would not be enough to allow the processing of such data by another controller.

The processing of health data is also allowed when necessary for reasons of 'substantial public interest'.[124] It should be noted that the GDPR does not require the processing merely in the 'public interest'; the public interest must be 'substantial'. What constitutes 'substantial public interest' is not defined in the GDPR. Moreover, the GDPR allows the processing of health data when necessary,

> for the purposes of preventive or occupational medicine, for the assessment of the working capacity of the employee, medical diagnosis, the provision of health or social care or treatment or the management of health or social care systems and services.[125]

Finally, the GDPR provides that Member States can maintain or introduce further conditions, including limitations, with regard to the processing of health, genetic data and biometric data.[126] This might contribute to the further fragmentation of the health data landscape in the EU and increase uncertainties.

3.4 'Public health' exceptions and restrictions

The GDPR enshrines several exemptions and restrictions of data protection rules for public health purposes. The processing of sensitive data – including health data – is allowed for reasons of public interest in the area of 'public health'.

'Public health' refers to:

> all elements related to health, namely health status, including morbidity and disability, the determinants having an effect on that health status, health care needs, resources allocated to health care, the provision of, and universal access to, health care as well as health care expenditure and financing, and the causes of mortality.[127]

Article 35 of the EU Charter of Fundamental Rights (EUCFR) guarantees a 'right of access to preventive health care and the right to benefit from medical treatment under the conditions established by national laws and practices' and provides that 'a high level of human health protection shall be ensured in the definition and implementation of all the Union's policies and activities'.

More particularly, the GDPR permits the processing of health data when this is necessary to protect against 'serious cross-border threats to health or ensuring high standards of quality and safety of health care and of medicinal products or medical devices'.[128] The public interest in the area of public health does not have to be 'substantial',[129] and this provision provides a basis for the processing of health data without needing any other legal basis (such as the data subject's explicit consent).[130] The GDPR warns, however, that such processing of health data for reasons of public interest should not result in personal data being processed for other purposes by third parties such as employers or insurance and banking companies.[131] Recital 46 GDPR states that '[s]ome types of processing may serve both important grounds of public interest and the vital interests of the data subject as for instance when processing is necessary for humanitarian purposes, including for monitoring epidemics and their spread'.[132] The current COVID-19 pandemic would be an example of such processing of personal health data that would be considered in the public interest in the area of public health and, therefore, permitted.[133]

The GDPR allows restrictions to data protection principles and data subjects' rights taken on the basis of 'public health' purposes.[134] Such restrictions can be imposed by EU or Member States' law by way of a 'legislative measure' that respects the essence of the fundamental rights and freedoms and is necessary and proportionate in a democratic society.[135] The GDPR also includes a 'public health' exemption to the right to erasure ('right to be forgotten') that obliges controllers to erase personal data concerning a data subject if requested to do so.[136] This means that if further retention of the personal data is necessary for public health reasons, the controller is not obliged to erase them even if the data subject has exercised her right to erasure. Furthermore, the GDPR provides a number of derogations from the general rule that personal data can be transferred to third countries outside the EU only when these provide an adequate level of protection[137] or appropriate safeguards, including binding corporate rules.[138] A case where such international transfer can take place without appropriate safeguards or an adequacy decision is when the transfer is 'necessary for important reasons of public interest'[139] that include 'public health, for example in the case of contact tracing for contagious diseases'.[140] Such derogation could be used, for instance, to allow for the transfer of EU originating personal data to countries that do not guarantee an adequate protection to combat the COVID-19 pandemic and trace the contacts' spread of this virus.

Finally, the GDPR makes clear that it applies to personal data processed for 'scientific research purposes', including technological development and demonstration, fundamental research, applied research and privately funded research.[141] According to the GDPR, 'scientific research purposes' also include studies conducted in the public interest in the area of public health.[142] If the result of scientific research in the health context gives reason for further measures in the interest of the data subject, the general rules of the GDPR are also applicable to those measures.[143]

3.5 Assessing the GDPR's health-related legislative choices

Overall, it is clear that the GDPR's provisions examined previously constitute a legislative attempt to *balance* two distinct forms of fundamental values and interests: those of data privacy and those of public health. Whether the GDPR achieves a fair balance in this respect, is a question that remains to be answered. However, a number of points can be raised in this regard.

First, the GDPR takes a clear position on the question 'for the benefit of whom' the balancing between the fundamental interests of data privacy and public health should be taking place. As Recital 53 puts it,

> Special categories of personal data which merit higher protection should be processed for health-related purposes only where necessary to achieve those purposes *for the benefit of natural persons and society as a whole* . . .[144]

This is a significant choice made by the EU legislator that provides the benchmark for the balancing exercise; this must always be undertaken for the benefit of individuals and the society as a whole.

Second, the question of balancing between data privacy interests on the one hand, and public health interests on the other hand, is a context-dependent one. These interests are prioritised differently depending on the context within which they arise: In situations- where the monitoring of epidemics and their spread is required – much like the current COVID-19 pandemic – public health interests are prioritised over data privacy. Under normal processing circumstances, data privacy interests are prioritised and the GDPR recognises increased levels of protection of 'health data' compared to normal sensitive data. There are exemptions, restrictions and exceptions under normal processing circumstances as well – these prioritise, in particular cases, public health interests. In this respect, the GDPR has done a good job, as it adopts a degree of flexibility when considering the different interests at stake.

Third, where public health restrictions are required, these must be prescribed by law, be necessary in a democratic society, respect the principle of proportionality and be accompanied with appropriate (data protection) safeguards. Such safeguards are crucial and must be respected even in exceptional times, such as the ongoing COVID-19 pandemic.[145]

What makes the GDPR's legislative choices more problematic, however, is their *binary* nature. This brings me to the fourth point I would like to make. The GDPR follows a 'black/white approach'[146] regarding health data privacy. The data are either sensitive or not; if they are, then they enjoy increased protections. They are either personal or not, and if they are, the data protection rules apply; if not, they fall altogether outside the scope of the GDPR. Such distinctions and dichotomies based on a binary approach are difficult to maintain in the big data analytics environment. They often make little sense and entail a risk of both regulatory overinclusiveness and underinclusiveness. Strict and rigid rules based on binary choices might not be necessary at every instance;[147] conversely, the GDPR's rules and protections regarding health data might fall short in effectively protecting individual and societal interests in certain cases.

4. Conclusion

The COVID-19 pandemic has brought forward a plethora of challenges, both known and unknown, that data privacy faces.[148] Health surveillance, however, is hardly new. This has often taken place also outside the traditional healthcare context through a variety of mHealth apps, devices and social media platforms.

The GDPR contains a broad definition of data concerning health and recognises augmented protection to these as sensitive data. This illustrates that the EU legislator considers health data privacy as an important interest, often at risk, that merits additional protection. At the same time, the GDPR includes several exemptions and restrictions to health data privacy interests. Some of these are based on the individual circumstances of data subjects (e.g., 'explicit consent' or to protect the 'vital interests' of the data subject), but most of them concern public health interests.

The GDPR's provisions balancing data privacy with public health interests appear flexible and context dependent. In this regard, data protection rules 'can in no manner be an obstacle to saving lives'[149] and 'do not hinder measures taken in the fight against the coronavirus pandemic'.[150] At the same time, exceptional measures should be adopted only when it is necessary and must be proportionate and followed by data privacy safeguards. This demonstrates that the GDPR enshrines the rule of law principle. Exceptional circumstances measures cannot appear and operate in a democracy vacuum; they must be taken in accordance with the rule of law and the principle of proportionality as they operate in a democratic society. This also confirms that the GDPR does not allow the exploitation of exceptional circumstances introduced to combat COVID-19 'to usher in an era of biosurveillance' that will persist even after the pandemic has ended.[151]

While the GDPR can be applauded for striking a reasonably fair balance between data privacy and public health interests, the binary, black/white approach it adopts regarding sensitive (health) / non-sensitive (non-health) is problematic. Such distinctions are difficult to make in a big data context using AI analytics and entail the risk of rendering the GDPR's rules both overinclusive and underinclusive.

Notes

1 Anita L. Allen, *Unpopular Privacy: What Must We Hide?* (New York: Oxford University Press, 2011).

2 Ibid.

3 For an overview of COVID-19 restrictive measures across the world, see Oxford University's COVID-19 Government Response Tracker project. Hale Thomas et al., 'Oxford COVID-19 Government Response Tracker', Blavatnik School of Government, 2020. Data use policy: Creative Commons Attribution CC BY standard <www.bsg.ox.ac.uk/research/research-projects/oxford-covid-19-government-response-tracker>.

4 See also Rebecca Ratcliffe, 'Teargas, Beatings and Bleach: The Most Extreme Covid-19 Lockdown Controls around the World', *The Guardian*, 1 April 2020 <www.theguardian.com/global-development/2020/apr/01/extreme-coronavirus-lockdown-controls-raise-fears-for-worlds-poorest>.

5 Alison Hills, '"Can I Sunbathe in the Park?" Is Now a Deep Moral Question', *The Guardian*, 10 April 2020 <www.theguardian.com/commentisfree/2020/apr/10/sunbathing-park-deep-moral-questions-philosophers-coronavirus-individual>.
6 Jack Nicas and Daisuke Wakabayashi, 'Apple and Google Team Up to "Contact Trace" the Coronavirus', *The New York Times*, 10 April 2020 <www.nytimes.com/2020/04/10/technology/apple-google-coronavirus-contact-tracing.html>.
7 Alex Hern, 'Experts Warn of Privacy Risk as US Uses GPS to Fight Coronavirus Spread', *The Guardian*, 2 April 2020 <www.theguardian.com/technology/2020/apr/02/experts-warn-of-privacy-risk-as-us-uses-gps-to-fight-coronavirus-spread>.
8 Regulation (EU) 2016/679 of the European Parliament and of the Council of 27 April 2016 on the protection of natural persons with regard to the processing of personal data and on the free movement of such data, and repealing Directive 95/46/EC (General Data Protection Regulation), Official Journal of the European Union, L 119/1, 4 May 2016.
9 Gillian Cleary, 'Mobile Privacy: What Do Your Apps Know About You?', 16 August 2018 <www.symantec.com/blogs/threat-intelligence/mobile-privacy-apps>.
10 Art 29WP Opinion 02/2013 on apps on smart devices, WP 202, Adopted on 27 February 2013.
11 European Commission, 'Digital Single Market Policy: The Internet of Things', <https://ec.europa.eu/digital-single-market/en/internet-of-things>.
12 The European Commission estimates that the number of IoT connections will raise to 6 billion by 2020. Commission Staff Working Document, Advancing the Internet of Things in Europe, Accompanying the document Communication From the Commission to the European Parliament, the Council, the European Economic and Social Committee and the Committee of the Regions Digitising European Industry Reaping the full benefits of a Digital Single Market {COM(2016) 180 final}, Brussels, 19.4.2016 SWD(2016) 110 final. See also, Art 29 WP, *Opinion 8/2014 on Recent Developments on the Internet of Things*, adopted on 16 September 2014; Samuel Greengard, *The Internet of Things* (Cambridge, MA: MIT Press, 2015).
13 Kari Paul, 'Teen Claims to Tweet from Her Smart Fridge – But Did She Really?', 13 August 2019 <www.theguardian.com/technology/2019/aug/13/teen-smart-fridge-twitter-grounded>.
14 On the meaning of 'data' and 'information' in the law in general and in data protection laws see Lee Bygrave, 'Information Concepts in Law: Generic Dreams and Definitional Daylight' (2015) 35 (1) *Oxford Journal of Legal Studies*, 91.
15 EDPS, Opinion 7/2015 *Meeting the Challenges of Big Data: A Call for Transparency, User Control, Data Protection by Design and Accountability*, 7.
16 Ibid.
17 Kitchin argues that there are seven dimensions to big data, including exhaustivity, resolution and indexicality, relationality and extensionality and scalability. Rob Kitchin, *The Data Revolution: Big Data, Open Data, Data Infrastructures and their Consequences* (London: Sage, 2014). Rob Kitchin and Gavin McArdle, 'What Makes Big Data, Big Data? Exploring the Ontological Characteristics of 26 Datasets' (2016) 3 (1) *Big Data and Society*, 1.
18 Variability is also often mentioned. This means that data captured may vary from time to time or place to place. Anil Jain, 'The 5 V's of Big Data', 17 September 2016 <www.ibm.com/blogs/watson-health/the-5-vs-of-big-data/>.
19 Sander Klous, 'Sustainable Harvesting of the Big Data Potential', in Bart van der Sloot et al. (eds.), *Exploring the Boundaries of Big Data* (Amsterdam: Amsterdam University Press, 2016), 27, 28.
20 UK Government Office for Science, *Artificial Intelligence: Opportunities and Implications for the Future of Decision Making*, 9 November 2016, 5.
21 John Danaher et al., 'Algorithmic Governance: Developing a Research Agenda through the Power of Collective Intelligence' (2017) *Big Data & Society*, 1, 2.

22 UK Government Office for Science, n 20, 5.
23 Ibid, 6.
24 Ibid, 7.
25 Ibid, 4.
26 Information Commissioner's Office (ICO), *Big Data, Artificial Intelligence, Machine Learning and Data Protection*, 20170904 Version: 2.2, para 11.
27 Sarah Perez, 'IDC: Apple Led Wearables Market in 2018, with 46.2M of the Total 172.2M Devices Shipped', 5 March 2019 <https://techcrunch.com/2019/03/05/idc-apple-led-wearables-market-in-2018-with-46-2m-of-the-total-172-2m-devices-shipped/>.
28 Oliver Wainwright, 'KGoal: Introducing the Fitness Tracker for your Vagina', *The Guardian*, 4 July 2014 <www.theguardian.com/artanddesign/architecture-design-blog/2014/jul/04/kgoal-fitness-tracker-vagina-pelvic-floor>.
29 Arwa Mahdawi, 'Is Buying a "Smart Nappy" Really Such a Clever Idea?', *The Guardian*, 24 July 2019 <www.theguardian.com/commentisfree/2019/jul/24/is-buying-a-smart-nappy-really-such-a-clever-idea?CMP=Share_AndroidApp_Gmail>.
30 Richard Godwin, '"You Can Track Everything": The Parents Who Digitise their Babies' Lives', *The Guardian*, 2 March 2019 <www.theguardian.com/lifeandstyle/2019/mar/02/apps-that-track-babies-and-give-data-to-tech-firms-parents>.
31 See Quantified Self, 'Self Knowledge Through Numbers' <https://quantifiedself.com/>.
32 Deborah Lupton, *The Quantified Self* (Cambridge: Polity Press, 2016).
33 See <www.patientslikeme.com/about>.
34 Ibid. 'Today, PatientsLikeMe is the world's largest personalized health network . . . Everything members have shared empowers the community with personal agency, establishing PatientsLikeMe as a clinically robust resource that has published more than 100 research studies.'
35 European Commission, Green Paper on mobile Health ("mHealth"), Brussels, 10.4.2014, COM(2014) 219 final, 4.
36 Deborah Lupton, 'Quantifying the Body: Monitoring and Measuring Health in the Age of mHealth Technologies' (2013) 23 (4) *Critical Public Health*, 393.
37 EDPS, Opinion 1/2015 *Mobile Health: Reconciling Technological Innovation with Data Protection*, 21 May 2015, 3.
38 Commission, Green Paper on mHealth, n 35, 5.
39 Kate Crawford and Jason Schultz, 'Big Data and Due Process: Toward a Framework to Redress Predictive Privacy Harms' (2014) 55 *B.C.L. Rev.*, 93, 102 <http://lawdigitalcommons.bc.edu/bclr/vol55/iss1/4>.
40 Nicola Davis, 'AI Equal with Human Experts in Medical Diagnosis, Study Finds', *The Guardian*, 24 September 2019 <www.theguardian.com/technology/2019/sep/24/ai-equal-with-human-experts-in-medical-diagnosis-study-finds?CMP=Share_AndroidApp_Gmail>.
41 Ian Sample, '"It's Going to Create a Revolution": How AI is Transforming the NHS', *The Guardian*, 4 July 2018 <www.theguardian.com/technology/2018/jul/04/its-going-create-revolution-how-ai-transforming-nhs>.
42 EDPS, Opinion 1/2015 *Mobile Health*, n 37, 9.
43 Directive 95/46/EC of the European Parliament and of the Council of 24 October 1995 on the protection of individuals with regard to the processing of personal data and on the free movement of such data, OJ L 281, 23/11/1995, p. 31.
44 Article 4 (15) GDPR.
45 Directive 2011/24/EU of the European Parliament and of the Council of 9 March 2011 on the application of patients' rights in cross-border healthcare, OJ L 88, 4.4.2011, p. 45.
46 Article 4 (13) GDPR. Emphasis added.
47 Antoinette Rouvroy, '"Of Data and Men" Fundamental Rights and Freedoms in a World of Big Data', Bureau of the Consultative Committee of the Convention for the

Protection of Individuals with regard to Automatic Processing of Personal Data [ETS 108], p. 27.

48 EDPS, Opinion 1/2015 *Mobile Health*, n 37, 6.

49 Kashmir Hill, 'How Target Figured Out a Teen Girl Was Pregnant Before Her Father Did', *Forbes*, 16 February 2012 <www.forbes.com/sites/kashmirhill/2012/02/16/how-target-figured-out-a-teen-girl-was-pregnant-before-her-father-did/#d4fc43566686>.

50 Mr Dehaye, a Belgian national, received an email from The Weather Company, owned by IBM, that informed him that 'based on hot weather conditions in Mr Dehaye's area he was likely to have an "overactive bladder" – and buy more drinks' 9 June 2019. See Aliya Ram and Madhumita Murgia, 'Data Brokers: Regulators Try to Rein in the "Privacy Deathstars"', *Financial Times*, 8 January 2019 <www.ft.com/content/f1590694-fe68-11e8-aebf-99e208d3e521>.

51 See Matthew Jones, 'What We Talk About When We Talk About (Big) Data' (2019) 28 *Journal of Strategic Information Systems*, 3. Jones argues that '[r]ather than being a referential, natural, foundational, objective and equal representation of the world, . . ., data are partial and contingent and are brought into being through situated practices of conceptualization, recording and use.'

52 Shoshana Zuboff, 'Big Other: Surveillance Capitalism and the Prospects of an Information Civilization' (2015) 30 *Journal of Information Technology*, 75, 79.

53 ICO, *Big Data, Artificial Intelligence, Machine Learning and Data Protection*, n 26, 13.

54 Ibid.

55 See Art 9 GDPR.

56 EDPS, Opinion 1/2015 *Mobile Health*, n 37, 6.

57 Helen Nissenbaum has stated 'anything about an individual that can be rendered in digital form can be stored over indefinitely long periods and be readily retrieved.' See Helen Nissenbaum, 'Privacy as Contextual Integrity' (2004) 79 *Wash. L. Rev.*, 119, 129.

58 Recital 71 GDPR explains that profiling 'consists of any form of automated processing of personal data evaluating the personal aspects relating to a natural person, in particular to analyse or predict aspects concerning the data subject's performance at work, economic situation, health, personal preferences or interests, reliability or behaviour, location or movements, where it produces legal effects concerning him or her or similarly significantly affects him or her.' For further details on the challenges posed by profiling, see Tzanou's chapter in this book.

59 OECD, 'Exploring the Economics of Personal Data: A Survey of Methodologies for Measuring Monetary Value', OECD Digital Economy Papers, No. 220, OECD Publishing, 2013 <http://dx.doi.org/10.1787/5k486qtxldmq-en>, 10.

60 Ibid.

61 Ibid.

62 The Commission states that mHealth covers 'medical and public health practice supported by mobile devices, such as mobile phones, patient monitoring devices, personal digital assistants (PDAs), and other wireless devices. It also includes . . . lifestyle and wellbeing apps that may connect to medical devices or sensors (e.g. bracelets or watches) as well as personal guidance systems, health information and medication reminders provided by sms and telemedicine provided wirelessly.' See Commission, Green Paper on mHealth, n 35, 3.

63 For a theoritisation of the mHealth phenomenon, see Lupton, n 36.

64 For a very interesting empirical study, see Quinn Grundy et al., 'Data Sharing Practices of Medicines Related Apps and the Mobile Ecosystem: Traffic, Content, and Network Analysis' (2019) 364:1920 *BMJ*, 1.

65 John Danaher, Sven Nyholm and Brian D. Earp, 'The Quantified Relationship' (2018) *The American Journal of Bioethics*, 3.

66 Ali Shameli et al., 'How Gamification Affects Physical Activity: Large-Scale Analysis of Walking Challenges in a Mobile Application' (2017) *Proc Int World Wide Web Conf.*,

455; Rekesh Corepal et al., 'Exploring the Use of a Gamified Intervention for Encouraging Physical Activity in Adolescents: A Qualitative Longitudinal Study in Northern Ireland' (2018) *BMJ Open*, 0:e019663.

67 Danaher et al., n 21.

68 Shoshana Zuboff, 'Big Other: Surveillance Capitalism and the Prospects of an Information Civilization' (2015) 30 *Journal of Information Technology*, 75. See also Tereza Hendl, Bianca Jansky, and Verina Wild, 'From Design to Data Handling. Why mHealth Needs a Feminist Perspective', in Loh, J. and Coeckelbergh, M. (eds.), *Feminist Philosophy of Technology* (Techno:Phil – Aktuelle Herausforderungen der Technikphilosophie, vol. 2) (Stuttgart: J.B. Metzler, 2019), 77.

69 Deborah Lupton, 'Quantified Sex: A Critical Analysis of Sexual and Reproductive Self-Tracking Using Apps' (2014) 17 *Culture, Health & Sexuality*, 440.

70 Frank Pasquale and Tara Adams Ragone, 'Protecting Health Privacy in an Era of Big Data Processing and Cloud Computing' (2014) 17 *Stan. Tech. L. Rev.*, 595, 632.

71 PatientsLikeMe, 'Privacy Policy' <www.patientslikeme.com/about/privacy>.

72 According to Article 4 (2), 'processing' means 'any operation or set of operations which is performed on personal data or on sets of personal data, whether or not by automated means, such as collection, recording, organisation, structuring, storage, adaptation or alteration, retrieval, consultation, use, disclosure by transmission, dissemination or otherwise making available, alignment or combination, restriction, erasure or destruction'.

73 According to Article 4 (1), 'personal data' means 'any information relating to an identified or identifiable natural person ("data subject"); an identifiable natural person is one who can be identified, directly or indirectly, in particular by reference to an identifier such as a name, an identification number, location data, an online identifier or to one or more factors specific to the physical, physiological, genetic, mental, economic, cultural or social identity of that natural person'.

74 Art 1 (1) GDPR.

75 Art 2 (2) GDPR.

76 Chris Jay Hoofnagle, Bart van der Sloot and Frederik Zuiderveen Borgesius, 'The European Union General Data Protection Regulation: What it is and What it Means' (2019) 28 (1) *Information & Communications Technology Law*, 65, 67.

77 Art 4 (7) GDPR.

78 See Article 51 GDPR.

79 Hoofnagle, van der Sloot and Borgesius, n 76, 67.

80 Article 5 (1) (a): Personal data should be 'processed lawfully, fairly and in a transparent manner in relation to the data subject'.

81 Article 5 (1) (b): Personal data should be 'collected for specified, explicit and legitimate purposes and not further processed in a manner that is incompatible with those purposes; further processing for archiving purposes in the public interest, scientific or historical research purposes or statistical purposes shall, in accordance with Article 89 (1), not be considered to be incompatible with the initial purposes'.

82 Article 5 (1) (c): Personal data should be 'adequate, relevant and limited to what is necessary in relation to the purposes for which they are processed'.

83 Article 5 (1) (d): Personal data should be 'accurate and, where necessary, kept up to date; every reasonable step must be taken to ensure that personal data that are inaccurate, having regard to the purposes for which they are processed, are erased or rectified without delay'.

84 Article 5 (1) (e): Personal data should be 'kept in a form which permits identification of data subjects for no longer than is necessary for the purposes for which the personal data are processed'.

85 Article 5 (1) (f): Personal data should be 'processed in a manner that ensures appropriate security of the personal data, including protection against unauthorised or unlawful processing and against accidental loss, destruction or damage, using appropriate technical or organisational measures'.

86 Article 5 (2) GDPR.

87 Articles 13 and 14 GDPR.
88 Article 15 GDPR.
89 Article 16 GDPR.
90 Article 17 GDPR. Article 17 is entitled 'Right to erasure ("right to be forgotten").
91 Article 20 GDPR.
92 Article 18 GDPR.
93 Article 21 GDPR.
94 Article 22 GDPR.
95 Article 34 (1) GDPR.
96 The processing may give rise to 'discrimination, identity theft or fraud, financial loss, damage to the reputation, loss of confidentiality of personal data protected by professional secrecy, unauthorised reversal of pseudonymisation, or any other significant economic or social disadvantage; . . . data subjects might be deprived of their rights and freedoms or prevented from exercising control over their personal data; . . . personal data are processed which reveal racial or ethnic origin, political opinions, religion or philosophical beliefs, trade union membership, and the processing of genetic data, data concerning health or data concerning sex life or criminal convictions and offences or related security measures; . . . personal aspects are evaluated, in particular analysing or predicting aspects concerning performance at work, economic situation, health, personal preferences or interests, reliability or behaviour, location or movements, in order to create or use personal profiles; . . . personal data of vulnerable natural persons, in particular of children, are processed; or . . . processing involves a large amount of personal data and affects a large number of data subjects'.
97 Articles 35, 36 GDPR and Recital 76. For an ethical and social impact assessment see Alessandro Mantelero, 'AI and Big Data: A Blueprint for a Human Rights, Social and Ethical Impact Assessment' (2018) 34 *Computer Law & Security Review*, 754.
98 Article 35 (1) GDPR.
99 Articles 33 and 34 GDPR.
100 Article 34 (1) GDPR.
101 Article 9 GDPR.
102 According to Recital 53 '[s]pecial categories of personal data . . . merit higher protection'.
103 Article 9 (1) GDPR.
104 Recital 75 GDPR.
105 Article 35 (3) (b) GDPR.
106 Ibid. See also Article 29 Working Party, Guidelines on Data Protection Impact Assessment (DPIA) and determining whether processing is 'likely to result in a high risk' for the purposes of Regulation 2016/679, WP248, 4 April 2017.
107 Hoofnagle, van der Sloot and Borgesius, n 76, 87.
108 Recital 91 GDPR.
109 According to Article 4 (4) GDPR 'profiling' means any form of automated processing of personal data consisting of the use of personal data to evaluate certain personal aspects relating to a natural person, in particular to analyse or predict aspects concerning that natural person's . . . health . . . '
110 Article 22 (4) GDPR.
111 Recital 71 GDPR.
112 Article 35 (3) (a) GDPR.
113 Recital 63 GDPR.
114 Article 30 (5) GDPR.
115 Article 37 (1) (c) GDPR.
116 Article 27 (2) (a) GDPR.
117 Article 9 (2) GDPR. Only the ones most relevant to health data are discussed here.
118 Article 9 (2) (a) GDPR.
119 See Hoofnagle, van der Sloot, and Borgesius, n 76, 72.

120 Article 9 (2) (a) GDPR.
121 Article 9 (2) (c) GDPR.
122 Article 9 (2) (e) GDPR.
123 See Hoofnagle, van der Sloot and Borgesius, n 76, 83.
124 Article 9 (2) (g) GDPR. Such processing must be undertaken on the basis of Union or Member State law, must be proportionate to the aim pursued, respect the essence of the right to data protection and provide for suitable and specific measures to safeguard the fundamental rights and the interests of the data subject.
125 Article 9 (2) (h) GDPR. Such processing must be undertaken on the basis of Union or Member State law or pursuant to contract with a health professional and subject to the conditions and safeguards referred to in Article 9 (3).
126 Article 9 (4) GDPR.
127 Regulation (EC) No 1338/2008 of the European Parliament and of the Council of 16 December 2008 on Community statistics on public health and health and safety at work, OJ L 354, 31.12.2008, p. 70. See also Recital 54 GDPR.
128 Article 9 (2) (i) GDPR. Such processing must be undertaken on the basis of Union or Member State law which provides for suitable and specific measures to safeguard the rights and freedoms of the data subject, in particular professional secrecy.
129 The European Data Protection Board (EDPD) seems to be requiring a 'substantial' public interest in this case too although this is not explicitly stated in Article 9 (2) (i) GDPR. See EDPD, Statement on the processing of personal data in the context of the COVID-19 outbreak, Adopted on 19 March 2020, 2.
130 Article 9 (2) (i) GDPR requires that professional secrecy requirements, such as patient doctor confidentiality, should be respected in this case.
131 Recital 54.
132 See also Recitals 45, 52 and 54.
133 EDPD, n 129, 2.
134 Article 23 (1) (e) GDPR. See also Recital 73.
135 Ibid. According to Article 23 (2) GDPR such measures should 'contain specific provisions at least, where relevant, as to: (a) the purposes of the processing or categories of processing; (b) the categories of personal data; (c) the scope of the restrictions introduced; (d) the safeguards to prevent abuse or unlawful access or transfer; (e) the specification of the controller or categories of controllers; (f) the storage periods and the applicable safeguards taking into account the nature, scope and purposes of the processing or categories of processing; (g) the risks to the rights and freedoms of data subjects; and (h) the right of data subjects to be informed about the restriction, unless that may be prejudicial to the purpose of the restriction.'
136 Article 17 (3) (c) GDPR. See also Recital 65.
137 Article 45 (3) GDPR.
138 Article 46 GDPR.
139 Article 49 (1) (d) GDPR. See also Article 49 (1) (f) that allows the transfer if it 'is necessary in order to protect the vital interests of the data subject or of other persons, where the data subject is physically or legally incapable of giving consent'.
140 Recital 112 GDPR.
141 Recital 159 GDPR. See also Article 179 (1) TFEU.
142 Ibid.
143 [Endnote text is missing].
144 Emphasis added.
145 See EDPD, n 129, 1.
146 Nikolaus Forgo, 'My Health Data – Your Research: Some Preliminary Thoughts on Different Values in the General Data Protection Regulation' (2015) 5 (1) *International Data Privacy Law* 54, 59.
147 See, for example, Forgo who discusses medical research and argues that in certain cases this might produce (incidental) findings with relevance to the participants. 'In such

cases it might be necessary for the physician as an investigator to re-identify the trial participant'. Ibid, 58.

148 See, for instance revelations, that the UK government is sharing confidential National Health Service (NHS) patient data with private tech firms to build 'a COVID-19 datastore'. Paul Lewis, David Conn, and David Pegg, 'UK Government Using Confidential Patient Data in Coronavirus Response', *The Guardian*, 12 April 2020 <www.theguardian.com/world/2020/apr/12/uk-government-using-confidential-patient-data-in-coronavirus-response>.

149 Joint Statement on the right to data protection in the context of the COVID-19 pandemic by Alessandra Pierucci, Chair of the Committee of Convention 108 and Jean-Philippe Walter, Data Protection Commissioner of the Council of Europe, Strasbourg, 30 March 2020.

150 EDPD, n 129.

151 This was argued by Edward Snowden. See David Pegg and Paul Lewis, 'NHS Coronavirus App: Memo Discussed Giving Ministers Power to "De-Anonymise" Users', *The Guardian*, 13 April 2020 <www.theguardian.com/world/2020/apr/13/nhs-coronavirus-app-memo-discussed-giving-ministers-power-to-de-anonymise-users>.

2 Attribution of responsibility under the GDPR in the context of health data processing

Yordanka Ivanova[1]

1. Introduction

Roles and responsibilities for compliance with data protection law and the General Data Protection Regulation (GDPR)[2] are traditionally distributed based on the primary distinction between *data controllers*, who determine the purposes and means of the data processing, and *data processors*, who are only acting on behalf of the controller(s) and under their instructions. To cater to more complex scenarios where various actors bear collective responsibility for certain data processing operations, the concept of joint controllership enables two or more controllers to determine jointly the purposes and means of the processing, with their additional obligations now explicitly regulated in Article 26 GDPR. These concepts, inherited from the repealed Directive 95/46/EC, have been significantly enhanced with novel and stronger obligations, as provided for in the GDPR. However, legal uncertainty continues to prevail as to the exact criteria used for defining correctly the legal capacity of the data processing actor, which is of key importance in correctly assigning the tasks, responsibilities and liability under GDPR. This uncertainty is largely due to sometimes conflicting guidelines given by Working Party Article 29 (WP29)[3] and some national data protection authorities (DPAs), which are now further convoluted with a number of new criteria forged by the Court of Justice of the EU (CJEU) in its most recent case law.

The purpose of this chapter is to analyze the existing legal definitions of (joint) controller and processor and their differing interpretation by the competent DPAs and the CJEU. In addition, the chapter will examine three concrete examples demonstrating how responsibility for compliance with the GDPR is attributed in the context of health data processing, including by means of new digital technologies. In particular, the chapter will analyze the roles and responsibilities of the actors involved in case of 1) clinical trials, 2) health data processing within the global platforms, and 3) wearables at the workplace. In conclusion, some general observations will be made, emphasizing the need for greater legal certainty in defining the capacity of the data processing actors and advocating for a change in the Court's approach in defining the scope of joint controllership from 'single phase' to 'value chain'.

2. Defining the capacity of a data processing actor

This section will present the existing distinct model for compliance with GDPR, where data processing actors are assigned different responsibilities depending on whether they act as a controller, joint controller or processor. These concepts are crucial because they allocate responsibilities for compliance with data protection law and determine how data subjects can exercise their rights, which is the applicable national law and how effective are the enforcement powers of the DPAs.[4] The next sections will examine the criteria derived from the relevant GDPR provisions and how these provisions have been interpreted and applied by the CJEU and the WP29.

2.1 Definition of data controller

Data controllers are the main actors who bear the most stringent obligations for compliance with the GDPR, ranging from responsibilities to ensure lawfulness of the processing and compliance with all data processing principles[5] up to general accountability and responsibility obligations to take appropriate measures to protect data subjects' fundamental rights and be able to demonstrate compliance,[6] including by means of new tools such as data protection impact assessments[7] and the novel data protection by design and by default principle.[8]

A data controller is defined in Article 4 (7) GDPR as

> the natural or legal person, public authority, agency or other body which, alone or jointly with others, determines the purposes and means of the processing of personal data; where the purposes and means of such processing are determined by Union or Member State law, the controller or the specific criteria for its nomination may be provided for by Union or Member State law.

Apparently, this provision is formulated rather widely to encompass both public and private actors, including individual persons, for example, when processing data with connection to a professional or commercial activity,[9] or data that is not purely personal or household in nature.[10] The crucial element in establishing the controllership is to identify who determines 'the purposes and means of the processing' or in other terms, *why* and *how* the processing takes place. In its opinion, WP29 has essentially advocated for a functional concept of controllership that allocates 'responsibilities where the factual influence is, and thus based on a factual rather than a formal analysis' which may follow from explicit or implicit legal competence or factual influence exercised over the processing.[11]

The CJEU has also upheld this functional approach and has interpreted rather broadly the concept of controllership in a series of important rulings where the principle of 'effective and complete protection of data subjects'[12] was upheld and new criteria for defining the controller's capacity developed.

In the *Facebook fan page* judgment, the Court ruled that a controller 'who exerts influence over the processing of personal data for his own purposes, [. . .] participates, as a result, in the determination of the purposes and means of that processing'.[13] The CJEU also confirmed that 'no actual control or access to the personal data' is necessary for an entity to be qualified as a controller.[14] In the subsequent *Yehovah's witnesses* case,[15] this broad interpretation was further applied in practice where a religious community was found to be a controller only because the processing of personal data of persons contacted by door-to-door preachers 'help to achieve the objective of the religious community' and because it 'organises and coordinates the preaching activities of its members.' In the most recent *Fashion ID* judgment,[16] the Court went even further by concluding that the Fashion ID company is a controller because it has embedded on its website the Facebook 'Like' social plugin. The CJEU ruled that by simply choosing to integrate a third-party service processing personal data, the website operator 'exerts a decisive influence over the collection and transmission of the personal data of visitors to that website to the third party service provider,' which would not have occurred without that service, thus determining 'the "means" at the origin of the collection and transmission of personal data'.[17] As regards the purposes of processing, the CJEU concluded that these are jointly determined because the processing operations are performed 'in the economic interests' of both Fashion ID and Facebook.[18] This case law shows that the Court focuses on the individual data processing operations within the value chain to assess who acts as a controller, which according to Mahieu et al.[19] is a significant expansion of the interpretation of 'determines the purposes and means' beyond WP29's opinion.

A final key element to be considered is the possibility of controllers to determine the purposes and means 'alone or jointly with others', which presupposes two types of controllers – independent or joint.

a. Independent controller(s)

According to WP29[20]:

> The mere fact that different subjects cooperate in processing personal data, for example in a chain, does not entail that they are joint controllers in all cases, since an exchange of data without sharing purposes or means in a common set of operations should be considered only as a transfer of data between separate controllers.

This interpretation is, however, questioned by the recent *Fashion ID* judgment,[21] where simply agreeing to use third-party services was ruled to involve joint controllership for the collection and transmission of the personal data when both controllers have (economic) interests in the processing, while for any subsequent or preceding processing they should preserve the quality of independent controllers, if they are not in a position to influence that processing.[22]

b. Joint controllers

The concept of joint controllership implies the idea of 'pluralistic control', where a controller determines the purposes and means of the processing 'jointly with others'. Joint controllers are subject not only to the general controller's obligations, but also bear additional responsibility to arrange their relationship in terms of distribution of responsibilities, transparency and communication with the data subjects, as stipulated in Article 26 GDPR.

Applying the functional approach, WP29 has argued that joint control should not be primarily determined by what the contract or the agreement between the parties states, but by the factual control they yield over the purposes and means of processing.[23] Joint control is thus said to follow from various circumstances, including use of centralized or shared infrastructure/databases, e.g., common Internet platform, shared database of customers or joint purpose(s) pursued at macro-level of separate data processing operations (e.g., behavioral advertising).[24]

In its case law, the CJEU has also ruled that:

> The existence of joint responsibility does not necessarily imply equal responsibility of the various operators engaged in the processing of personal data. On the contrary, those operators may be involved at different stages of that processing of personal data and to different degrees, so that the level of responsibility of each of them must be assessed with regard to all the relevant circumstances of the particular case.[25]

Based on the Court's case law, it can be concluded that two or more controllers determine the 'purpose(s) of processing' jointly when they are pursuing a common purpose,[26] a purpose of their own,[27] or have some legitimate interest (economic or other) in the processing of the personal data.[28] Two or more controllers determine the 'means of processing' jointly when they are organizing or coordinating the activity of other controllers processing personal data[29] or when they exert some influence over the processing operation,[30] including by simply initiating the collection or transmission of the data when using the service of another controller.[31]

While contributing to enhanced protection of the data subjects, such a wide interpretation of joint controllership may also lead to legal uncertainty as to its exact scope of application, which the CJEU has tried to limit in its most recent *Fashion ID* ruling. In contrast with the WP29's macroscopic interpretation of what it means to determine the purpose and means jointly, the Court has ruled that joint controllership must be limited only to the set of operations in which the joint controllers are actually involved (e.g., collection and transmission of data), while for any subsequent data processing operation, Facebook should be considered an independent controller.[32] As suggested by Mathieu and Hoboken,[33] the Court has thus introduced a phase-oriented approach in determining the purposes and means of processing and, hence, delineating the scope of application of joint controllership from the individual responsibility of each controller – which may in fact contradict with the WP29's broader interpretation discussed earlier. As I have argued elsewhere,[34] such a microscopic 'phase-oriented' approach may, however, lead to ineffective distribution of data protection responsibilities between (joint) controllers as well as weaker protection of data subjects whose rights and control over the processing across the value chain may be significantly diminished as a consequence.

2.2 Definition of data processor

Data processors are secondary actors in data protection law, with lower responsibility in comparison with controllers. Article 4 (8) GDPR defines *processor* as 'a natural or legal person, public authority, agency or other body which processes personal data on behalf of the controller.' The main purpose of this concept is therefore to distinguish between those responsible as controller(s) and those that are only acting on their behalf, thus being subject to strict but lower obligations, so as to ensure that the controller essentially preserves the control over the processing. In its opinion, WP29 has compared the controller–processor relation with the legal concept of delegation, whereby the delegated processing activity may be limited to a very specific task or context or may be more general and extended.[35] The legal requirements for the mandate of the processor are now provided for in Article 28 GDPR, which requires a written contract between the parties to specify the subject matter, purpose, scope and other key elements of the delegation and the processor's obligations, as stipulated in Article 28(3), e.g., obligations to only process data on the basis of documented instructions from the controller, to ensure security and integrity of the processing, to delete or return the data at the request of the controller, to assist the controller in its obligations, etc. The processor must act only within the mandate and on the instructions given by the controller with regard to the purpose of the processing and the means and may not sub-delegate its tasks to another sub-processor without prior specific or general written authorization of the controller and subject to the same legal obligations.[36]

Furthermore, the processor must not play any role in determining the purposes and means of the processing mandated by the controller, as then it would become a (joint) controller rather than a processor. For example, if a processor uses the data provided by the controller for its own purposes or outside the mandate, then it automatically becomes a controller in respect of that processing.[37] While determining the means certainly turns the processor into a (joint) controller, WP29 has argued that the delegation may imply a certain degree of discretion about how to best serve the controller's interests, allowing the processor to choose the most suitable means of processing as long as these are nonessential (e.g., not defining the categories of data, retention period, etc.).[38] Such understanding is also shared by the European Data Protection Supervisor,[39] although in the case law cited previously, the CJEU does not draw a distinction between essential and nonessential means and adopts instead a wide interpretation of the notion of controller.

WP29 has also provided a list of examples of potential processors, e.g., mailing services, payroll, hosting or cloud providers, computer grids, operation of video surveillance, call centers acting on behalf of a controller, accounting services acting under the strict supervision of controllers.[40] Still, some of these service providers have been interpreted differently by national DPAs, treating them as processors in some Member States and as controllers in others.[41] The qualification of these service providers as processors also can be questioned in the light of the recent CJEU case law that has enforced a rather broad interpretation of the concept of (joint) controller and what it means to 'determine the purpose and means of processing', including by simply pursuing any (economic) interest and exercising influence over the individual data processing operations.

3. Attribution of responsibility in the context of health data processing

The purpose of this section will be to examine concretely a number of case studies to clarify how the general concepts of joint (controller) and processor are applied in practice in the context of health data processing and how responsibilities for compliance with the GDPR are attributed to the different actors involved. To this end, three specific cases will be analyzed, including 1) clinical trials; 2) health data processing within the global platforms; and 3) wearables at the workplace.

3.1 Clinical trials

The first example concerns clinical trials, which in principle involve the cooperation between the medical centers responsible for the collection and storage of patients' health data and the sponsor(s) of the clinical trial – the pharmaceutical companies – which define the trial protocol, provide the necessary guidance to the centers with regard to data processing and monitor their compliance with the trial protocol and the internal procedures.

WP29 has already advised that clinical centers and sponsors are likely to be considered joint controllers given that the sponsor sets the trial protocol and acquires the patients' data as collected by the medical centers, and processes those data for its economic and research purposes in different ways (evaluating the information contained in the medical documents; receiving the data of adverse reactions; entering these data in the relevant database; performing statistical analyses to achieve the trial results).[42] On the other hand, the trial center is also said to carry out the trial autonomously – albeit in compliance with the sponsor's guidelines; it provides the information notices to patients and obtains their consent as also related to processing of the data concerning them; it allows the sponsor's collaborators to access the patients' original medical documents to perform monitoring activities; and it handles and is responsible for the safekeeping of those documents.[43] Against this distribution of tasks, WP29 has concluded that both the medical center and the sponsor make important determinations with regard to the way personal data relating to clinical trials are processed, and they should be accordingly regarded as joint controllers. However, it has also advised that the relation could be interpreted differently in cases where the sponsor determines the purposes and the essential elements of the means and the medical center is left with a very narrow margin of manoeuvre. It should be noted, however, that some DPAs may exclude the possibility for a medical center to act as a processor. For example, the Bulgarian DPA has issued an opinion[44] that the medical center can only act as a data controller, given that it is obliged to comply with specific legal obligations, in particular with the Clinical Trial Regulation.[45] The medical center is thus subject to existing health regulations prescribing how to carry out scientific health research and clinical trials with live persons (e.g., seeking obligatorily patients' consent, reviews from ethical research boards, etc.) and comply with specific prohibitions by law under what circumstances such medical research and trials are explicitly not allowed. On this basis, the Bulgarian DPA has concluded that it is not possible to be acting as a processor on behalf of the sponsor and solely on the basis of its instructions.

A more complex scenario for distribution of responsibilities in clinical trials arises where a Contract Research Organisation (CRO) acts as an intermediary between a number of medical centers and the sponsor(s). The CRO's role is usually to provide research support services to the sponsors and to coordinate and manage the clinical trials on their behalf, including by monitoring centers' compliance with the trial protocol and procedures. In principle, these intermediaries are regarded as processors, given that they act on behalf of the sponsors and are obliged to comply strictly with their guidelines and instructions. However, the CROs' coordinating function, and the fact that they also aggregate the patients' health data from a number of medical centers involved in the clinical trial, may justify CROs' own responsibility as joint controllers, as it could be assumed from the WP29's opinion and the national research laws mentioned therein.[46] Recent case law such as the *Yehovah's witnesses* judgment also suggests that under specific circumstances it may be possible for the CROs to act as joint controllers, considering their specific role in coordinating and organizing the work of the medical centers and the fact that they exercise some influence over the patients' data by verifying and aggregating it, while pursuing their own economic interest from this activity.

3.2 Health data within the global platforms

Global platforms such as Google, Facebook, YouTube and Twitter have become the key public fora in the digital society, allowing every citizen to exercise their right to freedom of expression and information by sharing and accessing online information and other content that may often relate to identified or identifiable individual(s) and thus constitute personal data, as defined in Article 4(1) GDPR. The advent of these platforms and new technologies inevitably poses the question of whether regular Internet users act as controllers when processing others' personal information online, or whether they can benefit from the so-called 'household exemption', which excludes processing by natural persons in the course of a purely personal or household activity.[47] Already in 2003, the CJEU replied to this question in the *Bodil Lindqvist*[48] judgment when it ruled that Ms. Lindqvist, who posted on Facebook information about the broken leg of a colleague, had in fact processed sensitive health data and acted as a data controller who could not benefit from the household exception because she made that data accessible to an unrestricted number of people. Such limited interpretation of the household exception has been recently confirmed in the *Buivids* case,[49] which shows that many Internet users who share online personal data with an unrestricted number of people are data controllers subject to the full GDPR application.

Irrespective of the household exemption for private users, Recital 18 of the GDPR states that the Regulation does apply to the controllers or processors that provide the means for processing personal data for such personal or household activities. The CJEU has already confirmed this in its famous *Google Spain* judgment, where by applying the principle of 'effective and complete protection of data subjects', the search engine was famously qualified as a data controller because its data processing 'can be distinguished from and is additional to that of' the original publisher and that its 'data processing [. . .] affects the data subject's rights additionally'.[50] Google was furthermore not allowed to benefit from the journalistic exemption under Article 85 GDPR, which allows certain derogations from the data protection requirements where necessary to reconcile the right to data protection with the fundamental right to freedom of expression.[51] More recently in *GC*, the Court still tempered slightly the search engines' obligations when processing sensitive personal data, taking account of the search engine's '*responsibilities, powers and capabilities*' and concluding that the restrictions for processing sensitive data under Article 9 GDPR are applicable to Google only 'on the basis of a request by the data subject'[52] and not prior to that. Where the operator of a search engine receives a request under Article 17 GDPR for de-referencing,

> the operator must, on the basis of all the relevant factors of the particular case and taking into account the seriousness of the interference with the data subject's fundamental rights to privacy and protection of personal data laid down in Articles 7 and 8 of the Charter, ascertain [. . .] whether the inclusion of that link in the list of results displayed following a search on the basis of the data subject's name is strictly necessary for protecting the freedom of information of internet users potentially interested in accessing that web page by means of such a search, protected by Article 11 of the Charter.[53]

Having said that global platforms and Internet users act as controllers when making personal data accessible to an unrestricted number of persons, a logical question is whether they act as joint or independent controllers. While this issue has not been specifically addressed by the CJEU, the WP29 has advised that Internet users (not benefitting from the household exemption) and social networks should be regarded as joint controllers.[54] Support for such interpretation can be also found in the *Fashion ID* judgment, considering that both the platform and the user exercise influence over the processing of the same personal data for their own economic or other legitimate interests. However, if Facebook alone further processes the personal data for any purpose of its own (e.g., for ad profiling of users or machine learning of algorithms), Facebook should be rather regarded as an independent controller for this subsequent processing, to the extent that the Internet user is not in a position to actually influence this further processing.

A final hypothesis to be analyzed is where the data uploaded in the global platform are accessed and further processed by third-party organizations for their own purposes. One illustrative example is the app developed by the UK Samaritans charity organization, which was launched in 2014 to screen public posts in Twitter in order to predict the suicidal propensity of Twitter users and send warnings to their 'friends' in the network as a preventive measure.[55] While the overall purpose of suicide prevention seems noble at first sight, this app raised serious privacy concerns because Twitter users were not informed about this highly sensitive processing of information about their mental state of mind and the interests of the persons blacklisted as suicidal were not sufficiently safeguarded, considering all the adverse social, emotional and other harms this processing may cause them. With regard to their responsibility, the Samaritans have contested the applicability of the data protection legislation to their activity, arguing that the data used were already made public.[56] However, the Information Commissioner's Office (ICO) has confirmed that the data protection legislation continues to apply also in cases where the personal data are public, and concluded that the Samaritans acted as a data controller given that they had determined the purpose and the manner of the subsequent processing of the Twitter users' health data. While not specifically addressed by the ICO, it is suggested that in this particular case the Samaritans acted as an *independent* controller, because there was no legal relationship between the charity organization and the global platform. Still, it is possible that if such a legal relationship existed or Twitter had given the Samaritans access to the non-public profiles of the users without seeking their prior consent, the two organizations would have acted as joint controllers who determine jointly the purpose and means of the subsequent processing.

3.3 Wearables at the workplace

The third and final example concerns popular health wearable devices such as fitness trackers, smartwatches, chips or other items, which enable in real time the collection and processing of large quantities of personal data, often including highly sensitive data about one's health condition such as blood pressure, pulse, dietary habits, calories burnt, quality of sleep and stress levels. The personal data are usually recorded in an accompanying application that is synchronised to the user's smartphone and also may be uploaded to their computer or accessed online if the data are stored in a cloud system. According to WP29, the information and communications technology (ICT) provider of the wearable service would act as a data controller in respect to the data subjects' data generated as a result of the wearable's use.[57]

The situation may become more complicated as these high-tech devices for health monitoring have also entered the corporate sphere, with an increasing number of companies subsidizing their employees to buy and use them, while at the same time gaining access to that sensitive information and often using it for surveillance or as input into employees' insurance plans, incentive schemes and wellness packages.[58] Such practices raise serious concerns for their privacy and data protection implications, considering the purposes for which those data are used by the employers who act as data controllers, given that they determine the purpose and means of the processing of their employees' health data. Accordingly, employers' access to and use of the sensitive information should be based on a specific legal ground under article 9(2) of the GDPR which would most probably require employees' explicit consent, because the use of these tech devices could not be justified as necessary for the purposes of traditional occupational health medicine. However, given the unequal relationship between employers and employees and the sensitive nature of the health data, it is highly unlikely that legally valid consent can be given for the tracking or monitoring of those data, as employees are essentially not 'free' to give such consent in the first place.[59] In its opinion, WP29 has reached a similar conclusion: Even if the employer uses a third party to collect the health data, which would only provide aggregated information about general health developments to the employer, the processing would still be unlawful.[60] Hence, any corporate gifts for employees in the form of smart wearables or other new technologies should under no circumstances involve any access on behalf of the employer to the health data generated.

An interesting question in terms of responsibility and liability arises also in the case where the employer shares the unlawfully collected employees' health data with an insurance company that may use it afterward to calculate the insurance premiums of the employees. In this relation, a recent report of the UK Center of Data Ethics and Innovation illustrates how insurance companies use new AI and big data technologies to collect, share and analyze large troves of personal data from social platforms, wearables, GPS locations, etc., which is usually done without the express consent of customers and may lead to hyper-personalised risk assessments, potentially leaving some individuals 'uninsurable' by revealing previously unseen indicators of risk – an outcome highly likely in the case of health data processing.[61] The question thus arises: Would the insurance company act as an independent controller for the subsequent processing of the employees' health data, or would the employer be jointly responsible? Considering the CJEU's reasoning in the *Fashion ID* judgment, the employer would be jointly responsible with the insurance company for the collection and transmission of the employees' health data but not for the subsequent data processing performed by the insurance company, because the employer would not be really in a position to influence the way the insurance company sets the premiums. Insurance companies are also subject to strict market regulations,[62] so it is more likely that they are treated by the DPAs as independent controllers. However, it must be noted that the employer would also gain benefit from the way insurance premiums are set, which also explains why it has transferred the data to the insurance company on purpose, as the final outcome would be also in its economic interest. Hence, it is suggested that recognizing the employer and the insurance company as joint controllers for the subsequent processing in relation to the premium setting would more effectively protect the employees and provide them with more just and complete compensation for the unlawful processing of their health data obtained through the wearables.

4. Conclusion

The analysis in the previous sections has explained the key criteria used for attributing responsibility under data protection law based on the distinction between (joint) controller and processor. On a positive side, recent case law of the CJEU has advanced quite a broad interpretation of the notion of controller, which may help to ensure more complete and effective protection of data subjects and their fundamental rights. However, the criteria developed by the Court and the 'phase-oriented' approach in defining the scope of joint controllership differ substantially from the macroscopic view and the clearer distinction between controllers and processors, proposed by the WP29. These differences inevitably lead to inconsistent interpretation of the notions of (joint) controller and processor and legal uncertainty that is even further exacerbated because of the existing divergent interpretations given by the national DPAs. An updated guidance of the European Data Protection Board is therefore of paramount importance to solve the inconsistencies between the two approaches and provide a unified interpretation of how to define the role and the scope of joint controllers' responsibility.

The case studies analyzing the distribution of responsibilities in the context of health data processing have also shown that the 'phase-oriented' approach adopted by the Court may absolve from responsibility and liability actors who, even if not in a position to influence the subsequent processing, have implicitly agreed with its purpose and outcome. This may therefore pose the question of whether the scope of joint controllership should not be extended by the Court to all actors across the value chain who explicitly or implicitly agree with the overarching purpose of the processing, as proposed by the WP29. Arguably, such a 'value chain' approach is more incentivizing and suited to the current economic and technological reality, and more appropriate to ensure effective protection of the data subjects and enhanced accountability of the multiple actors involved that is of even greater importance in the case of highly sensitive health data processing.

Notes

1 The chapter reflects the author's personal opinion as a researcher and is in no way engaging or presenting the position of the EU Institutions.
2 Regulation (EU) 2016/679 of the European Parliament and of the Council of 27 April 2016 on the protection of natural persons with regard to the processing of personal data and on the free movement of such data, and repealing Directive 95/46/EC (General Data Protection Regulation) (Text with EEA relevance), OJ L 119, 4.5.2016, p. 1–88.
3 Article 29 Working Party, Opinion 1/2010 on the concepts of "controller" and "processor", 00264/10/EN WP 169, 2010.
4 WP29, Opinion 1/2010, p. 2.
5 Article 5 GDPR.
6 Article 24 GDPR.
7 Article 35 GDPR.
8 Article 25 GDPR.
9 Recitals 18 and 91 GDPR.
10 Article 2 (2) (c) GDPR and Recital 18 GDPR.
11 WP29, Opinion 1/2010, pp. 9–10.
12 CJEU, C-131/12, *Google Spain*, ECLI:EU:C:2014:317, paras. 34 and 38; C-210/16, *Wirtschaftsakademie Schleswig-Holstein (Facebook fan page)*, EU:C:2018:388, para. 28; C-40/17, *Fashion ID GmbH & Co. KG*, ECLI:EU:C:2019:629, para. 66.
13 CJEU, C-210/16, *Facebook fan page*, para. 68.
14 Ibidem, para. 38; Case C-25/17, *Yehovah's witnesses*, para. 69.
15 CJEU, C-25/17, *Yehovah's witnesses*, ECLI:EU:C:2018:551, para. 71.
16 CJEU, C-40/17, *Fashion ID GmbH & Co. KG*, ECLI:EU:C:2019:629.
17 Ibidem, paras. 78–79.
18 Ibidem, para. 80.
19 R. Mahieu, J. Hoboken, & H. Asghari, "Responsibility for Data Protection in a Networked World: On the Question of the Controller, 'Effective and Complete Protection' and Its Application to Data Access Rights in Europe", *JIPITEC*, Vol. 10 (2019), p. 86.
20 WP29, Opinion 1/2010, p. 16.
21 CJEU, C-40/17, *Fashion ID*, paras. 78–80.
22 Ibidem, paras. 74–75.
23 WP29, Opinion 1/2010, pp. 18–20.
24 Ibidem.
25 CJEU, C-210/16, *Facebook fan page*, paras. 28, 43, and 44; CJEU, C-25/17 *Yehovah's witnesses*, para.66; CJEU, C-40/17, *Fashion ID*, para. 70.
26 CJEU, C-25/17, *Yehovah's witnesses*, para. 71.
27 CJEU, C-210/16, *Facebook fan page*, para. 68.
28 CJEU, C-40/17, *Fashion ID*, para.80.
29 CJEU, C-25/17, *Yehovah's witnesses*, para.71.
30 CJEU, C-210/16, *Facebook fan page*, para.36.
31 CJEU, C-40/17, *Fashion ID*, paras.78–79.
32 Ibidem, para.76.
33 R. Mahieu & J. Hoboken, "Fashion-ID: Introducing a Phase-Oriented Approach to Data Protection?", *The Europeanlawblog*, 20 September 2019. Retrieved from <https://europeanlawblog.eu/2019/09/30/fashion-id-introducing-a-phase-oriented-approach-to-data-protection/>.
34 Y. Ivanova, "Data Controller, Processor, or Joint Controller: Designing the Right Way for Reaching Compliance with the GDPR in a Data- and Technology-Driven World" (Forthcoming), in Tzanou, M. (ed.), *Personal Data Protection and Legal Developments in the European Union* (IGI Global, 2020).
35 WP29, Opinion 1/2010, p. 25.
36 Article 28 (2) and (4) of the GDPR.

37 Article 28 (10) GDPR. CJEU, C-101/01 *Bodil Lindqvist*, EU:C:2003:596, para. 47; CJEU, C-73/07 *Satakunnan Markkinapörssi and Satamedia*, EU:C:2008:727, para. 44; CJEU, C-212/13 *Ryneš*, EU:C:2014:2428, paras. 31 and 33, CJEU C-25/17 *Tietosuojavaltuutettu Jehovan todistajat (Yehovah's witnesses)*, ECLI:EU:C:2018, para. 40.
38 WP29, Opinion 1/2010, p. 25.
39 European Data Protection Supervisor, Guidelines on the concepts of controller, processor and joint controllership under Regulation (EU) 2018/1725, 2019.
40 WP29, Opinion 1/2010, pp. 24–30.
41 For example, according to the UK Information Commissioner's Office (ICO), accounting firms act always as independent controllers given that they have specific professional obligations, while the Bulgarian DPA has issued guidelines that accounting firms should instead be considered processors. Postal services are treated by WP29 as processors for the content of the messages and controllers when processing the personal data of the sender and recipient (e.g., names, contact details). By contrast, according to ICO, postal services do not have any capacity in relation to the content of the postal packages, as these are not considered to be data processing activities. By contrast, the Bulgarian DPA entirely treats postal services as independent controllers, given their obligations by law to ensure security and confidentiality of the delivery.
42 WP29, Opinion 1/2010, p. 32.
43 Ibidem.
44 Bulgarian Commission for Personal Data Protection, Opinion № НДМСПО-01–190/2019 Specifically on the Capacity of Data Controller or Processor in Clinical Trials and More Generally about the Distinction Guidelines on the GDPR, 2016. Retrieved from <www.cpdp.bg/index.php?p=element&aid=1163>.
45 Regulation (EU) No 536/2014 of the European Parliament and of the Council of 16 April 2014 on clinical trials on medicinal products for human use, and repealing Directive 2001/20/EC Text with EEA relevance, OJ L 158, 27.5.2014, p. 1–76.
46 WP29, Opinion 1/2010, p. 30.
47 Article1 (2) c) of the GDPR.
48 CJEU, C-101/01, *Bodil Lindqvist*, EU:C:2003:596.
49 CJEU, C – 345/17, *Buivids*, ECLI:EU:C:2019:122.
50 CJEU, C- 131/12, *Google Spain SL and Google Inc. v Agencia Española de Protección de Datos (AEPD) and Mario Costeja González*, ECLI:EU:C:2013:424, paras. 34–38.
51 Ibidem, para. 85.
52 CJEU, C-136/17, *GC and others v CNIL*, ECLI:EU:C:2019:773, paras. 45–47.
53 Ibidem, para.68.
54 Article 29 Working Party, Opinion 5/2009 on online social networking, WP 163, 2009.
55 P. Bernal, *The Internet, Warts and All: Free Speech, Privacy and Truth* (Cambridge: Cambridge University Press, 2018), p. 157.
56 J. Baines, "ICO: Samaritans Radar Failed to Comply with Data Protection Act", 25 April 2015. Retrieved From <https://informationrightsandwrongs.com/2015/04/25/ico-samaritans-radar-failed-to-comply-with-data-protection-act/>.
57 Article 29 Working Party, Opinion 2/2017 on data processing at work, 17/EN WP 249, 2017, p. 18.
58 Kathryn Montgomery, Jeff Chester and Katharina Kopp, "Health Wearables: Ensuring Fairness, Preventing Discrimination, and Promoting Equity in an Emerging Internet-of-Things Environment", *Journal of Information Policy*, Vol. 8 (2018), pp. 34–77.
59 Recital 43 of the GDPR states that 'consent should not provide a valid legal ground for the processing of personal data in a specific case where there is a clear imbalance between the data subject and the controller, in particular where the controller is a public authority and it is therefore unlikely that consent was freely given in all the circumstances of that specific situation. Consent is presumed not to be freely given if it does not allow separate consent to be given to different personal data processing operations

despite it being appropriate in the individual case, or if the performance of a contract, including the provision of a service, is dependent on the consent despite such consent not being necessary for such performance'.

60 Article 29 Working Party, Opinion 2/2017, p. 19.

61 Center of Data Ethics and Innovation, CDEI Snapshot Series, AI and Personal Insurance, September 2019.

62 See, for example, Directive (EU) 2016/97 of the European Parliament and of the Council of 20 January 2016 on insurance distribution (recast)Text with EEA relevance, OJ L 26, 2.2.2016, pp. 19–59.

3 Healthcare data about children in social media

The challenges raised under the GDPR

Rosemary Jay

Introduction

Since the General Data Protection Regulation (GDPR) and the UK Data Protection Act 2018 came into effect, there has been a significant focus on the processing of children's data. The UK Information Commissioner issued guidance on the processing of personal data relating to children[1] and published a draft Code on the design of online services directed at children.[2] Just prior to the implementation date, the Article 29 Working Party (now replaced by the European Data Protection Board [EDPB]) published its Guidelines on Consent.[3] This has been mirrored by an increase in interest in how "sharenting" is treated by the law.[4] This chapter reviews those developments.

While the focus of the chapter is health data about children, the use of social media by those with parental responsibility raises broader questions around who has the right to control that data, and around the rights of children to the privacy of such data. This chapter reviews the application of data protection rights. It should be noted that children may have other remedies for excessive sharenting – for example, applying the law of confidence or seeking tortious remedies for misuse of private information.[5] In this chapter, the term "parent" is occasionally used as a shorthand but always refers to the person with parental responsibility.

The chapter does not address those cases where personal data about children is posted, shared or otherwise made public by persons other than parents, although some of the discussion may be relevant to such cases.

The GDPR

On 27 April 2016, the European Commission published two instruments:

- Regulation (EU) 2016/679 on the protection of natural persons with regards to the processing of personal data and the free movement of such data and repealing Directive 95/46/EC (General Data Protection Regulation)(GDPR); and
- Directive (EU) 2016/680 on the protection of personal data by competent authorities for the purposes of the prevention, investigation, detection or

prosecution of criminal offences or the execution of criminal penalties and on the free movement of such data and repealing Council Framework Decision 2008/977 (Data Protection Law Enforcement Directive) (DPLED)

Although the GDPR is directly applicable law, there are elements of the package, such as the powers of the supervisory authority, which require national implementation. The DPLED, being a directive, requires national implementation. In addition, Member States have had to consider how they will deal with the data protection regulation of those areas of activity which are not covered by either instrument, being outside the DPLED and European Union (EU) competence and hence outside the scope of the GDPR.

The UK has elected to address the areas outside DPLED and EU competence by applying data protection standards, consistent with the GDPR, to all such data save that processed by the UK intelligence services. The UK Data Protection Act (UK Act) (DPA 2018):

- implements those provisions of the GDPR which require Member State implementation;
- inserts a number of additional data protection provisions which supplement the GDPR;
- implements the DPLED in Part 3 of the DPA 2018;
- applies a separate data protection regime based on the Council of Europe Convention for the Protection of Individuals with Regards to the Automatic Processing of Personal Data (Treaty 108) to the supervision of processing by the intelligence services in Part 4 of the DPA 2018; and
- applies the provisions of the GDPR, with minor amendments, to processing otherwise outside EU competence (the applied GDPR).[6]

Post-Brexit, the UK Government proposes to merge the provisions of the GDPR and applied GDPR into one regime which will remain consistent with the GDPR. The provisions of Parts 3 and 4 of the DPA 2018 will remain unchanged. Neither Part 3 nor 4 is relevant to the discussion in this chapter.

Sharenting

The term "sharenting" (or "over-sharenting") has now reached Wikipedia, which describes it as the overuse of social media by parents to share content based on their children's activities. Wikipedia notes that the original use of the term has been attributed to *The Wall Street Journal* in 2013, and has since given rise to an ongoing debate about how the parent's rights to share their personal and family information can be balanced with the child's right to privacy. There are now numerous studies on the extent of sharenting[7] and the potential impact of sharenting on children.[8] The focus in this chapter is not on the nature or effects of sharenting but on the application of the GDPR rights to allow children to control the personal data posted about them by those with parental responsibility, and in particular, personal data about the child's health.

Children under the GDPR

The GDPR, in common with previous data protection legislation, seeks to safeguard the data protection rights of individuals (data subjects) and to provide them with remedies for breaches of those rights. The GDPR imposes stronger controls on those who process and use personal data and gives stronger rights and remedies than the laws which it has replaced.

There is no age restriction on when an individual is considered to be a data subject with rights under the law. Children are data subjects from birth. The importance of the protection of children's rights is recognized in the EU legal order under Article 24 of the EU Charter of Fundamental Rights.[9] As data subjects, children have all the rights available to data subjects under the law. They cannot utilise those rights on their own behalf until they have the legal competence to do so. Nevertheless, Article 24 argues that their views should be taken into account even if they are not sufficiently mature to take full responsibility for decisions.

Provisions of the GDPR relevant to children[10]

Article 6(1)(f) sets out the balancing test which permits data controllers to process personal data based on their legitimate interests, except where those interests are overridden by the interests or fundamental rights and freedoms of data subjects. The provision makes specific reference to the interests of children, "in particular where the data subject is a child".

Article 8 restricts the use of information society services offered directly to children where consent is the basis for the processing and requires that the service has reasonably verifiable parental consent. There is a degree of leeway for Member States on the age level at which the verifiable parental consent must be required. It cannot be lower than 13 years or higher than 16 years. The UK has selected the age of 13 years, on the basis, it appears, that this has become a de facto standard, having been adopted under the US Children's Online Privacy Protection Act of 1998. The GDPR refers to the processing of personal data relating to counselling and preventative services in Recital 38. The UK Act has formalized this and provides that parental consent is not required for information society services to children under 13 where those services consist of "preventative or counselling services".

Article 12 requires that data controllers provide transparent information to data subjects about the processing of personal data using plain and clear language and refers specifically to information available to children, "in particular for any information addressed specifically for a child".

The same statement appears in the relevant recital, Recital 58.

Article 17(1) provides data subjects with rights to have personal data erased in certain cases. One of those cases is where the personal data was collected "in relation to the offer of information society services referred to in Article 8(1)"; that is, such services offered directly to a child under the specified age. The importance of the right being available to children is emphasized by Recital 65 which states that,

> That right is relevant in particular where the data subject has given his or her consent as a child and is not fully aware of the risks involved by the processing, and later wants to remove such personal data, especially on the internet. The data subject should be able to exercise that right notwithstanding the fact that he or she is no longer a child.

References to the importance of considering the position of children occur in several recitals and additional articles. Recital 38 relates to the broad, overarching provisions in Article 5 which set out the principles of fairness, proportionality and accuracy. It states,

> Children merit specific protection with regard to their personal data, as they may be less aware of the risks, consequences and safeguards concerned and their rights in relation to the processing of personal data. Such specific protection should, in particular, apply to the use of personal data of children for the purposes of marketing or creating personality or user profiles or the collection of personal data with regard to children when using services offered directly to a child. The consent of the holder of parental responsibility should not be necessary in the context of preventative or counselling services offered directly to a child.

Recital 75, which relates to the general obligations of data controllers to take account of and address risks to data subjects arising from their processing of personal data, recognizes children as being among the vulnerable. It notes, ". . . where personal data of vulnerable natural persons, in particular of children, are processed" as an area of data processing which may give rise to specific risks.

References to the importance of the protection of children also occur in:

- Recital 71, with reference to Article 22 on automated decision-making, where it is noted such decisions should not concern children;
- Article 40(2)(g) on codes of conduct, where it is noted that such codes may specify the application of the GDPR with regard to the protection of children; and
- Article 57(1)(b), which states that activities of data controllers addressed specifically to children shall receive the special attention of supervisory authorities.

Provisions of the DPA 2018 relevant to children

There are a number of provisions in the DPA 2018 which have relevance to the position of children; for example, there are extensive exemptions which protect the privacy of children in adoption, family and other proceedings. In this chapter, the focus is on the specific provision requiring regulatory guidance in respect of the processing of children's personal data online.

Section 123 of the DPA 2018 requires the Information Commissioner to prepare a code of practice on age-appropriate design. This provision owes nothing to the GDPR. It was added to the UK Act during its passage through Parliament and reflects a growing concern in the UK about the protection of children online. During the passage of the Bill, Baroness Kidron[11] proposed an amendment to the GDPR which would have required the provision of "minimums standards of age-appropriate design as determined by the Commissioner" to be in place before a website could seek the consent of children over the age of 13 to the use of information society services.

Those proposing the amendment argued that it would require the Information Commissioner to create guidance on age-appropriate design, taking into account such matters as,

> a child's need for high privacy settings by default, not revealing their GPS location, using their data only to enable them to use a service as they wish and no more, and not automatically excluding them if they will not give up vast swathes of data however nicely you ask. If the commissioner so wished, it could also mean giving a child time off by not sending endless notifications during school hours or sleep hours and deactivating features designed to promote extended use; making commercially driven content, whether a vlogger or a direct marketing campaign, visible to and understood by a minor; and insisting on reporting processes with an end-point and a reasonable expectation of resolution.

The amendment was initially opposed by the Government. Eventually, however, the Lords achieved a partial success. The code was de-coupled from Article 8 GDPR, the Government arguing successfully that the addition of a further constraint would undermine Article 8, but the code itself reached the statute book. A draft code was issued by the Information Commissioner in April 2019, with consultation closing at the end of May 2019. At the time of writing, the revised code has not been published.[12] It is notable that the scope of the proposed code is extremely wide and encompasses areas that are difficult to regard as related to the design of online services. The starting point of the code is that the best interests of the child should always be the primary consideration for those providing online services to children: "The best interests of the child should be a primary consideration when you design and develop online services likely to be accessed by a child".[13]

In relation to the sharing of personal data about children, it counsels online service providers as follows: "Do not disclose children's data unless you can demonstrate a compelling reason to do so, taking account of the best interests of the child".[14]

In relation to geolocation,

> Switch geolocation options off by default (unless you can demonstrate a compelling reason for geolocation, taking account of the best interests of the child), and provide an obvious sign for children when location tracking is active. Options which make a child's location visible to others should default back to off at the end of each session.[15]

These examples are of interest because they illuminate the fact that a number of the potential harms that the code addresses, and against which service providers will have to apply safeguards, mirror those that may arise as a result of sharenting.[16] Yet there is nothing in the draft code which deals with the potential for harms arising from the behavior of those with parental responsibility. To date, this approach is seen in all the guidance that has been produced by regulators in relation to the position of children under the GDPR.

Health data under the GDPR

Data concerning health is defined as "personal data relating to the physical or mental health of a natural person, including the provision of health care services, which reveal information about his or her health status".

The relevant recital (35) expands on the definition and provides:

> Personal data concerning health should include all data pertaining to the health status of a data subject which reveal information relating to the past, current or future physical or mental health status of the data subject. This includes . . . information derived from the testing or examination of a body part or bodily substance, including from genetic and biological samples; and any information on, for example, a disease, disability, disease risk, medical history, clinical treatment or the physiological or biomedical state of the data subject independent of its source, for example from a physical or other health professional, a hospital a medical device or an in vitro diagnostic test.

This is a wide definition, and it is easy to see how a parent could share health data without necessarily realizing it. Data concerning health is one of the classes of special category personal data under the GDPR. Such special category personal data are subject to more stringent requirements than other categories of information before processing can take place and must be protected with adequate safeguards, e.g., for the security of the data.

Individual safeguards and rights under the GDPR

Under the GDPR, individuals have the following main safeguards and rights:

1 Personal data in the special categories cannot be processed by a data controller unless the controller can point to a clear and specific justification based on one of the listed grounds (grounds for processing).[17] These include the explicit, specific consent of the data subject or that the processing is necessary for health-related reasons or areas such as public health. In order for consent to be valid and explicit it must be clear that the data subject has had a proper explanation of the purposes of the processing and has the knowledge and understanding to consent to it.[18] Consent may be withdrawn by the data subject at any time but such withdrawal does not affect the lawfulness of processing based on consent prior to the withdrawal.[19]
2 Individuals have the right to know what personal data about them are held,[20] to object to its processing,[21] to have the use of the personal data restricted in certain cases and to have information erased (the right to be forgotten).[22] In the case of the right to be forgotten, under Article 17 this includes a specific right to erasure where the personal data have been collected in relation to an "offer of information society services referred to in Article 8(1)." This refers to the provision explained previously, under which an information society service which is offered directly to a child requires the reasonably verifiable consent of the person with parental responsibility where the child is under 13.

Overview of protective provisions for children's health data and social media

On the face of it, the GDPR regime should offer a level of protection to children in respect to health data and social media. A child should not be able to provide consent to the use of such services under the age of 13 without the reasonably verifiable consent of the parent. Over the age of 13, the processing of health data should require explicit consent, which requires the child to fully understand the nature of the processing taking place. If the child does place such data on social media, then the right in Article 17 should be applicable to ensure it can be removed once the child changes his or her mind.

In addition, the unauthorised logging of health data about a child by a third party on social media should give rise to the possibility of action by the child, or the parent acting on the child's behalf, to have it taken down under the right to erasure.

This analysis, however, omits an extremely significant point. Health data about children, as so much personal data about children, may be disclosed on social media sites by parents rather than by children or by third parties. This leads to two questions:

1 Can parents be restricted under the GDPR from posting information about a child under the age of capacity, where that information concerns

the child's health and is inappropriate, intrusive and likely to breach the child's rights to privacy or cause detriment to the child?

2 If personal data about health has been posted by a parent before the child has data protection capacity (increasingly referred to as digital capacity), can the child enforce the removal of the data after reaching the age of capacity?

Personal and household exclusion under the GDPR

The first question involves a consideration of the scope of the GDPR and the applied GDPR. Both exclude processing by a natural person in the course of a purely personal or household activity.[23]

Recital 18 provides,

> This regulation does to apply to the processing of personal data by a natural person in the course of a purely personal or household activity and thus with no connection to a professional or commercial activity. Personal or household activities could include correspondence and the holding of addresses, or social networking and online activity undertaken in the context of such activities. However this regulation applies to controllers or processors which provide the means for processing personal data for such personal or household activities.

The recital makes a distinction between the users and providers of social media sites. The users may claim the exclusion but the providers may not.

The provision is an exclusion rather than an exemption. In other words, personal data falling under this description is not covered at all by the GDPR or applied GDPR. The powers of the regulator do not apply unless national legislation includes a specific power to the regulator to review the facts to see if the exclusion applies. Under the DPA 2018, the Commissioner has the power to serve Information Notices in order to determine whether the processing being carried out falls within the exclusion.[24] If the Commissioner determines that the exclusion does not apply to sharenting, then potentially she will be able to use her enforcement powers against parents.

The question therefore arises of whether sharenting of a child's health data falls within the exclusion for personal and household activities (often referred to as the domestic purposes exemption). The equivalent provision in Directive 95/46/EC has been considered by the European Court in several cases. The provision came to the attention of the Court in one of the earliest cases, *Lindqvist*.[25] Mrs. Lindqvist had posted information, which included health information, about members of her church congregation on a website and had been prosecuted under the Swedish legislation for doing so without having notified the processing to the Swedish regulator. In her defence, it was argued that the posting was carried out "by a natural person in the course of a purely personal or household activity".

The European Court held that her actions did not fall within the domestic purposes exclusion, stating that it,

> must therefore be interpreted as relating only to activities which are carried out in the course of private or family life of individuals which is clearly not the case with the processing of personal data consisting in publication on the internet so that those data are made accessible to an indefinite number of persons.

It appears from *Lindqvist*, therefore, that a narrow interpretation should be placed on the exclusion. It might be argued that *Lindqvist* suggests that the exclusion does not apply where any information is posted on the Internet. However, such an interpretation would run counter to the interpretative provision in Recital 18 quoted earlier, which appears to accept that at least some level of online activity can relate to private or family life and can fall within the exclusion.

During the passage of the GDPR, the Article 29 Working Party (WP) reviewed the difficulties that DPAs faced in applying the domestic purposes exemption and proposed the provision be amended and clarified to deal with them. The lobbying was not wholly successful; however, the resulting documentation provides a helpful view of some of the difficult legal and factual points that can arise in the application of the provision.[26] The areas of concern it highlighted included the relationship between the exclusion for personal use and the exemption which protects freedom of expression.

The WP noted that historically, the personal and domestic exemption has been distinct from the exemption for freedom of expression; however, this has increasingly ceased to be the case as the power of individuals to publish material has increased. It noted that,

> It is certainly the case that an inappropriate level of scrutiny and regulation of natural persons' personal or household processing activities by DPAs could inhibit individuals' freedom of speech and could in itself constitute a breach of the individual's right to privacy.[27]

In general terms this is no doubt a fair comment, but the relevant case law suggests that it is unlikely that posting intrusive personal health data about individual children will be regarded as involving a level of freedom of expression worthy of the protection of the law.

The relation between the two exemptions has been raised in a case before the CJEU and in a case under the UK 1998 DPA. In *Serjejs Buivids v Datu valsts inspekcija*,[28] the CJEU considered whether a video made by Mr. Buivids and uploaded to YouTube could claim either the domestic purposes exemption or, if covered by the law, an exemption for freedom of expression. Mr. Buivids had filmed police officers in a Latvian police station in their work while he was making a statement in administrative proceedings brought against him. The

Latvian data protection authority held that he had acted in breach of data protection law by failing to tell the officers of the filming, and ordered him to take the film down from YouTube. The Court held that the personal and household exclusion under the Directive had to be strictly interpreted as it is a full carve out. It took into account the fact that there was no restriction on the dissemination of the personal data by Mr. Buivids and held that the exclusion did not apply. It also rejected the application of the journalistic exemption. It confirmed that it is necessary to interpret the notion of journalism in a broad manner, and that the journalism derogation cannot be confined to professional practice but is applicable to every person engaged in journalism. However, it went on to hold that not everything published online comes under the concept of journalistic activity. The question was whether the material was intended solely to disclose information, opinions or ideas to the public. It held that this was not the purpose of Mr. Buivids' publication and the exemption was not applicable to him.

The exemption was considered by the UK courts under the 1998 Act in *The Law Society v Kordowski*.[29] In the *Kordowski* case, the judge held that the domestic purpose exemption did not apply to a website called "Solicitors from Hell", which purported to expose the behavior of solicitors with whom clients were (to put it mildly) dissatisfied. It appeared from a letter read out in court that the Information Commissioner had suggested that the relevant exemption in the 1998 Act[30] would apply to the website. The letter was quoted in the judgment. In it, the Commissioner had said that the exemption was

> intended to balance the individual's rights to respect for his/her private life with freedom of expression. . . . The situation would clearly be impossible were the Information Commissioner be expected to rule on what it is acceptable for one individual to say about another individual. That is not what my office is established to do.

In its judgment, the court made clear that it considered the Commissioner's view to be wrong. The website was moderated, was run as a commercial venture and clearly included third-party material. Equally, the journalistic exemption under the 1998 DPA could not be applicable to the site.

The application of the domestic exclusion to the use of CCTV cameras was considered by the CJEU in the case of *Rynes v Urad pro ochranuosobnichudaju*.[31] Mr. Rynes and his family had been subject to harassment by persons unknown, so he fixed a CCTV camera to film the entrance to the family home. The camera also took in footage of the public entrance area. The perpetrators were caught and prosecuted on the basis of the footage. They sought to challenge the conviction on the basis that the film had been obtained in breach of data protection. The Court again applied a strict interpretation of the domestic purposes exemption and held that the CCTV footage was caught by the data protection regime as it covered a public area, not only a private area.

The UK courts further consider the domestic exclusion in the joined cases of *Ittihadieh v 5–11 Cheyne Gardens & Ors.* and *Deer v Oxford University*.[32]

In the *Ittihadieh* case, there was no disclosure of personal data, unlike the other cases. In this case, the applicant was at odds with the management company that ran the block of flats in which he resided. He had made a subject access request to the management company. The directors of the company were all neighbours of the applicant, living in the same block. The directors held some information about the applicant separately from the management company and claimed the domestic purposes exemption under the 1998 Act in respect to the information that they held personally about the applicant. The Court accepted that the domestic purposes exemption could apply to information held by one neighbour about another in a personal capacity in connection with the block of flats in which they both resided.

Applying these cases to the position of a parent sharenting a child's health data is not wholly straightforward. There is no prohibition on a parent disclosing any particular type of personal data about a child, including special category personal data such as health data, on social media. The proviso is that the processing must be purely for a personal and household purpose. Given the narrow view taken by the CJEU under the previous law to the equivalent exemption, it would appear that a narrow approach should be taken to the exclusion, particularly where the activity involves widespread publication of personal data about children and involves special category personal data.

Clearly, any particular case will be fact dependent. It is suggested that relevant issues would include:

- The nature of the personal information and the level of intrusion into the child's privacy;
- The extent of the sharing;
- How far other participants were required to observe privacy or confidentiality rules;
- The reason for the sharing;
- The age and capacity of the child and whether the child had the capacity to understand and be consulted about the sharing;
- The sheer amount of material placed online;
- Any restrictions on further dissemination of the material; and
- Any retention periods applicable to the material posted.

As an example, some limited sharing of health information on a closed site intended for families of children with a particular health problem, with appropriate safeguards to restrict further dissemination, would appear to qualify as being a purely personal use to support the family by sharing relevant information, and hence within the exclusion. On the other hand, posting of specific, identifiable intrusive health information on a site open to a wide range of people, for broader purposes – for example, to raise awareness of the issue or as part of a fundraising campaign – without any safeguards against inappropriate use or access, could reasonably be regarded as being outside the terms of the exclusion because such sharing would not be limited to purely personal and household purposes.

This appears to be in accord with the interpretation applied by the CJEU so far, although whether the Court would apply a restrictive interpretation where issues for decision involved family information is open to question. Supervisory authorities may also be reluctant to venture into the domestic sphere of family life, despite the fact that the failure to do so arguably leaves children without the privacy protection that the GDPR should be affording to them. Under the previous law, the Information Commissioner took a clear line that he would not look at any complaints about individual postings on social media on the grounds that the processing would always be exempt under the relevant section:

> The ICO will not consider complaints made against individuals who have posted personal data whilst acting in a personal capacity, no matter how unfair, derogatory or distressing the posts may be. This is because where an individual is posting for the purposes of their personal, family, household or recreational purposes the section 36 exemption will apply.[33]

This guidance was issued under the DPA 1998, which had a somewhat wider exemption provision; however, the policy position may well remain attractive to regulators who (understandably) wish to avoid being drawn into mediation on individual disputes.

Impact of the GDPR

If the GDPR applies to sharenting parents as data controllers, the question arises as to whether any other broad exemptions are available to protect them from the potential reach of regulatory supervision or actions by data subjects. As noted earlier, the Article 29 Working Party suggested that an element of freedom of expression may come into play.

Application of the exemption for freedom of expression under the DPA 2018

Under the DPA 2018, the exemption for the protection of freedom of expression is found in Schedule 2 Part 5 and applies only to personal data processed for the purposes of journalistic, literary, artistic or academic purposes. The exemption is subject to a number of conditions:

- The processing must be carried out with a view to the publication by a person of journalistic, literary, artistic or academic material;
- The controller must reasonably believe that the publication of the material would be in the public interest;
- The controller must consider the GDPR conditions which he or she is disapplying and reasonably believe that the relevant conditions would be incompatible with the purpose of the publication; and

- In determining whether the publication would be in the public interest, the controller must take into account the special interest in freedom of expression and also any of the following relevant codes and guidelines:

    - BBC Editorial Guidelines;
    - Ofcom Broadcasting Code; or
    - Editors' Code of Practice.

In effect, therefore, a parent wishing to lay claim to the journalistic exemption for sharenting would have a significant evidential burden to meet. It may be unlikely that the terms of the exemption could be met in most cases.

If there is no exemption, the terms of the GDPR apply. A parent would have to show that he or she was processing the personal data of the child on the basis of consent provided on the child's behalf. However, a right exercised on behalf of a child must be exercised in the child's best interests.[34] As has been noted in relation to the growing body of analysis and research in this area, the consensus appears to be that sharenting of sensitive information, particularly about health, is not necessarily in the best interests of a child. Without a lawful basis for processing the personal data, the parent could be at risk of action taken by the regulator to require removal of material and potentially impose a fine to deter further publication. On first sight this may appear to be an unlikely outcome, particularly as a child below the age of capacity will be unable to make a complaint. However, complaints could be made by others – for example, one parent in contested proceedings about material posted by the other parent. At the very least, it should be recognized as a potential risk.

The current thinking from regulators and others appears to be an assumption that parents can post almost anything about their children without risk of action by regulators, as exemplified by the ICO guidance from 2014. The previous analysis suggests that this is not the case under the GDPR. On the contrary, parents should be able to justify how their posting falls within the personal and household exemption, in particular before any sensitive material – such as health information about a child below the age of capacity – is placed online.

This conclusion is in line with the United Nations (UN) Convention on the Rights of the Child, and the European Charter, and reflects the restrictions placed on the publication of information about children in other areas, such as publication by the press under the Editors' Code of Practice.

It could be further argued that, if the purported consent of the parent is invalid, the processing involved in sharenting would be unlawful unless an alternative ground for processing could be found. The only alternative ground would appear to be Article 6(1)(f), that the processing is in the legitimate interest of the parent (to exercise a right of freedom of expression to the extent that can be said to apply) and not out-weighted by detriment to the rights and freedoms of the child (the rights to privacy and data protection). If the balance was held to favour the child, the parent would be left with no ground for the processing.

If this is the case, it is possible that a child could later argue that all such processing had been unlawful *ab initio* and seek erasure and damages in respect to the posting.

Can children enforce the removal of posted personal data after capacity?

Turning to the second question, this involves consideration of digital capacity and the application of the individual rights under the GDPR.

Capacity under the GDPR

Under the GDPR, the only hard provision on age is the Article 8 provision applicable to access to information society services, as described earlier. Capacity is not covered otherwise in the GDPR. Under UK law, once a child has mental capacity, he or she can exercise any of the individual rights. In Scotland, a person over the age of 12 is presumed to have sufficient age and maturity to exercise their data protection rights unless the contrary is shown.[35] In England, Wales and Northern Ireland, capacity is not hard-linked to a specific age but the ICO view is that generally by the age of 12, a child should be able to make up their own mind and exercise their own data protection rights:[36]

> A child may exercise the above rights on their own behalf as long as they are competent to do so. . . . A child should not be considered to be competent if it is evident that he or she is acting against their own best interests.[37]

It may be difficult to draw an absolutely hard edge here, as there may be some rights that a child is capable of understanding but others that are not as clear; however, once the child has capacity, he or she is able to exercise rights personally.

The law provides for different capacity at different ages. In the UK, a child may marry at 16 with parental consent. The UN Convention on the Rights of the Child treats anyone under 18 as being a child. Under the GDPR and DPA 2018, the following factors appear to be relevant to the question of the age of capacity:

- The acceptance in the UK Act and regulatory guidance that a child over the age of around 12 is deemed to be able to exercise the data subject rights on their own behalf;
- The fact that the rights exercisable include the rights to erasure and objection to processing;
- The acceptance in Article 8 GDPR that 13 is a reasonable starting point at which a child can consent on his or her own behalf to online activity; and

- The fact that a child who has given a legitimate consent following the Article 8 age level has an absolute right to withdraw consent to the processing.

These indicate that the age of digital capacity generally lies at around 13 years. Applying these as guidelines, it would seem logical that the same approach should be taken to assessing whether a child has the data protection capacity to raise objections to processing and to withdraw a consent previously provided on his or her behalf by the parent.

Position of the social media site

As we have seen from the Recital, the social media site will be subject to the GDPR, irrespective of whether the parent is or is not so subject. The accepted view is that social media sites are data controllers of the personal data posted, as they benefit from advertising, etc. around the posted data.

As noted earlier, a parent may legitimately post special category personal data about children online in reliance on the personal and household exclusion. Equally, a parent who has engaged in sharenting may be directly subject to the GDPR himself or herself. While the child is under the age of digital capacity, the parent has the right to consent on behalf of the child (subject to the caveat that the action must be taken in the best interests of the child). Where there is sharenting it can be taken that, to the extent that the personal data also concerns the parent, the parent is giving clear and explicit consent on his or her own behalf, and giving, or purporting to give, such consent on behalf of the child, to the processing of the personal data via social media.

However, once the child is over the age of capacity, what is the position, particularly in relation to special category personal data such as health data?

The general rights of objection which all data subjects have against data controllers will not be applicable against the activities of the parent who is acting within the personal and household exemption. The rights will be applicable against a sharenting parent who has overstepped the terms of the exemption and become subject to the GDPR. In reality, children are unlikely to use GDPR rights directly against a parent. The child can, however, use his or her rights directly against the social media site and can do so irrespective of whether the parent has acted in reliance on the domestic exclusion or has overstepped the terms of the exclusion.

If the child had posted the material directly onto social media while they were a child, they would have an acknowledged right to its removal. Article 17(1)(f) provides that there is a right to erasure of personal data (subject always to the tests of an overriding listed interest) where the personal data have been collected by the data controller in relation to the offer of information society services referred to in Article 8(1).

The position is not quite so clear if the personal data about the child has been posted by the parent. As we have seen, the social media site will rely on parental consent given on behalf of the child as the basis for its processing. Once the child has reached the age of capacity, there is generally a presumption that the consent endures. This appears to be an accepted position. The Article 29 Working Party Guidelines on Consent[38] put the point as follows:

> With regard to the data subject's autonomy to consent to the processing of their personal data and have full control over the processing, consent by a holder of parental responsibility or authorized by a holder of parental responsibility for the processing of personal data can be confirmed, modified or withdrawn once the subject reaches the age of digital consent.
>
> In practice this means that, if the child does not take any action consent given by a holder or parental responsibility or authorized by a holder of parental responsibility for the processing of personal data given prior to the age of digital consent, will remain a valid ground for processing.

This does not appear to be an unreasonable position. The guidance suggests that the holder of the parental consent should give the child notice and inform the child of the right to withdraw consent on reaching capacity. In practical terms, this may be unlikely; but a child who has reached digital capacity clearly has the capacity to withdraw consent to the processing.

If the material has been posted after the age of capacity, the child can clearly state that the parent is no longer empowered to give consent on his or her behalf. Once this happens, the social media site has no obvious ground on which to process the data and the child can then activate the rights of objection in Article 17(1)(b), which provides for the erasure of material where the processing was based on consent, the data subject has withdrawn that consent and there is no other legal ground for the processing.

Can a child withdraw consent to processing given by the parent on their behalf when the child was without capacity? The answer is clearly "yes". The act of processing the personal data posted is a continuing one. The definition of processing is a wide one and includes the storage, retrieval, consultation, use, disclosure by transmission, dissemination or otherwise making available of data.[39]

This view is supported by the ICO Guidance:[40]

> The right to erasure does not necessarily have to be exercised by the same person as provided the original consent. If consent was originally provided by a holder of parental responsibility this does not mean that they will also have to request the erasure. If the data subject is no longer a child, or if they are now competent to exercise their rights on their own behalf then you should usually accept their request for erasure without needing to involve the parent.

As has been noted previously, the Article 17 right is not an absolute one. A data controller can resist an application for erasure where the data controller can show that the continued processing is necessary for:

- Exercising rights of freedom of expression and information;
- Compliance with a legal obligation to which the controller in subject or exercising a task in the public interest or pursuance of official authority;
- Reasons of public interest in the area of public health;
- Archiving or statistical purposes or the establishment, exercise or defence of legal claims.

The final three grounds are unlikely to be raised in a dispute about the removal of personal health data; however, it should be noted that freedom of expression and information are recognized as interests which may override the right to erasure. This is a freestanding exemption under the GDPR. It is not subject to the rules on the application of the exemption for journalism, academic, literary or artistic works, described earlier. It may therefore offer some protection to the data controller. Unfortunately, it is not clear whether the parent who posted the information could claim the exemption. Article 17 does not make it explicit that the exemption can only be claimed by the data controller against whom the erasure request is made. If this is the case, the exemption will be nugatory as, by analogy to the Google case on search engines under Directive 95/46/EC, the social media site, as publisher rather than producer of the information, will not be entitled to claim an interest in freedom of expression and information.[41] This would suggest that the exemption may be claimed by the person who published the information – in this case, a parent responsible for sharenting who falls within the GDPR.

If this is the case, and the remedy is adopted by children to remove embarrassing material sharented by parents, social media providers may find themselves in the unenviable position of having to adjudicate between the rights of the parent to freedom of expression and the rights of the child to privacy. A consideration of the cases referred to earlier in this chapter, together with the importance attached to the protection of the position of children under the GDPR, would suggest that the child's rights would trump any right of the parents in any but the most unusual cases.

Conclusions

In the real world, of course, one hopes that parents will be willing to remove postings to which their children object. Nevertheless, family relationships are not always as harmonious as might be hoped. In such cases, the existence of a GDPR remedy that a child can evoke once they reach capacity to have sharented material removed, may prove extremely useful. It may not, however, overcome the problem that once something has been shared, it may be copied and remain online despite the individual's efforts to have it removed.

Notes

1 Children and the GDPR <www.ico.org.uk>.

2 Age Appropriate Design: A Code of Practice for Online Services. Draft code available at <www.ico.org.uk>.

3 April 2018.
4 See paper Stacey B. Steinberg, 'Sharenting: Children's Privacy in the Age of Social Media' (2017) 66 *Emory L.J.* 839 for a US perspective.
5 For an analysis of the potential application of the law of confidence, tortious remedies, including Misuse of Private Information, see Claire Bessant, 'Sharenting: Balancing the Conflicting Rights of Parents and Children' (2018) 23 (1) *Communications Law*, 7–24, 1746–7616.
6 Schedule 6 DPA 2018. None of the amendments are relevant for the issues under consideration in this paper.
7 For example, OFCOM Communications Market report 2017 cited 42% of UK parents admitted to regularly sharenting.
8 The range of potential impacts is impressive, from embarrassment, shame and anxiety, concerns at the appropriation and misuse of images in pornography, concerns at children being targeted because their location is known, the use of information gleaned from posted material to groom children online and concerns about fraud and identity theft. There are also potentially positive outcomes, such as support for parents facing difficulties. See studies cited in Bessant (fn 4) and Steinberg (fn 3).
9 "Children shall have the right to such protection and care as is necessary for their well-being. They may express their views freely. Such views shall be taken into consideration on matters which concern them in accordance with their age and maturity. In all actions relating to children, whether taken by public authorities or private institutions, the child's best interests must be a primary consideration".
10 I am indebted to the White Paper produced by the Centre for Information Policy Leadership on Children and the GDPR for the material in this section.
11 6 November 2017 House of Lords Committee session.
12 20 September 2019.
13 Age Appropriate Design: A Code of Practice for Online Services – Consultation document April 2019 issued by the UK Information Commissioner <www.ico.org.uk>.
14 Ibid page 51.
15 Ibid page 54.
16 See FN 7.
17 GDPR Article 9.
18 Ibid Article 7.
19 Ibid Article 7 (3).
20 Ibid Article 15.
21 Ibid Article 21.
22 Ibid Article 17.
23 GDPR Article 2 (2)© DPA 2018 s.21(3).
24 DPA 2018 s.142(1)(b) (ii).
25 *Bodil Lindqvist v Kammar Aklagaren* (C-101/01) [2003] E.C.R.
26 See <https://ec.europa.eu/justice/article-29/documentation/other-document/files/2013/20130227_statement_dp_annex2_en.pdf>.
27 See fn 26.
28 Case C- 345/17 CJEU 14 February 2019.
29 [2011] EWHC 3185.
30 DPA 1998 s.36.
31 Case C-212-13.
32 [2017]EWCA Civ.
33 ICO, 'Social Networking and On-line Forums – When Does the DPA Apply?', 2014.
34 *Re D (A Child)*[2014] EWCA Civ 315, 'the concept of parental responsibility describes an adult's responsibility to secure the welfare of their child which is to be exercised for the benefit of the child not the adult. The all-encompassing nature of the responsibility underpins one of the principles of the Act which is the 'no order' principle in section

1(5) CA 1985: the expectation that all other things being equal parents will exercise their responsibility so as to contribute to the welfare of their child without the need for a court order defining or restricting that exercise.' per Ryder LJ.

35 DPA 2018 s.208.

36 Children and the GDPR <www. Ico.org.uk>.

37 Ibid page 41.

38 Final issued April 2018.

39 GDPR Article 4 (2).

40 See fn 36.

41 *Google Spain SL v AEPD C 131–12.*

4 European-wide big health data analytics under the GDPR

Jos Dumortier and Mahault Piéchaud Boura

Introduction: the AEGLE project

Under which rules and conditions can health data be brought together on a European-wide platform for the purpose of Big Data analytics? This question was one of the challenges of the AEGLE innovation action, funded by the European Commission under the Horizon 2020 programme.[1] The objective of AEGLE, to which the authors of this chapter contributed as legal experts, was to develop an online platform to which health researchers can submit health datasets for carrying out Big Data analytics. The function of the proposed platform essentially consists in providing algorithms, software tools and a service package, to facilitate Big Data analytics.[2] For the development of the AEGLE platform, a limited set of health data were used to test and demonstrate its functioning. The development team worked with three use cases: a) data relating to chronic lymphocytic leukaemia (CLL) patients; b) intensive care unit (ICU) data, combining clinical information with data streams from ICU devices; and c) data relating to diabetes patients with longitudinal electronic health records. For carrying out these use cases, the AEGLE development team made use of medical data obtained from patients in hospitals located in Greece, Italy, Sweden and the United Kingdom.

While providing legal assistance to the AEGLE developers in overcoming legal and ethical hurdles to bring health data from four countries together on one European-wide platform, it soon became clear that the rules and procedures applicable in each country were very different. This could partly be explained by the fact that AEGLE started in 2014, when the GDPR was still under discussion and the legal landscape on personal data protection was very fragmented in Europe. The GDPR was enacted in May 2016, while the AEGLE project was still running, and it was therefore interesting to examine if the GDPR would solve this fragmentation.[3] Did the GDPR result in one harmonised set of rules to be followed by researchers all over the European Union, if they wish to reuse health data for Big Data analytics purposes?

To investigate this question, national legal experts from 30 European countries were asked during the spring of 2018 to draft a report on the status of the legal framework in their country. The reports collected in the framework of the

AEGLE project describe the national rules and procedures applicable to the use of health data for research purposes before and after the entry into force of the GDPR. The entire collection of 30 national reports is available online.[4] When reading through these national reports, it appears clearly that the legal rules and procedures remain very divergent, notwithstanding the entry into force of the GDPR. What is the reason for this remaining fragmentation? Did the GDPR not create "a more coherent data protection framework in the Union" as it was intended by the European legislator?[5]

The GDPR: a fair balance between individual rights and research needs

The GDPR, as any other legal text, serves multiple objectives at the same time and the ultimately adopted version is, as usual for European Union legal instruments, the result of a political compromise. One of the key objectives of the GDPR is to foster innovation while strengthening the data protection rights of individuals.[6] This is expressed in Recital 159 of the GDPR, which states that, under the Regulation, the processing of personal data for research purposes should take into account the Union's objective under Article 179(1) of the Treaty on the Functioning of the European Union (TFEU), of achieving a European Research Area. Additionally, the importance of Big Data analytics, particularly in the health sector, is explicitly underlined in Recital 157:

> By coupling information from registries, researchers can obtain new knowledge of great value with regard to widespread medical conditions such as cardiovascular disease, cancer and depression. On the basis of registries, research results can be enhanced, as they draw on a larger population.

It must be emphasized that the term "scientific research" has to be interpreted in a broad sense under the GDPR. Recital 159 of the GDPR states that "processing of personal data for scientific research purposes should be interpreted in a broad manner including for example technological development and demonstration, fundamental research, applied research and privately funded research". In essence, scientific research is any process aiming at the discovery of new knowledge and new know-how.[7] Yet, the notion of "scientific research" should not be unreasonably stretched. This is why the former Article 29 Working Party has put a caveat on the notion: scientific research must be pursued in accordance with sector-related methodological and ethical standards.[8]

The GDPR defines data concerning health as "personal data related to the physical or mental health of a natural person, including the provision of health care services, which reveal information about his or her health status'". The inclusion of the definition of health data in the European data protection legal framework has been welcomed, as it ensures a uniform interpretation of this term throughout the Union.[9] Health data belong to the category of special personal data. Because of their sensitive nature, such data are subject to stricter rules than common personal data such as names, addresses, telephone numbers, etc. It should also be noted from the beginning that the GDPR does not apply to anonymized data, i.e., personal data rendered anonymous in such a manner that the data subject is not or no longer identifiable directly or indirectly by means "reasonably likely to be used". Recital 26 of the GDPR specifies that

> to ascertain whether means are reasonably likely to be used to identify the natural person, account should be taken of all objective factors, such as the costs of and the amount of time required for identification, taking into consideration the available technology at the time of the processing and technological developments.

Big Data analytics is not always carried out for scientific research purposes. The objective can also be to produce statistics as a support for management decisions. Recital 162 provides some clarification about the concept of statistics:

> Statistical purposes mean any operation of collection and the processing of personal data necessary for statistical surveys or for the production of statistical results. Those statistical results may further be used for different purposes, including a scientific research purpose. The statistical purpose implies that the result of processing for statistical purposes is not personal data, but aggregate data, and that this result or the personal data are not used in support of measures or decisions regarding any particular natural person.

Generally speaking, most of the rules about scientific research – which will be further explained in this chapter – also apply to the processing of personal data for statistical purposes. However, to simplify, this chapter will focus only on Big Data analytics for health research purposes.

While the initial text of the GDPR, as it was proposed by the Commission in 2012, provided the option to carry out scientific research on a legal basis other than consent, the Civil Liberties Committee (LIBE) of the European Parliament proposed a revision requiring that "consent should always form the correct basis for the processing of personal health data in a research context unless such research serves a purpose of 'exceptionally high public interest'". The LIBE Committee justified its revision by arguing that

> the current proposal for Article 83 appears to allow processing of health data, in identifiable form, for research purposes without reference to consent. The only safeguards (that identifiable data must be kept separate and that researchers can use identifiable data only if research cannot be fulfilled by using non-identifiable data) significantly lowers the protection of health data. There is a risk that the current proposal will allow for researchers to use identifiable data without consent.[10]

The amendment proposed by the European Parliament Committee raised serious concerns that this would hinder health research significantly.[11] Finally, the Council of Ministers did not agree with the approach favoured by the Parliament and the text of the GDPR, as it was ultimately adopted in 2016, provides for major derogations.

Yet, GDPR commentators still often refer to consent as the first possible legal ground for the processing of health data and all other grounds as exceptions.[12] The assumption that consent of the data subject is always necessary for the processing of health data may also find its roots in the culture of consent developed in the context of clinical trials. Consent to the participation in a study or a trial must be distinguished from the consent to the processing of personal data.[13] Data protection legislation only governs the processing of personal data, not the actual participation of individuals in research projects. This participation is subject to other legal rules, in particular the European Clinical Trial Regulation[14] and to ethical standards, such as the Declaration of Helsinki on Ethical Principles for Medical Research Involving Human Subjects of the World Medical Association.[15]

To understand how the GDPR regulates the processing of health data for research purposes, a distinction must be made between research as a primary purpose of processing and research as a secondary purpose. Research as a primary purpose refers to the situation where research is the primary purpose for which health data are collected from the data subject. This occurs, for example, when researchers ask volunteers to fill in a questionnaire providing information about their health status, or to agree with the transfer of health data from wearables. Secondary use, on the other hand, refers to situations where health data are initially not collected for research purposes but, for instance, for the provision of health care.

Collecting health data specifically for research purposes

Collecting health data specifically for research purposes is regulated by Article 9 of the GDPR. This article deals with special categories of personal data, namely

> personal data revealing racial or ethnic origin, political opinions, religious or philosophical beliefs, or trade union membership, and the processing of genetic data, biometric data for the purpose of uniquely identifying a natural person, data concerning health or data concerning a natural person's sex life or sexual orientation.

Article 9 essentially states that the processing of such "sensitive" personal data is prohibited except if the processing can be justified under one of 10 exceptions listed in that article. One of these exceptions, overruling the prohibition to process sensitive personal data, is the necessity of the processing "for archiving purposes in the public interest, scientific or historical research purposes or statistical purposes" (Art. 9.2 (j)). As a consequence of this article, the prohibition to process health data does not apply if the processing of the health data is necessary for scientific research and under the condition that all other provisions of the GDPR are respected. In other words: if scientific research is the purpose of the processing, health data can be processed under the similar conditions as "common" personal data.

One of the first conditions for the processing of "common" personal data is the requirement to designate a "legal basis". Article 6 of the GDPR determines that processing of personal data is only lawful if it is based on one of the six legal grounds listed in that article. Among those six possible legal grounds, the most obvious one when collecting health data specifically for research purposes is the consent of the data subject. Other legal grounds, listed in Article 6, may be applicable as well – such as the performance of a task carried out in the public interest or the legitimate interest of the controller – but in practice, these legal grounds are much less obvious in this situation. In most cases, researchers collecting health data in the context of the research project or a series of research projects will collect the data directly from the data subjects and there will be no practical obstacles to obtain consent for the processing of the data. Obtaining consent from a patient is mainly problematic where the researcher and the patient are not in contact with each other or where the decision to use the health data for research purposes is taken afterwards.

Consent as a legal basis for collecting health data for research

For consent to be a valid legal basis, it must be freely given, specific, informed and unambiguous. Recital 32 of the GDPR states that

> consent should be given by a clear affirmative act establishing a freely given, specific, informed and unambiguous indication of the data subject's agreement to the processing of personal data relating to him or her, such as by a written statement, including by electronic means, or an oral statement.

This could include ticking a box on an Internet website or another statement or conduct that clearly indicates in this context the data subject's acceptance of the proposed processing of his or her personal data. Silence, pre-ticked boxes or inactivity should not therefore constitute consent.[16]

The consent must further be informed. This means adequate information must be provided to the data subject to enable him or her to make an enlightened choice. Data subjects must at least have information on the controller's identity, the purpose of each of the processing operations for which consent is sought, the (type of) data collected and used, the existence of the right to withdraw consent, information about the use of the data for automated decision-making where relevant, as well as on the possible risks of data transfers outside of the European Economic Area due to absence of an adequacy decision and of appropriate safeguards.

Finally, consent must be specific for a particular purpose. This may be problematic in the context of research, as health data may be collected from data subjects at a moment when the specific research project for which the data will be used is not yet fully clear. In other cases, health data may be collected in view of a long-term research programme or to feed a repository of health data to be made available to the research community. The GDPR recognises this problem. Recital 33 admits a certain flexibility in the specification of the research purpose, stating that

> it is often not possible to fully identify the purpose of personal data processing for scientific research purposes at the time of data collection. Therefore, data subjects should be allowed to give their consent to certain areas of scientific research when in keeping with recognised ethical standards for scientific research.

This is often qualified as "broad consent"', but it should be kept in mind that it "does not disapply the obligations with regard to the requirement for specific consent to the processing of data for scientific research purposes". The data protection supervisory authorities assembled in the former Article 29 Working Party have specified in one of their opinions that broad consent may be an option, when explaining that the purpose cannot be fully determined at the onset of the project, but that this should be strictly interpreted in the case of processing of sensitive data and will be the object of a high degree of scrutiny.[17]

Dynamic consent is another possible option. It often consists of using a technical solution, such as a mobile application or a server platform, to engage individual and active participants.[18] This allows researchers to easily inform research participants and ask for re-consent or additional consent. However, it is a solution which is not apt to apply in every research situation.

It should be kept in mind that, pursuant to Article 7 of the GDPR, the consent provided by data subjects for the processing of personal data may be withdrawn at any time. This can be a factor of uncertainty in a research project. However, the data subject's right to withdraw is not absolute. If a person volunteers to participate in a research project and afterwards withdraws his or her consent without any reason, the withdrawal can be qualified as an abuse of right. Volunteers participating in a research project may also be requested to sign a contract stipulating that they will receive some kind of compensation. They can be offered a fitness watch for free, membership of an online forum or free access to a health information website, in exchange for having their data transferred to a server of the research team. Such scenarios are now regulated by the Directive 2019/770 of 20 May 2019 on certain aspects concerning contracts for the supply of digital content and digital services.[19] This Directive also applies to any digital content or digital service that constitutes a medical device, such as health applications, which can be obtained by the consumer without being prescribed or provided by a health professional. Recital 37 of this directive states that its provisions are without prejudice to the application of the GDPR and that "in the event of a conflict between the directive and Union law on the protection of personal data, the latter should prevail". However, it also stipulates that

> the Directive does not regulate the consequences for the contracts covered by this Directive in the event that the consumer withdraws the consent for the processing of the consumer's personal data. Such consequences should remain a matter for national law.[20]

Apparently one must therefore make a distinction between the right to withdraw consent for the processing of personal data, attributed to data subjects by the GDPR, and the right to terminate the contract.[21] A possible outcome could be to avoid the use of consent as a legal basis for the processing of the health data in this context but to consider the processing "necessary for the performance of a contract to which the data subject is party" (Art. 6.1(b) of the GDPR).

Secondary use of health data for scientific research

The framework outlined in the previous section applies when the data processed have been collected expressly for the purpose of scientific research. However, very often the data used for scientific research are not collected initially for research purposes, but researchers reuse health data that have been obtained from patients in a clinical context. Health data are often provided to researchers by hospitals, extracted from electronic health records or obtained from health data repositories set up by public authorities. In these situations, research is a secondary purpose of the data processing. The primary purpose, for which data have been collected, was the provision of health care.

As a general rule, secondary use of personal data is not prohibited by the GDPR insofar as the secondary purpose for which data are reused is not incompatible with the original purpose for which the data have initially been obtained. For example, if a patient contacts the hospital to make an appointment for receiving care and provides his or her contact data, the hospital can use these contact data afterwards to send the bill to the patient. This secondary purpose (invoicing) is not incompatible with the purpose (making an appointment) for which the patient provided his/her contact data. The limit between what is qualified as compatible and from which stage a secondary purpose becomes incompatible, is not always easy to determine. Article 6.4 of the GDPR contains some guidelines on how to ascertain whether processing for another purpose is compatible with the purpose for which the personal data are initially collected.

Yet, if the secondary purpose of the processing of personal data is scientific research, compatibility with the initial purpose is legally presumed. In other words, health data initially collected from patients for the provision of health care (primary purpose) can be reused for scientific research purposes (secondary purpose). Article 5.1(b) of the GDPR contains a legal presumption that reuse for scientific research is always compatible with the initial purpose for which the data have been collected.

The main consequence of this legal presumption is that no separate legal basis is needed for the secondary use of health data for scientific research purposes. Recital 50 of the GDPR provides that "no legal basis separate from that which allowed the collection of the personal data is required". In other words, the processing can be done on the same legal basis as the one used for the primary processing. In practice this means that, in the case of secondary use for research purposes, the initial legal basis for which health data have been collected – the provision of health care – remains valid. In many European Member States where the provision of health care is legally qualified as a contract between the health care provider and the patient, the most obvious legal basis for the initial processing in such situations is the necessity of the data processing for the performance of a contract to which the data subject is party (Article 6.1(b) of the GDPR).

Duty to inform the data subject

Simplifying what has been explained earlier, the rules regarding processing of health data for research purposes could be summarised as follows: Consent of the data subject is required if health data are collected specifically to be used for research but not if researchers reuse health data that have initially been collected in a clinical context. Yet, with regard to this latter situation, questions are often raised about the legal duty of the controller to inform the data subject. Does the researcher who reuses health data initially collected for the provision of health care not have the obligation to inform the patient that his or her data will be reused for a research project?

This problem is dealt with in Articles 13 and 14 of the GDPR, regulating the duty of the controller to inform the data subject. The articles make a distinction between two situations: a) the controller obtains the data from the data subject, or b) the data have not been obtained from the data subject by the controller. In a research context, the first situation will most often occur if health data are specifically collected to be used for research. Data subjects must evidently always be informed in this case. This rule also applies if a hospital providing health care to a patient wishes to further process the health data collected in the clinical context for its own research projects or to transfer this data to someone else. As a controller, the hospital has obtained the health data from the patient, and consequently must inform this patient about, e.g., the purposes for which this data will be used. It is also important to emphasize that the information to be provided to the patient must include information about his or her data subject rights. One of these rights, pursuant to Article 21.6 of the GDPR, is the right of the data subject, on grounds relating to his or her particular situation, to object to processing of personal data concerning him or her, unless the processing is necessary for the performance of a task carried out for reasons of public interest. As will be explained further in this chapter, Member States have the possibility to provide for a derogation from this right "in so far as such rights are likely to render impossible or seriously impair the achievement of the specific purposes, and such derogations are necessary for the fulfilment of those purposes" (Art. 89.2 of the GDPR). Not all Member States have provided such a derogation – which explains why, for example, in the Netherlands the law stipulates that health data obtained in a clinical context can only be reused for research purposes if, among other conditions, the patient did not explicitly object.[22]

If the hospital provided the health data, collected in a clinical context, to another controller – for example, to a private or public research institution – the question further comes up of whether the latter institution, the receiver of the data, also has a duty to inform. This other controller did not obtain the data from the data subject and, consequently, Article 14 of the GDPR comes into play. Article 14.5(b) of the GDPR waives controllers from the obligation to inform the data subject if one of the following two conditions is fulfilled: a) "the provision of such information proves impossible or would involve a disproportionate effort, in particular for processing for archiving purposes in the public interest, scientific or historical research purposes or statistical purposes"; or b) the duty to inform "is likely to render impossible or seriously impair the achievement of the objectives of that processing". The provision stipulates in addition that, "in such cases the controller shall take appropriate measures to protect the data subject's rights and freedoms and legitimate interests, including making the information publicly available".

The first condition is often present when researchers process large volumes of historical health data, relating to patients who cannot be contacted anymore, either because their contact details are outdated or not known or because the patients are deceased. In this context it is also important to refer to Article 11.1 of the GDPR. This provision states that

> if the purposes for which a controller processes personal data do not or do no longer require the identification of a data subject by the controller, the controller shall not be obliged to maintain, acquire or process additional information in order to identify the data subject for the sole purpose of complying with this Regulation.

In other words, controllers are not obliged to collect updated contact details exclusively for the purpose of addressing information to the data subject about the personal data processing. The second condition refers, for example, to research projects including double-blind tests. Providing prior and full information to the data subject would result in biases and account for other effects that might influence results such as the placebo effect, where the belief that one is being treated has an effect on the results.

Other research exemptions in the GDPR

Besides the rules already explained, the GDPR contains a series of other so-called research exemptions, i.e., provisions that lower the threshold for GDPR compliance in order to facilitate scientific research. One of these exemptions relates to the so-called principle of storage limitation. Article 5.1(e) of the GDPR stipulates that personal data must be

> kept in a form which permits identification of data subjects for no longer than is necessary for the purposes for which the personal data are processed; personal data may be stored for longer periods insofar as the personal data will be processed solely for archiving purposes in the public interest, scientific or historical research purposes or statistical purposes.

As a result, health data may be stored for longer periods than strictly necessary for the purpose for which they have been collected if they will be further processed for research purposes.

Another exemption relates to the exercise of data subject rights, in particular the so-called "right to be forgotten". A data subject should have the right to have his or her personal data erased and no longer processed where the personal data are no longer necessary in relation to the purposes for which they are collected or otherwise processed, where a data subject has withdrawn his or her consent or objects to the processing of personal data concerning him or her or where the processing of his or her personal data does not otherwise comply with the GDPR. Yet, according to Article 17.3(d) of the GDPR, the right to have personal data erased does not apply to the extent that processing is necessary for research purposes. On the other hand, it should be mentioned that, pursuant to Article 21.6 of the GDPR,

> where personal data are processed for scientific or historical research purposes or statistical purposes pursuant to Article 89(1), the data subject, on grounds relating to his or her particular situation, shall have the right to object to processing of personal data concerning him or her, unless the processing is necessary for the performance of a task carried out for reasons of public interest.

Finally, Article 89.2 of the GDPR states that additional derogations from certain data subject rights, such as the right of the data subject to have access to the data relating to him or her, can be provided by Union or Member State law if the personal data are processed for research purposes. As will be explained in the following paragraph, a derogation from the right of the data subject to access his or her data is in many cases necessary because researchers often work with pseudonymised data and are not able themselves to identify the data subject, and consequently unable to retrieve the data to respond to an access request.

Appropriate safeguards to be implemented by controllers

Article 89.1 of the GDPR states that the processing of personal data for scientific research purposes

> shall be subject to appropriate safeguards, in accordance with this Regulation, for the rights and freedoms of the data subject. Those safeguards shall

> ensure that technical and organisational measures are in place in particular order to ensure respect for the principle of data minimisation. Those measures may include pseudonymisation provided that those purposes can be fulfilled in that manner. Where those purposes can be fulfilled by further processing which does not permit or no longer permits the identification of data subjects, those purposes shall be fulfilled in that manner.

The decision of which safeguards are appropriate in given circumstances belongs to the controller. The GDPR refers to "technical and organisational measures, in particular to ensure respect for the principle of data minimisation". Pseudonymisation is mentioned as one possible measure in this respect. Pursuant to Article 4(5) of the GDPR, "pseudonymisation" means:

> the processing of personal data in such a manner that the personal data can no longer be attributed to a specific data subject without the use of additional information, provided that such additional information is kept separately and is subject to technical and organisational measures to ensure that the personal data are not attributed to an identified or identifiable natural person.

Some Member States have inserted further guidance in their national data protection law, but it is important to emphasize that the decision about the measures to be taken has not been delegated to national legislators but is a duty that the GDPR imposes directly on the controller.

This is perfectly illustrated by Article 22, § 2 of the German federal data protection law which provides, by way of example, a list of 10 possible measures that controllers can implement to comply with Article 89.1 of the GDPR, such as keep an audit trail, organise awareness raising, designate a data protection offer, provide adequate access control, encrypt the data, implement pseudonymisation, apply control procedures, take measures to guarantee confidentiality, integrity and availability of the data, etc.[23] Correctly, the German federal legislator did not impose these measures because Article 89.1 of the GDPR delegates the power to decide which measures are most appropriate, directly to the controller.

How can the persistent fragmentation be explained?

The European legal framework for the processing of personal data for scientific research purposes after the entry into force of the GDPR, explained in the previous paragraphs, may seem complex but altogether it remains reasonably clear. Nevertheless, our AEGLE study of the national rules applicable to the processing of health data for research purposes in 30 European countries has shown that these rules are very different in each of the European countries. Researchers who are planning to use health data from multiple European countries are in the first place confronted with rules and procedures imposed on the national, regional or local level. In practice, the GDPR did not result in a harmonised European legal framework in this domain.

The remaining fragmentation can be explained by various factors. The most obvious one is the competence of the Member States to further regulate the processing of health data. Article 9.5 of the GDPR states that "Member States may maintain or introduce further conditions, including limitations, with regard to the processing of genetic data, biometric data or data concerning health". The European Union has only limited competences in the field of healthcare. These can particularly be found within the domains of "common safety concerns in public health matters" and "the protection and improvement of human health".[24] Those are domains where the competence of the European Commission is concurrent to that of the Member States. This means that, apart from three topics in the field of public safety, the Union can support, coordinate and complement but not harmonize the regulatory framework.[25] Because of the difficulty in effectively separating regulation of health care from regulation of health data processing, the GDPR had to leave a margin for Member States to adapt the data protection rules to the particularities of their national healthcare systems.

A second explanation has to be sought in the ambiguity of certain provisions of the GDPR.[26] Article 9.2(j), for example, states that the processing of sensitive data is not prohibited if the processing is necessary for archiving purposes in the public interest, scientific or historical research purposes or statistical purposes in accordance with Article 89.1,

> based on Union or Member State law which shall be proportionate to the aim pursued, respect the essence of the right to data protection and provide for suitable and specific measures to safeguard the fundamental rights and the interests of the data subject.

This provision, explicitly referring to "Union or Member State law", seems to contradict the text of Article 89.1 where, as already explained, the choice of appropriate safeguards has been delegated directly to the controller. This ambiguity resulted in the creation or maintenance of very specific national legal frameworks regulating the processing of health data for research purposes. For example, in France, the applicable legislation has little or no connection anymore with the provisions of the GDPR explained in this chapter. One requirement is that a processing for scientific research purposes must be approved to be in conformity with methodologies of reference established by the supervisory authority (the Commission Nationale de l'Informatique et des Libertés [CNIL]) or must otherwise apply for an authorisation to the CNIL.[27] The most obvious explanation for the complexity and fragmentation, however, is the fact that, besides the legal rules and procedures established in the GDPR and the national data protection laws, additional regulatory requirements are imposed for the use of specific health data sources. Sometimes these requirements are anchored in formal national legislation. Austria, for example, has specific legal rules applicable to researchers who wish to use data repositories set up by public authorities.[28] These rules are particularly relevant for the access of researchers to the national electronic health record system (elektronische Gesundheitsakte, or "ELGA").[29] Specific rules and procedures govern the access for researchers to National Health Service (NHS) data in the UK.[30] Terms and conditions can also be prescribed by healthcare institutions directly. In order to transfer health data to a research team, hospitals are often bound by specific legal rules related to hospital security. In Germany, for example, these rules are different depending on the public or private character of the hospital and may be established at the regional level. Moreover, hospitals generally do not provide clinical data for research purposes without the approval of an ethics committee. The organisation of ethics committees is different in each European country. They sometimes operate at a national or regional level but frequently at the local level, within a particular hospital. Ethics committees often include their own interpretation of applicable data protection rules in their deliberations and sometimes impose standards that are stricter than those which are legally required. To avoid this, it would be appropriate to establish a clear distinction between ethical standards and legal rules. Ethics committees should judge the compliance of a proposed research plan with ethical principles. Data protection officers or supervisory authorities should advise about the legal compliance of the personal data processing in the context of the research project. This task division is embedded in the procedures of the French data protection law.[31]

Conclusion

The main lesson learnt from our legal research in the context of the AEGLE project is that the GDPR has not resulted in a harmonised regulatory framework for researchers who wish to perform research based on health data to be collected in multiple European countries. The study also shows that the complexity and fragmentation of the regulatory landscape is not in the first place a consequence of the GDPR having failed to reach its ambitions. Rules and procedures to be respected by researchers planning to use health data for research purposes are not exclusively imposed by data protection law but they are more often related to data ownership. In practice, researchers are requested to meet the conditions set by the health data owners, in the first place by healthcare institutions and private or public health data repositories.

To overcome the complexity with which researchers are confronted, recent initiatives of the European Commission to promote the creation of European-wide repositories, for example of health images or digital pathology slides, must be welcomed.[32] If successful, such initiatives can shift the burden of bringing health data from different countries together from the researcher to the repository owners.

Notes

1 Grant Agreement n°644906.; <www.aegle-uhealth.eu/en/>; In Greek mythology, "Aegle" is said to be one of the daughters of Asclepius and Epione. Her name has derived from "Αἴγλη" ("Aegle"), meaning "brightness," or "splendour," either from the beauty of the human body when in good health, or from the honour paid to the medical profession.
2 The platform is currently accessible at <www.biolytica.eu/>.
3 Regulation (EU) 2016/679 of the European Parliament and of the Council of 27 April 2016 on the protection of natural persons with regard to the processing of personal data and on the free movement of such data, and repealing Directive 95/46/EC (General Data Protection Regulation).
4 <www.timelex.eu/en/horizon-projects/aegle>.
5 As stated in Recital 7 of the GDPR. See also Donnelly, M., & McDonagh, M. (2019). Health Research, Consent and the GDPR Exemption. *European Journal of Health Law*, 26(2), 97–119.
6 Molnár-Gábor, F. (2018). Germany: A Fair Balance Between Scientific Freedom and Data Subjects' Rights? *Human Genetics*, 137(8), 619–626.
7 Datatilsynet. (January 2018). Artificial Intelligence and Privacy, Report. *The Norwegian Data Protection Authority*, p. 17, available here: <www.datatilsynet.no/globalassets/global/english/ai-and-privacy.pdf>.
8 Article 29's Working Party, Guidelines on Consent under Regulation 2016/679, WP 259, p. 27. See also Shabani, M., & Borry, P. (2018). Rules for Processing Genetic Data for Research Purposes in View of the New EU General Data Protection Regulation. *European Journal of Human Genetics*, 26(2), 149.
9 European Parliament, Panel for the Future of Science and Technology, European Parliamentary Research Service. (July 2019). How the General Data Protection Regulation Changes the Rules for Scientific Research. Report, available here: <www.europarl.europa.eu/RegData/etudes/STUD/2019/634447/EPRS_STU(2019)634447_EN.pdf>.
10 European Parliament, Committee on Civil Liberties, Justice and Home Affairs. Report on the Proposal for a Regulation of the European Parliament and of the Council on the Protection of Individuals with Regard to the Processing of Personal Data and on the Free Movement of Such Data (General Data Protection Regulation) (COM(2012) 0011-C7-0025/2012-2012/0011(COD)). Rapporteur: Jan Phillip Albrecht, p. 24, available here: <www.europarl.europa.eu/sides/getDoc.do?type=REPORT&reference=A7-2013-0402&language=EN>.
11 M. Ploem, Essink-Bot, M. & Stronks, K. (2013). Proposed EU Data Protection Regulation is a Threat to Medical Research. *British Medical Journal*, 346, 3534; Dove, Edward S. *et al.* (September 6, 2014). Data Protection and Consent to Biomedical Research: A Step Forward? *The Lancet*, 384, 855.
12 Dove, E. & Laurie, G. (2015). Consent and Anonymisation: Beware Binary Constructions. *British Medical Journal*, 350, 1139.
13 EDPB, Opinion 3/2019 concerning the Questions and Answers on the interplay between the Clinical Trials Regulation (CTR)[284] and the General Data Protection Regulation (GDPR), available here: <https://edpb.europa.eu/sites/edpb/files/files/file1/edpb_opinionctrq_a_final_en.pdf>.
14 Regulation (EU) No 536/2014 of the European Parliament and of the Council of 16 April 2014 on clinical trials on medicinal products for human use, and repealing Directive 2001/20/EC (OJ L 158, 27.5.2014, p. 1). See also Recital 161 of the GDPR: *"For the purpose of consenting to the participation in scientific research activities in clinical trials, the relevant provisions of Regulation (EU) No 536/2014 of the European Parliament and of the Council (1) should apply"*.
15 See <www.wma.net/policies-post/wma-declaration-of-helsinki-ethical-principles-for-medical-research-involving-human-subjects/>.

16 See also the European Court of Justice judgment of 1 October 2019 in Case C-673/17 (Bundesverband der Verbraucherzentralen und Verbraucherverbände – Verbraucherzentrale Bundesverband eV v. Planet49 GmbH).
17 Article 29 Working Party, Guidelines on consent under Regulation2016/679, WP 259 rev. 01, pp. 27–29.
18 Kaye, J., Whitley, E., Lund, D. *et al.* (2015). Dynamic Consent: A Patient Interface for Twenty-first Century Research Networks. *European Journal of Human Genetics*, 23, 141–146. See also Megan Prictor *et al.* (2019). Consent for Data Processing under the General Data Protection Regulation: Could 'Dynamic Consent' be a Useful Tool for Researchers? *Journal of Data Protection & Privacy*, 3(1), 93–112(20).
19 Directive (EU) 2019/770 of the European Parliament and of the Council of 20 May 2019 on certain aspects concerning contracts for the supply of digital content and digital services, ELI: <http://data.europa.eu/eli/dir/2019/770/oj>.
20 Recital 12 of Directive (EU) 2019/770.
21 This opinion seems to shared by the European Data Protection Board in the Guidelines 2/2019 on the processing of personal data under Article 6(1)(b) GDPR in the context of the provision of online services to data subjects, 9 April 2019, p. 7: "*It is important to distinguish between entering into a contract and giving consent within the meaning of Article 6(1)(a), as these concepts are not the same and have different implications for data subjects' rights and expectations*".
22 Nederland Burgerlijk Wetboek (Dutch Civil Code), Book 7, Titel 7, Art. 458. For an English translation of the entire provision, see <www.dutchcivillaw.com/civilcode book077.htm>.
23 German federal data protection law, Section 22, § 2. An English translation, provided by the German federal Ministry of Interior, is available here: <https://iapp.org/media/pdf/resource_center/Eng-trans-Germany-DPL.pdf>.
24 Articles 4 (2) (k) and 6 of the Treaty on the Functioning of the European Union (TFEU), *OJ* C 326 of 26.10.2012, 47–390.
25 These three topics are: 1) organs and substances of human origin and blood and blood derivatives; 2) measures in the veterinary and phytosanitary fields; 3) medicinal products and devices for medical use. See article 168 TFEU.
26 See also van Veen, Evert-Ben. (November 2018). Observational Health Research in Europe: Understanding the General Data Protection Regulation and Underlying Debate. *European Journal of Cancer*, 104, 70–80, <https://doi.org/10.1016/j.ejca.2018.09.032>.
27 See Chapter IX of the French data protection law (Loi Informatique et Libertés); an English translation is available on the website of the CNIL: <www.cnil.fr/sites/default/files/typo/document/Act78-17VA.pdf>.
28 <www.registerforschung.at/ressourcen>.
29 The debate in Austria about the proposed access for research purposes to the electronic health record data has, according to the press media, resulted in over 5,000 patients opting out from the system. See <www.derstandard.at/story/2000079259475/5-000-elga-abmeldungen-wegen-forschungsdaten-debatte>.
30 See the Health Data Access Tool Kit, made available to researchers by the Medical Research Council, <https://hda-toolkit.org/story_html5.html>.
31 See Article 54 of the French law, available here: <www.cnil.fr/sites/default/files/typo/document/Act78-17VA.pdf>.
32 See, for example, the call for proposals DT-TDS-05–2020 under the Horizon 2020 programme (AI for health imaging), available here: <https://ec.europa.eu/info/funding-tenders/opportunities/portal/screen/opportunities/topic-details/dt-tds-05-2020>; also the call IMI2–2019–18–01 (Central repository of digital pathology slides to support the development of artificial intelligence tools), available here: <https://ec.europa.eu/info/funding-tenders/opportunities/portal/screen/opportunities/topic-details/imi2-2019-18-01>.

5 Privacy issues in eHealth and mHealth apps

Beatriz Sainz-de-Abajo, Isabel de la Torre-Díez, Susel Góngora-Alonso and Miguel López-Coronado

1. Introduction

In the last 30 years, there has been a significant advance in the fields of telecommunications and information technology (IT). This has resulted in improvement in mobile communications and wireless networks. The explosive growth of mobile communications offers new hope for the promotion of quality healthcare.[1]

With millions of smartphones and tablets in use worldwide, these devices can be a valuable tool in healthcare management.[2] 5G, a new generation of mobile broadband (MBB) network, working in different countries, has opened opportunities for innovative means of healthcare delivery.[3] In the field of health, it is vital to obtain the right information at the right time, regardless of time and location.[4]

eHealth uses advanced and reliable communication techniques to deliver signals, and it is important to have a good understanding of the systems involved.[5] Advances in microelectronics and integrated circuits, wireless communication and low-power smart sensors have enabled the realization of a wireless body area network (WBAN), which transmits our health data.[6] Remote monitoring of these biomedical signals allows attention to a physically distant patient.[7]

In the field of telecommunications, there has been an evolution: from voice services to data services.[8] The sale of mobile phones, especially smartphones, has skyrocketed.[9] They are devices with new features capable of taking full advantage of 3G, 4G and 5G networks,[10] and that combine a large number of transistors, powerful GPUs and a compact design.[11,12,13,14]

The smartphone market has created a new software industry based on the creation of applications for smartphones,[15] which leads to endless opportunities for socioeconomic development. This industry has expanded exponentially and is in constant progression.[16] And it is estimated that by 2026, the mHealth applications market will reach $236 billion.[17] All of these apps are included in what is known as mHealth or mobile health, defined by the World Health Organization (WHO) as "medical and public health practice supported by mobile devices, such as mobile phones, patient monitoring devices, personal digital assistants, and other wireless devices".[18]

However, in this race to be the first in developing and releasing a new app, some aspects have not been adequately considered. Every wireless system is sensitive to privacy and security issues.[19] Privacy and security are of primary importance, especially with those apps concerned with personal and non-transferable data, such as health apps, which store an electronic register of the patient´s health or other information relative to their health.

In accordance with the definitions adopted by the National Committee on Vital and Health Statistics (NCVHS) of the department of Health and Human Services of the United States of America,[20] "Privacy is an individual's right to control the acquisition, uses, or disclosures of his or her identifiable health data. Confidentiality, which is closely related, refers to the obligations of those who receive information to respect the privacy interests of those to whom the data relates. Security is altogether different. It refers to physical, technological, or administrative safeguards or tools used to protect identifiable health data from unwarranted access or disclosure".

On the part of the EU General Data Protection Regulation (GDPR), in relation to the security of personal data, it also indicates the following: "The personal data that you collect should be pseudonymised and/or encrypted. Although it is central to protecting data and can help protect the privacy and security of personal data, pseudonymisation has its limits, which is why the GDPR also mentions encryption. Organisations that fail to do this will face severe disciplinary action from data protection authorities".[21]

One of the conclusions of the study[22] undertaken by IBM and the Ponemon Institute demonstrated that 50% of the biggest mobile app development companies have no security budget and are not taking the necessary precautions to protect the mobile apps being developed for their customers. The study shows that the number of cyberattacks related to the security of mobile devices continues to increase. We must be careful when connecting to open public Wi-Fi networks. Mobile device data is exposed and vulnerable to hacker attacks.

Doctors and patients are adopting mobile technology at a faster rate than that at which the providers can protect their security and privacy, converting this into a significant problem because companies are giving more importance to release dates and user experience, ignoring security issues, which opens doors to the access of confidential business and personal information by hackers and cyber delinquents. During the development of mobile applications, aspects such as the usefulness for the end user are put above security and privacy. Security is often compromised by customer requirements. "The race to release" is the principal reason for why the apps contain vulnerable code. Of those companies which currently analyse vulnerabilities prior to launching apps in the marketplace, only 15% test them with the necessary frequency to check that they are safe and effective.

The phenomenon of Bring Your Own Device[23] (BYOD) is becoming increasingly popular; indeed, in many cases it is becoming a necessity for those health-related companies and organizations that have finally accepted this approach, given the ease and potential savings which go with allowing the employees to take their own devices to work, despite the potential risks.[24,25]

Disterer defines BYOD in his work[26] as “a megatrend occurring in IT that requires sweeping changes to the way devices are used in the workplace [. . .]. It is about end users being able to use the compute and communication devices they choose to increase productivity and mobility”.

These personal devices access the information and use the corporate network. There is no control over the applications used by the employee for private use, and there is no separation between personal and professional information within the device. For all this, it is necessary to establish adequate security policies and mechanisms. The doctors and medical students are not aware of the security and privacy aspects of the mobile applications that they use daily.[27] This is a problem that affects us globally.

Additionally, in the field of mobile health, a great amount of work needs to be done to overcome the legal and cultural differences relating to privacy between different countries and regions of the world. Here, where two fields are converging – doctors and telecommunications – the regulators are fighting to stay up to speed. There is a problem, and policies and regulations are being developed to face the challenges of personal security and privacy in the era of smartphones and mobile applications.[28]

In the paper “The role of privacy protection in healthcare information systems adoption”,[29] the need to adopt systems to protect the privacy of data in mobile health applications is analysed. Safeguarding the privacy of patient data is the most important obstacle to overcome.[30,31] Although there are few investigations with respect to privacy and security rules for mobile health[32,33] there are many about specific privacy and security techniques, such as the authentication protocol for ubiquitous health monitoring systems.[34,35,36,37,38]

In this chapter, a revision of eHealth and mHealth privacy laws in developed countries is undertaken, centred on the European Union and the United States, with the aim of establishing the main aspects which should be taken into account by application developers.

2. Review of privacy laws in Europe and the United States

As mobile app usage grows in popularity, the number of app downloads increases, based on a study made in 2019 by Ian Blair.[39]

The patient must have the last word concerning the use of their health data. In the GDPR – Data Protection Impact Assessments – Art. 35,[40] we found that although there is no law, administrations and companies throughout the world that deal with huge quantities of data should be obligated to draw up a text called “impact evaluation”. This must be completed before the collection of data or massive use of information, in which it is analysed whether or not privacy norms would be respected, and how this would happen.

When one person gives their information to another, they should have previously been informed as to why the information was collected, how and where it will be used, in which files it will be stored and with what level of security. Once informed, the person consents to give this information, or not. Especially with health data,[41] express and written "explicit consent" must exist.[42] Their details can be seen by the entire medical team with the objective of finding a cure or palliative treatment, and professional confidentiality exists.

In the United States, the main law that applies to mHealth questions is the Health Insurance Portability and Accountability Act (HIPAA).[43] This law protects the privacy of information of digital health.[44] Another important law is section 5[45] of the Federal Trade Commission Act.[46] There is another significant law that only applies to minors of less than 13 years old – the Children's Online Privacy Protection Act (COPPA) of 1998,[47] which prohibits the collection of personal information about children without the express consent of their parents or legal guardians.

Regarding the fact that parents share information about their children online without their consent, there is a conflict. On the one hand, they are the guardians of their children's privacy;[48] and on the other hand, they are the narrators of their children's personal stories.[49]

In the EU, the GDPR (General Data Protection Regulation)[50] lays down rules relating to the protection of natural persons with regard to the processing of personal data and rules relating to the free movement of personal data. It protects fundamental rights and freedoms of natural persons, and in particular their right to the protection of personal data. The European Data Protection Regulation is applicable as of May 25, 2018 in all member states to harmonize data privacy laws across Europe. The privacy by default guarantees that the most stringent privacy settings are automatically applied to the incorporation of the client to a new service. This means that customer, as a user, is not requested to manually tamper with privacy settings as to achieve maximum personal data protection. In addition, automatically applied privacy settings must include a time-shift function, ensuring that personal information will be kept only for the period of time necessary to provide on-board service. Finally, and taking into account social networks, GDPR protects personal data access from an indefinite number of individuals.[51]

Regarding the security of the processing, adequate technical and organizational measures must be implemented to guarantee a level of security appropriate to the risk, such as: 1) the ability to guarantee the confidentiality, integrity, availability and continuous resistance of the processing systems and services; 2) the ability to restore the availability and access to personal data in a timely manner in the event of a physical or technical incident; and 3) a process to periodically test and assess the effectiveness of technical and organizational measures to ensure the safety of processing.[52]

In this way, when assessing the appropriate level of security, account shall be taken in particular of the risks that are presented by processing, in particular from accidental or unlawful destruction, loss, alteration, unauthorised disclosure of, or access to personal data transmitted, stored or otherwise processed.

While the Regulation applies mainly to the protection of natural persons, organizations may also benefit from knowing what personal data they have available to them and where they are located. On the other hand, there is an obligation to protect personal data, which will be the responsibility of the Data Protection Officer (DPO), designated by the controller and the processor.[53]

3. Privacy and security challenges in health apps

It is the responsibility of the consumer to protect their own information using passwords to open the device and further passwords within the apps to protect their private information. In order to reduce the security risks of health applications, a verification process is needed on the part of the app stores to detect malware in applications.

The confidential information collected by mobile health apps may be accessible by the patients, doctors, family members or scientific investigators, but it might also be shared with third parties, such as advertisers,[54] raising grave doubts about the confidentiality of the consumers' information.

Given the increasing use of Electronic Health Registers (EHRs) and electronic health care (eHealth), confidentiality, integrity and availability of consumer information are the main problems today for health service providers in terms of data security and privacy.[55]

According to Kumar,[56] "The health industry sector has been confronted by the need to manage the big data being produced by various sources, which are well known for producing high volumes of heterogeneous data".

As these systems manage personal and health-related data, protection of privacy is paramount.[57] For this reason, it is important that the data is secure, avoiding risks that could affect the privacy of people and the possible malicious use of that data.

How can this challenge be addressed from a technical point of view? This technological challenge involves redefining the architecture of communication networks – the technological infrastructures – not only to guarantee the current services and those being released but also those which will appear in the near future.[58]

The lack of standardized terms and of security involved in mHealth applications is a great barrier to their generalized use. The problems of security in mobile health applications are rising due to the lack of directives or standards in the development of applications. The Open Web Application Security Project (OWASP)[59] brings together in one list the ten security failures most commonly exploited in mobile applications, with the aim of bringing awareness to security and identifying said risks.[60]

In the insights guide "Evaluating Mhealth Adoption Barriers: Privacy and Regulation",[61] Kane stated that certain health applications make use of the Internet, connecting via Bluetooth sensors such as wearables or those integrated into the smartphone itself, which follow and monitor the health of the patient or the activities of a consumer. Health monitoring of the patient can take place in real time, with or without the participation of the patient or their constant approval. The author concentrated on information collected by health applications, which have open access to the patient and at the same time share information with others. The data collected by such health applications not only contains detailed information about the health of the person, but also about their habits and their location and movements, which may possibly put sensitive information about that person at risk, if that information becomes available.

McCarthy[62] highlighted the principal preoccupations relating to consumer information, which is generally poorly protected in health applications. In a study of 43 health and fitness applications, only 74% of the free apps and 60% of the paying apps had a privacy policy, available either within the app or on the website of the developer. However, only 25% of the free apps and 48% of the paying apps informed the consumers about the privacy policy. In addition, none of the free apps and only a few of the paying ones encrypted the information that the consumers introduced to be able to use the app. Encryption or cyphering is the conversion of information to a form which cannot be easily understood by non-authorized people. Hence, those health apps which do not encrypt consumer information suppose a risk to data privacy.

In a recent study[63] from the Privacy Rights Clearinghouse, Nasiri has also informed about the risks to privacy of information in health apps. It was found that many consumers use apps to interact with their health providers, such as undertaking monitoring to deal with symptoms and other information. He found that information shared with others can lead to security risks and reported that the investigators undertook a survey of 20 of the 23 most popular free health apps, and found that 50% of them sent information to third parties and 39% sent information to non-identified parties and with no type of encryption. It was found that paying apps were a little more secure in comparison to their free counterparts.

Data security breaches in the health sector have become common according to Figg and Kam,[64] with many providers of online mHealth, including doctors and scientific investigators, able to see a patient's clinical records without the knowledge of said patient. The authors also reported that the breaches in data security in the health sector are a threat to privacy which could lead to medical identity theft.

The World Privacy Forum describes medical identity theft as a situation in which one person uses the identity of another, such as their name or Medicare number, without the knowledge or consent of that person, which could affect the security of many consumers.[65,66]

According to the Federal Trade Commission, there were around 18,000 cases of medical identity theft between 2005 and 2011, giving rise to certain benefits for the delinquent. They can steal records and sell them on the black market; they can alter patient records just for amusement such as, for example, adding false entries relating to a diagnostic, blood type, allergies to certain medicines or other health information. Victims who have their medical files altered by delinquents could receive the wrong treatment, which may have disastrous consequences for their health, possibly leading to death.

Confidential medical data is exposed to threats such as hacking.[67] Fraud and identity theft caused by security failures could also lead to a breakdown in confidence between consumers and health providers. However, a safe mHealth environment, which generates confidence between consumers and health service providers, must adopt a regulation or standard to increase security and protect against any unauthorized attack.[68]

Storage of information in the cloud brings with it a raft of new problems, above all when it concerns the availability of services and the security and privacy of consumers.[69] Security problems are critical when a medical care provider decides to use a management system of healthcare establishments based in the cloud, because moving the patient information signifies that their files will end up housed in the servers of the service provider.[70]

According to Zhang and Liu,[71] by moving patient information to the cloud, health providers are leaving this information open to various external risks because the data is available through the Internet. Both the cloud service providers and the health service providers understand the consequences in relation to the risks to the privacy of sensitive consumer information. The health professional must guarantee the security of the patient information, ensuring that the platform in the cloud has all the necessary security measures in place.[72] The cloud provider is responsible for protecting the security and privacy of this information, providing the necessary security to avoid external attacks that may steal or erase the data.

A promising study explains that to protect an mHealth app against a wide range of attacks with negligible overload, it would be necessary to apply a Security Module Layer (SML) that implements the security-check modules, and a System Interface Layer (SIL) that interfaces SML to the Android operating system (OS).[73]

Cybercriminals are looking to exploit the inexperience and credulity of the user as well as the security failings of the very system and its applications. Protecting the security is very important and becoming a top priority for many organizations.[74] Understanding that the vulnerabilities and security failings of the platforms are beyond the control of the mobile device application developers, there are other aspects, such as the security of the very apps which they are developing, where the responsibility must lie with them.

Different methodologies exist, their maxim being "security by design", which allows for the evaluation of app security – such as the case of the OWASP,[75] which has as their objective to identify dangers related to the security of mobile devices and provide the necessary controls in development to reduce the impact and the probability of exploitation. These methodologies are independent of the platform for which the application is developed, and it is equally recommended that the guidelines be followed and controls put in place during development of another platform, above all if it involves any sort of application that manages sensitive health data.

4. Conclusions

Smartphone users download eHealth and mHealth applications for medical care thanks to their affordability and efficiency. Many of these applications are free. The problem is that these applications use confidential data. This involves a security and privacy risk. We do not know the use made with the data. None of the operating systems guarantee data security. Vulnerability news is ongoing despite security mechanisms. User acceptance will come with improved data security associated with eHealth and mHealth applications.

First of all, we must highlight the important technological revolution that we are experiencing today, and as with any self-respecting revolution, it has three characteristics. Whatever we do, it is now unstoppable; the revolution will follow its course. It is transformational, as the way we do things after the revolution will be completely different. And finally, there will be winners and losers. The first one to accept the inevitable and take the necessary steps to adapt will be the winners, and here the health industry is not lagging behind.

The health and well-being industry is conscious of the enormous potential for growth that exists in the smartphone and wearable market in society today, given the huge number of opportunities which are offered by socioeconomic development – and with that, the level of penetration of mobile applications in the day-to-day life of any person, both at a professional level or in another field (leisure, banking, health).

The huge importance that mobile applications related to mHealth are gaining must be highlighted, being the third category of highest growth, just behind games and services. More and more people are worried about their health and well-being, and mobile apps are playing a fundamental role.

The success of these apps is based on the fact that mobile devices these days can facilitate the job of collecting patient information in clinical tests and others. They can help in the early detection of outbreaks of illness related to environmental exposure or infectious agents, thanks to their numerous sensors. They also aid communication with health professionals, giving rise to a new form of relationship between doctor and patient and offering multiple benefits for both parties, from time saving during the consultation to the improvement in adherence to therapy and the monitoring of chronically ill patients.

However, in this race to win the health category and join in the digital health revolution, haste is no good thing, and being the first to develop and release a new app can lead to a lack of adequate consideration of certain aspects. Amongst them are privacy and security, which in this case have a particular importance, especially in those health applications which store the patient's electronic records or various information relative to their state of health.

It is such that amongst the huge quantity of data that is managed daily, medical information is a very juicy prize for cybercriminals, given that they can earn up to 10 times more money in the black market than with credit card details. If we add to this that the doctors and patients are adopting mobile technology faster than the providers are able to protect the privacy and security of these apps, security becomes a significant problem. The companies give priority to the release date and user experience without taking proper care of security, and the new, small software companies with novice programmers take no notice of it all.

Acknowledgments

This research has been partially supported by European Commission and the Ministry of Industry, Energy and Tourism under the project AAL-20125036 named "Wetake Care: ICT- based Solution for (Self-) Management of Daily Living".

Notes

1 Vital Wave Consulting, 'MHealth for Development: The Opportunity of Mobile Technology for Healthcare in the Developing World' (Washington, DC and Berkshire, UK: UN Foundation-Vodafone Foundation Partnership, 2009).

2 Borja Martínez-Pérez, Isabel de la Torre-Díez and Miguel López-Coronado, 'Mobile Health Applications for the Most Prevalent Conditions by the World Health Organization: Review and Analysis' (2013) 15 *Journal of Medical Internet Research* e120.

3 Basant Kumar, S.P. Singh and Anand Mohan, 'Emerging Mobile Communication Technologies for Health' (2010) *2010 International Conference on Computer and Communication Technology, ICCCT-2010.*

4 Mehdia Ajana El Khaddar and others, 'Emerging Wireless Technologies in E-Health: Trends, Challenges, and Framework Design Issues' (2012) *Proceedings of 2012 International Conference on Multimedia Computing and Systems, ICMCS 2012* 440.

5 Chin Feng Lin, 'Mobile Telemedicine: A Survey Study' (2012) 36 *Journal of Medical Systems* 511.

6 Sana Ullah and others, 'A Comprehensive Survey of Wireless Body Area Networks on PHY, MAC, and Network Layers Solutions' (2012) 36 *Journal of Medical Systems* 1065.

7 R. Gupta and M. Mitra, 'Wireless Electrocardiogram Transmission in ISM Band: An Approach Towards Telecardiology' (2014) 38 *Journal of Medical Systems* 90.

8 Neil Coleman, 'Mapping Subscribers for Better Mobile Networks' (2013) 12 *GEO: Connexion* 43.

9 Fabrizio Bert and others, 'Smartphones and Health Promotion: A Review of the Evidence' (2014) 38 *Journal of Medical Systems* 9995.

10 Farid Touati and Rohan Tabish, 'U-Healthcare System: State-of-the-Art Review and Challenges' (2013) 37 *Journal of Medical Systems* 9949.

11 Z. Xiao and F.E. Camino, 'The Fabrication of Carbon Nanotube Field-Effect Transistors with Semiconductors as the Source and Drain Contact Materials' (2009) 20 *Nanotechnology*.

12 Kenji Nakatani, 'New Technology Trends in Touch Panel Sensing' (2012) *Proceedings of the International Display Workshops*.

13 A. Benfdila and others, 'On the Drain Current Saturation in Carbon Nanotube Field Effect Transistors' (2010) 5 (3) *Nano* 161–165.

14 Matthias Bremer and others, 'The TV in Your Pocket: Development of Liquid-Crystal Materials for the New Millennium' (2013) 52 *Angewandte Chemie* 8880–8896.

15 Cynthia Kratzke and Carolyn Cox, 'Smartphone Technology and Apps Smartphone Technology and Apps: Rapidly Changing Health Promotion' (2012) 15 *International Electronic Journal of Health Education* 72–82.

16 J. Clement, 'Apple App Store: Quarterly Growth of Available Apps as 2015–2019' <www.statista.com/statistics/185722/apple-app-store-quarterly-growth-of-available-apps/> accessed 22 January 2020.

17 Research and Markets, 'MHealth Apps Market to Reach $236 Billion by 2026, Growing at a CAGR of 44.7% Over 2019–2026' (2019) <www.globenewswire.com/news-release/2019/08/21/1904780/0/en/mHealth-Apps-Market-to-Reach-236-Billion-by-2026-Growing-at-a-CAGR-of-44-7-Over-2019-2026.html> accessed 22 January 2020.

18 World Health Organization, 'MHealth: New Horizons for Health through Mobile Technologies' (2011) <www.who.int/goe/publications/goe_mhealth_web.pdf?ua=1> accessed 22 March 2020.
19 Hairong Yan and others, 'Wireless Sensor Network Based E-Health System – Implementation and Experimental Results' (2010) 56 (4) *IEEE Transactions on Consumer Electronics* 2288–2295.
20 Simon P. Cohn, 'Privacy and Confidentiality in the Nationwide Health Information Network', (*National Commitee on Vital and Health Statistics*, 2006).
21 Luke Irwin, 'The GDPR: What Exactly Is Personal Data?' <www.itgovernance.eu/blog/en/the-gdpr-what-exactly-is-personal-data> accessed 22 January 2020.
22 Ponemon Institute, '2017 Cost of Data Breach Study: Global Overview' (*IBM Security*, 2018), 47 <www.ibm.com/security/data-breach> accessed 4 April 2020.
23 Georg Disterer and Carsten Kleiner, 'BYOD Bring Your Own Device' (2013) 9 *Procedia Technology* 43.
24 The Wall Street Journal – Deloitte, 'Security and Privacy in Mobile Health' (2013) <http://deloitte.wsj.com/cio/2013/08/06/security-and-privacy-in-mobile-health/> accessed 22 March 2020.
25 Jennifer E. Moyer, 'Managing Mobile Devices in Hospitals: A Literature Review of BYOD Policies and Usage' (2013) 13 *Journal of Hospital Librarianship* 197 <www.tandfonline.com/doi/citedby/10.1080/15323269.2013.798768?scroll=top&needAccess=true>.
26 Disterer and Kleiner (n 23).
27 Elizabeth C. Whipple, Kacy L. Allgood and Elizabeth M. Larue, 'Third-Year Medical Students' Knowledge of Privacy and Security Issues Concerning Mobile Devices' (2012) 34 *Medical Teacher* e532.
28 Vodafone Global Enterprise, 'Evaluating MHealth Adoption Barriers: Privacy and Regulation – Protecting Your Patients Privacy in a Mobile World' (2013) <http://mhealthregulatorycoalition.org/wp-content/uploads/2013/01/VodafoneGlobalEnterprise-mHealth-Insights-Guide-Evaluating-mHealth-Adoption-Privacy-and-Regulation.pdf> accessed 27 March 2020.
29 Chien Lung Hsu, Ming Ren Lee and Chien Hui Su, 'The Role of Privacy Protection in Healthcare Information Systems Adoption' (2013) 37 *Journal of Medical Systems* 9966.
30 Benjamin P. Rosenbaum, 'Radio Frequency Identification (RFID) in Health Care: Privacy and Security Concerns Limiting Adoption' (2014) 38 *Journal of Medical Systems* 19.
31 Hays Green, 'Strategies for Safeguarding Security of Mobile Computing' (2013) 67 *Healthcare Financial Management* 88.
32 Syeda Uzma Gardazi, Arshad Ali Shahid and Christine Salimbene, 'HIPAA and QMS Based Architectural Requirements to Cope with the OCR Audit Program' (2012) *Proceedings – 2012 3rd FTRA International Conference on Mobile, Ubiquitous, and Intelligent Computing, MUSIC 2012*.
33 David D. Luxton, Robert A. Kayl and Matthew C. Mishkind, 'MHealth Data Security: The Need for HIPAA-Compliant Standardization' (2012) 18 *Telemedicine and e-Health* 284.
34 Chang Kuo Yeh, Hung Ming Chen and Jung Wen Lo, 'An Authentication Protocol for Ubiquitous Health Monitoring Systems' (2013) 33 *Journal of Medical and Biological Engineering* 415.
35 Jiankang Ren, Guowei Wu and Lin Yao, 'A Sensitive Data Aggregation Scheme for Body Sensor Networks Based on Data Hiding' (2013) 17 *Personal and Ubiquitous Computing* 1317.
36 Xuelei Li and others, 'Secure Privacy-Preserving Biometric Authentication Scheme for Telecare Medicine Information Systems' (2014) 38 *Journal of Medical Systems* 139.
37 Chin Ling Chen and others, 'A Privacy Authentication Scheme Based on Cloud for Medical Environment' (2014) 38 *Journal of Medical Systems* 143.

38 Jung Tae Kim, 'Enhanced Secure Authentication for Mobile RFID Healthcare System in Wireless Sensor Networks' (2012) *Computer Applications for Database, Education, and Ubiquitous Computing*.

39 Ian Blair, 'Mobile App Download and Usage Statistics (2019)' (2019) <https://buildfire.com/app-statistics/> accessed 27 February 2020.

40 EU. GDPR, 'Article 35. "Data Protection Impact Assessment"' <www.privacy-regulation.eu/en/article-35-data-protection-impact-assessment-GDPR.htm> accessed 29 March 2020.

41 EU. GDPR, 'Article 9. "Processing of Special Categories of Personal Data"' <www.privacy-regulation.eu/en/article-9-processing-of-special-categories-of-personal-data-GDPR.htm> accessed 22 January 2020.

42 EU. GDPR, 'GDPR: Guidance on Consent Requirements' (2018) <www.cooley.com/news/insight/2018/2018-03-09-gdpr-guidance-on-consent-requirements> accessed 22 January 2020.

43 Public Law, 'Health Insurance Portability and Accountability Act of 1996. No. 104–191, 110 Stat.'

44 Barbara L. Filkins and others, 'Privacy and Security in the Era of Digital Health: What Should Translational Researchers Know and Do about It?' (2016) 8 *American Journal of Translational Research* 1560.

45 Federal Trade Commission, 'Act. 15 U.S.C.'

46 FTC Staff Report, 'Mobile Privacy Disclosures: Building Trust Through Transparency' (2013) <www.ftc.gov/sites/default/files/ documents/reports/mobile-privacy-disclosures-building-trust- through-transparency-federal-trade-commission-staff-report/ 130201mobileprivacyreport.pdf> accessed 22 January 2020.

47 Public Law, 'Children's Online Privacy Protection Act of 1998 (COPPA). No. 105–277, 112 Stat.'

48 Timothy Phoenix Oblad and Elizabeth Trejos-Castillo, 'Children's Online Privacy Protection Act', in Marilyn Coleman and Lawrence Ganong (eds.), *The Social History of the American Family: An Encyclopedia* (Thousand Oaks, CA: SAGE Publications, Inc, 2014).

49 Stacey Steinberg, 'Sharenting: Children's Privacy in the Age of Social Media' (2017) 66 *Emory Law Journal* 839 <https://ssrn.com/abstract=2711442>.

50 EU. GDPR, 'General Data Protection Regulation (GDPR)' (2016) <https://gdpr-info.eu/> accessed 22 January 2020.

51 Eirini Mougiakou and Maria Virvou, 'Based on GDPR Privacy in UML: Case of e-Learning Program' (2018) *2017 8th International Conference on Information, Intelligence, Systems and Applications, IISA 2017*.

52 EU. GDPR, 'General Data Protection Regulation (GDPR)' (n 50).

53 A. Skendzic, B. Kovacic and E. Tijan, 'General Data Protection Regulation – Protection of Personal Data in an Organisation' (2018) *2018 41st International Convention on Information and Communication Technology, Electronics and Microelectronics, MIPRO 2018 – Proceedings*.

54 Vodafone Global Enterprise (n 28).

55 Jin Wang and others, 'A Research on Security and Privacy Issues for Patient Related Data in Medical Organization System' (2013) 7 *International Journal of Security and its Applications* 287.

56 Sunil Kumar and Maninder Singh, 'Big Data Analytics for Healthcare Industry: Impact, Applications, and Tools' (2018) 2 *Big Data Mining and Analytics* 48.

57 Milica Milutinovic and Bart De Decker, 'Privacy-Preserving Data Management in EHealth Systems' (2013) 9 *Procedia Technology* 1085 <https://doi.org/10.1016/j.protcy.2013.12.121%0A>.

58 Bahar Farahani and others, 'Towards Fog-Driven IoT EHealth: Promises and Challenges of IoT in Medicine and Healthcare' (2018) 78 *Future Generation Computer Systems* 659 <https://doi.org/10.1016/j.future.2017.04.036>.

59 OWASP, 'OWASP Mobile Security Project' (2015) <www.owasp.org/index.php/OWASP_Mobile_Security_Project#tab=Top_10_Mobile_Risks> accessed 22 January 2020.

60 Hadi Kharrazi and others, 'Mobile Personal Health Records: An Evaluation of Features and Functionality' (2012) 81 *International Journal of Medical Informatics* 579.
61 Vodafone Global Enterprise (n 28).
62 Michael McCarthy, 'Experts Warn on Data Security in Health and Fitness Apps' (2013) 347 *BMJ* (Clinical research ed.).
63 HealthCareBusinessTech, 'Mobile Health Apps Create Privacy Risk, Study Says' (2014) <www.healthcarebusinesstech.com/mobile-health-apps-privacy/> accessed 27 March 2020.
64 William Douglas Figg and Hwee Joo Kam, 'Medical Information Security' (2011) 5 *International Journal of Security (IJS)* 22.
65 ibid.
66 Pam Dixon, 'Medical Identity Theft – The Information Crime That Can Kill You' (2006) <www.worldprivacyforum.org/2006/05/report-medical-identity-theft-the-information-crime-that-can-kill-you/> accessed 9 February 2020.
67 M. Ahmed, M. Ahamad and T. Jaiswal, 'Augmenting Security and Accountability within the EHealth Exchange' (2014) *IBM Journal of Research and Development* <https://doi.org/10.1147/JRD.2013.2288068>.
68 B. Faudree and M. Ford, 'Security and Privacy in Mobile Health' (*CIO Journal*, 2013) <www.webcitation.org/6tp8fjE01> accessed 30 March 2020.
69 Qijun Gu and Mina Guirguis, *Secure Mobile Cloud Computing and Security Issues*, vol 9781461432 (2013).
70 John D. Piette and others, 'A Preliminary Study of a Cloud-Computing Model for Chronic Illness Self-Care Support in an Underdeveloped Country' (2011) 40 *American Journal of Preventive Medicine* 629.
71 Rui Zhang and Ling Liu, 'Security Models and Requirements for Healthcare Application Clouds' (2010) *Proceedings – 2010 IEEE 3rd International Conference on Cloud Computing, CLOUD 2010.*
72 Joel J.P.C. Rodrigues and others, 'Analysis of the Security and Privacy Requirements of Cloud-Based Electronic Health Records Systems' (2013) 15 *Journal of Medical Internet Research* e186.
73 Muzammil Hussain and others, 'A Security Framework for MHealth Apps on Android Platform' (2018) 75 *Computers and Security* 191.
74 Sahar Al-Dhahri, Manar Al-Sarti and Azrilah Abdul, 'Information Security Management System' (2017) 158 *International Journal of Computer Applications* 29.
75 OWASP (n 59).

Section 2

A critical assessment of the GDPR's regulatory solutions

6 Regulating non-personal data in the age of Big Data

Bart van der Sloot

1. Introduction

The right to privacy has been included in national constitutions for centuries, with the distinction between the private and the public domain, the sanctity of the body and the secrecy of communication as core pillars of constitutional democracies around the world. After World War II, a number of human rights instruments were drawn up, such as the Universal Declaration of Human Rights,[1] the International Covenant on Civil and Political Human Rights[2] and the European Convention on Human Rights (ECHR).[3] Each of those included a specific article on the protection of the right to privacy, guaranteeing the respect for every individual's private life, family life, home and communication.

Informational privacy is an uncontroversial element of the right to privacy. Still, the right to privacy traditionally only covers information that is either private (falling under the protection of communicational secrecy) or sensitive (falling under the protection of private life). Privacy does not apply, or applies only to a limited extent, to the processing of public or insensitive data. In addition, when processing of personal information only has a minor effect on a person's private life, such would not be said to pass the threshold of the so-called *de minimis rule*, which is formalised in article 35 § 3 ECHR, providing that the European Court of Human Rights (ECtHR) should declare inadmissible any individual application if the applicant has not suffered a significant disadvantage.

Such logic has been applied in the context of data processing throughout the ECtHR's history. For example, when the European Commission of Human Rights (ECmHR) was faced with a person who felt that a photo taken of his vehicle violated his right to privacy, as protected under Article 8 ECHR, the Commission declared the claim inadmissible:

> Afin de déterminer dans des cas similaires l'étendue de la garantie accordée par l'article 8 contre les ingérences des autorités publiques, la Commission examine si la prise de photographies constitue une intrusion dans la sphère privée d'un individu (par exemple lorsqu'elles sont prises à son domicile),

> si les photographies se réfèrent à des événements d'ordre privé ou public, et si elles sont destinées à servir à un usage limité ou susceptibles d'être portées à la connaissance du public. En l'espèce, la Commission relève que la photographie dont se plaint le requérant a été prise sur la voie publique, alors qu'il circulait en voiture, dans un but de preuve et d'identification. Rien n'indique que la photographie ait été portée à la connaissance du public ni utilisée à d'autres fins que celle des poursuites dont le requérant a fait l'objet. Faisant application des critères exposés ci-dessus, la Commission arrive à la conclusion qu'il n'y a pas eu ingérence dans la vie privée du requérant.[4]

With the rise of databases in which large numbers of insensitive and public data were included, both the United States,[5] a number of European countries[6] and the Council of Europe[7] adopted specific data protection laws in the 1970s. The novelty of these instruments was that they provided protection to personal information that was not necessarily private or sensitive; they also covered the processing of data concerning, for example, the number of dogs owned by a person, her place of birth, whether she has a drivers licence, etc. The material scope of the right to data protection is not dependent on the existence of individual harm, but determined by the question of whether the data can be used to identify a person. 'Do you see that man there, with the black hat on, next to the streetlight', is considered personal data, even if identification does not have any effect on that person's private life or affects him in any significant way.

In contrast to human rights instruments, data protection regimes, such as the General Data Protection Regulation (GDPR), do not only provide protection to individual interests but typically aim at reconciling two interests, as is exemplified by Article 1 of that Regulation, specifying:

> 1. This Regulation lays down rules relating to the protection of natural persons with regard to the processing of personal data and rules relating to the free movement of personal data. 2. This Regulation protects fundamental rights and freedoms of natural persons and in particular their right to the protection of personal data. 3. The free movement of personal data within the Union shall be neither restricted nor prohibited for reasons connected with the protection of natural persons with regard to the processing of personal data.

The goal of the European Union (EU) data protection framework lies in its ambition to take away restrictions for data processing operations, while at the same time assuring a high level of protection for data subjects. One of the problems that existed before the EU data protection framework had been put in place – in the form of the predecessor of the GDPR, the 1995 Data Protection Directive – was that each EU country adopted its own data protection standards. This hampered international data transfers and data-driven activities because an international organisation had to comply with multiple, sometimes conflicting, data protection requirements. By laying down a common data protection regime applicable throughout the EU, this problem is tackled, while at the same time providing protection to the interests of data subjects.

Two important developments have occurred since the 1970s.

First, the right to privacy and the right to data protection have grown apart. While initially, the right to data protection and the various data protection regimes were directly linked to and seen as a part of the right to privacy, at least within the EU, the right to data protection is now seen as a related though separate right. Inter alia, the Charter of Fundamental Rights of the European Union includes one article on the right to privacy and another on the right to data protection,[8] and while the Data Protection Directive from 1995 still held that the Directive provided protection in particular to the right to privacy,[9] the document that replaced it – the General Data Protection Regulation from 2016 – stresses that the instrument intends to provide further rules on the right to data protection, not the right to privacy, and has rephrased generally accepted terms such as 'privacy by design', 'privacy policy', 'privacy impact assessment' and 'privacy officer' to 'data protection by design', 'data protection policy', 'data protection impact assessment' and 'data protection officer'.[10]

Second, the material scope of data protection regimes has grown considerably over time. The Council of Europe adopted two Resolutions for data processing in 1973 and 1974, one for the private and one for the public sector, which defined 'personal information' simply as information relating to individuals (physical persons). Here, the individual and subjective element in the definition of personal data is still prominent. Already by 1981, however, in the subsequent Convention for the Protection of Individuals with regard to Automatic Processing of Personal Data, adopted by the Council of Europe, 'personal data' were defined as any information relating to an identified or identifiable individual.[11] An 'identifiable person' is an individual who at the present cannot be identified through the data, but in the future might be. This means that data that are not yet linked to an individual, but could be with relative ease in the future, already fall within the scope of the right to data protection. Under the subsequent Data Protection Directive, the scope of personal data was broadened, among others by including not only direct but also indirect identifiable data, and under the General Data Protection Regulation the definition was widened even further.

The reason for widening the scope of data protection regimes is that even data remotely connected to an individual can increasingly be used to gain insights on that person. While companies and governmental organizations used to be able to link data to a specific person only when they had direct identifiers, such as a name or an address, they are increasingly capable of connecting two or three indirect identifiers that in themselves do not refer to a specific person but might when combined. To accommodate this change, the concept of personal data has been broadened over time, to ensure that citizens are protected when organisations process these indirectly identifiable data. Some have suggested that the definition of personal data is now so broad that potentially all data could fall under its scope. Others have suggested that given that the technological capacities will only grow, it might be easier to simply let go of the notion of 'personal data' and regulate 'data' instead.[12]

Interestingly, the European Union has recently taken a contrary approach. Instead of broadening the scope of 'personal data' or accepting that the difference between personal data and non-personal data may be increasingly redundant, it has emphasised the polarity between the two types of data. In 2018, it adopted a Regulation on the transfer of non-personal data that only aims at stimulating cross-border data processing, without providing any form of protection to citizens. Where human rights documents aim at the protection of the interests of citizens and data protection regimes aim at reconciling the interests of citizens and the interests of organisations processing personal data, the Regulation on non-personal data only aims at protecting the interests of the latter. Article 1 of that Regulation specifies:

> This Regulation aims to ensure the free flow of data other than personal data within the Union by laying down rules relating to data localisation requirements, the availability of data to competent authorities and the porting of data for professional users.[13]

The material provisions of the Regulation do not aim at restricting or laying down conditions for the processing or transfer of non-personal data but in contrast, prohibit any type of restriction or limitation in national laws on the availability, transfer and processing of non-personal data.

This chapter will question the logic behind this choice. It will do so in three steps. First, it will discuss the tension between the current legal paradigm, which is grounded in a static conceptualisation of data, and the technological reality, in which the status of data is constantly in flux (Section 2). Second, it will argue why the boundaries between personal data and non-personal data, between metadata and content data, between anonymous and identifying data and between non-sensitive and sensitive data is increasingly difficult to draw (Section 3). Third, it will suggest why the logic underpinning the distinction between the various legal categories of data may no longer be valid in the age of Big Data (Section 4). Finally, the conclusion to this chapter will discuss the implications of these three arguments for the regulation of data (Section 5).

Two caveats are important. First, this chapter will mainly refer to and draw from legal definitions and examples from European legislative instruments. Although there may be some elements particular to the European situation, by and large, legal instruments around the world are based on much of the same premises and categorisations. Second, when referring to Big Data, this chapter will describe those processes in most simplistic terms, for example explaining how complex data analytics and computational modelling through self-learning algorithms work by referring to data analysis and profiling based on two or three data points; in reality, the number is usually closer to 200 or 300 data points that are interrelated in various ways. Although data analytics is consequently infinitely more complex than explained here, in essence it operates similarly to the examples provided here in basic terms for the sake of clarity and accessibility.

2. The status of data is unstable

Law works with definitions, categories and delineations. The moment something is defined, there is discussion about borderline cases. Does owning a tank fall under the right of the people to keep and bear arms as provided by the Second Amendment to the United States Constitution? Is shouting 'Fire, fire!' in a movie theatre covered by the freedom of expression? Should the Church of the Flying Spaghetti Monster be considered a religious institution for the purposes of the freedom of religion? These discussions are intensified when legal definitions and categories play a role in contexts in which rapidly evolving technologies and unforeseen applications emerge. When confronted with such questions and legal complexities, courts have generally adopted a flexible approach and opted for a broad understanding of subjective rights.

For example, the European Court of Human Rights has suggested that the protection of the home does not only apply to traditional houses, but will cover new forms of housing that have emerged since the 1950s, when the Convention was adopted. Among others, the right to home is not limited to residences which are lawfully established and may be invoked by a person living in a flat for which the lease is in the name of another tenant; the right to privacy may also be applied to social housing occupied by the applicant as a tenant, even though the right of occupation under domestic law has come to an end, or to the occupation of a flat for thirty-nine years without any legal basis. The protection offered under Article 8 ECHR is not limited to traditional residences and includes, for example, caravans and other non-fixed abodes, including cabins and bungalows occupying land, regardless of whether such occupation is lawful under domestic law; it may also cover second homes or holiday homes and even a legal person, such as a company, can invoke the right to 'home' when its business premises is entered.[14]

The right to data protection is no exception in this respect. As touched upon in the introduction, both legislators and courts have been prepared to widen the scope of the various definitions relevant to the right to data protection and have usually adopted a flexible approach when determining whether a certain data processing operation, technique or application would fall under a certain category or not. Not only has the scope of 'personal data' been broadened over time, the European Court of Human Rights has also accepted that under certain conditions, the secrecy of communication not only applies to the content of communication but also to communication data and metadata, because it is

> not persuaded that the acquisition of related communications data is necessarily less intrusive than the acquisition of content. For example, the content of an electronic communication might be encrypted and, even

> if it were decrypted, might not reveal anything of note about the sender or recipient. The related communications data, on the other hand, could reveal the identities and geographic location of the sender and recipient and the equipment through which the communication was transmitted. In bulk, the degree of intrusion is magnified, since the patterns that will emerge could be capable of painting an intimate picture of a person through the mapping of social networks, location tracking, Internet browsing tracking, mapping of communication patterns, and insight into who a person interacted with.[15]

Although the various legal categories are interpreted flexibly, they still guide and provide a basic framework for the reasoning of courts. Some of the most important legal differentiations are:

- *Personal data and non-personal data:* As explained, the distinction between personal data and non-personal data, even although the amount and type of data that are said to fall under the first category have grown exponentially over the last few decades, is determinative for the question of whether the General Data Protection Regulation applies. When non-personal data are processed, not only is there no protection for citizens but countries are prohibited from laying down restrictions and conditions for the processing and transfer of non-personal data. This has implications for two subsets of non-personal data:
    - *Identifying and anonymous data:* All anonymous data are non-personal data but not all non-personal data are anonymous data. Anonymous data are data that were personal data at one point but are no longer so, while non-personal data can also refer to data that never were personal data. Anonymisation is the process of stripping a dataset, however big or small, from all relevant identifiers. If the sentence 'Beppe Grillo is a dangerous politician' is changed to 'Mr. X. is a dangerous politician', where no other data are processed that could indirectly identify Grillo, the data are considered non-personal.
    - *Individual and aggregated data:* Aggregated data are non-personal data when the group of the category, the *n*, is large enough. If statistical analysis about 100,000 persons results in the profile '70% of the men who drive a yellow car are left-wing voters', such would not be considered personal data.
- *Personal data and sensitive personal data:* There is a special regime under the GDPR for 'sensitive data', which are personal data revealing racial or ethnic origin, political opinions, religious or philosophical beliefs or trade union membership, and the processing of genetic data, biometric data for the purpose of uniquely identifying a natural person, data concerning health or data concerning a natural person's sex life or sexual orientation. Because these data have a particularly close link to the individual, the GDPR

specifies that processing them is in principle prohibited.[16] Although there are exceptions, these are more limited and restrictive than the grounds that can be used for legitimizing the processing of non-sensitive personal data.[17]

Content data and metadata: Though processing of data will only fall under the protection of private life if it significantly affects or harms a person, there is no threshold for the secrecy of communications. 'The content and form of the correspondence is irrelevant to the question of interference. [] There is no de minimis principle for interference to occur: opening one letter is enough.'[18] This means that even if a private email is opened that reads 'Honey, I'm having train delay and will arrive 30 minutes late', such would be considered an interference with the right to privacy under Article 8 of the European Convention on Human Rights. Although the ECtHR has stressed that there are situations in which metadata are collected in bulk and consequently fall under the scope of the right to privacy, such will only be the case when trails of metadata can be used to create detailed insights in the private life of a person. Consequently, most cases that concern the collection of metadata are not covered or are only marginally covered by Article 8 ECHR.[19] Likewise, metadata can fall under the protective scope of EU data protection law, though when they do, they enjoy different levels of protection.[20]

In short, legal regimes differentiate between types of data and relate to them different levels of protection. The processing of personal data is regulated, the processing of non-personal data is not; processing sensitive personal data is regulated more tightly than the processing of non-sensitive personal data; the bulk collection and use of metadata can fall under the scope of Article 8 ECHR, but only if it paints a clear picture of a person's private life, while the collection and use of content communication data will always be covered by the right to privacy; etc.

Such an approach to data regulation works well in a world where the nature of the data is relatively stable. This presupposition is challenged by Big Data processes. Big Data, for the purposes of this chapter, will be understood as data-driven processes that run through three phases.

1 Gathering: With respect to the volume of data, the basic philosophy of Big Data is 'the more, the merrier'. The larger the data set, the richer the patterns and correlations that can be found and the more valuable the conclusions that can be drawn therefrom. Relying on smart computers and self-learning algorithms, artificial intelligence can learn from continuous data input and become 'smarter'. Big Data can not only work on collected data, it can also produce new, inferred and probabilistic information. With respect to the variety of data sources, Big Data can be used to link an existing database to a database of another organization or to enrich it with information scraped from the Internet. Because Big Data revolves around analysing large amounts of data and detecting general patterns and high-level correlations, the quality of specific data is said to become less and less important – quantity over quality. Because data gathering and storage

is so cheap, data are often gathered without a predefined purpose; often, organisations determine only afterwards whether data represent any value to them and if so, to what use the data can be put.

2 Analysing: Once the data have been collected, they will be stored and analysed. The analysis of data is typically focussed on finding general characteristics, patterns and group profiles (meaning groups of people, of objects or of phenomena). General characteristics can be gained from data analytics – for example, how earthquakes typically evolve, from which indicators can predict an upcoming earthquake and determine which type of building is relatively unaffected by an earthquake. An important characteristic of Big Data is that the computer programs used for analysing data are typically based on statistics – statistical correlations are produced, not causal relations. These correlations typically involve probabilities. For example, an algorithm can predict that of the houses built with a concrete foundation, 70% will remain intact after an earthquake, while of the houses without a concrete foundation, this only holds true for 35%; or that people who place felt pads under the legs of their chairs and tables on average repay their loans more often than people who do not use felt pads. This also brings another point to the fore, namely that with Big Data, information about one aspect of life can be used for predictions about other aspects that are normally conceived as unrelated or belonging to a different domain of life. It may appear, for example, that the colour of a person's couch has a predictive value for her future health, that the music taste of a person's friends on Facebook says something about her sexual orientation, or that the name of a person's cat has a predictive value for her career path.

3 Usage: The correlations gained through data analytics can be used at a general level. For example, when policy choices are based on the prediction that in 20 years' time, the majority of the population will be obese; they can be used to make predictions about groups of people, events or objects, such as bridges, immigrants or men with red cars and big houses; and they can be applied to specific, individual cases, projecting the general profile on a specific case. Well known data-driven applications include mass surveillance, predictive policing, smart cities, living labs, social credit scoring and personalised advertisements.

What is important to underline for the purpose of this chapter is that the nature of the data in Big Data processes is not stable, but highly volatile. A dataset that contains ordinary personal data may be linked and enriched with another dataset and become a set that contains sensitive data; the data may then be aggregated or stripped from their identifiers and become non-personal data; subsequently, the data may be deanonymised or integrated in another dataset containing personal data. The subsequent steps may happen in a split second. For example, when discussing the groups and categories in Big Data processes, it has been suggested that

> in the big data era, groups are increasingly fluid, not only through their changing membership, but also because of the changing criteria for the

> group itself. A group, the criteria for grouping people and the membership of a group might change in a split second. The purpose for which the group is designed may also change from day to day to adapt to new insights gained from data analytics, and groups may be formed and dissolved through the push of a button.[21]

This means that it becomes increasingly difficult to work with and uphold the various categories used in the law. The question is not only what falls under the definition of 'personal data', 'metadata', 'anonymous data' or 'sensitive personal data'; the point is that even though it might theoretically be possible to determine the status of a datapoint at every specific moment in time, this would be undoable in practical terms and defeat its purpose in legal terms, because applying a level of protection to a dataset at a specific moment in time is fruitless if its status is changed within a split second, potentially even a number of times. To draw a comparison: The question is not whether a caravan can, under specific conditions, also be considered a home deserving protection under the right to privacy, Article 8 of the European Convention on Human Rights. The question is whether it makes sense to work with a concept of a home, as distinguished from non-homes, when a specific building is to be considered a home at one moment in time, a business premises the next second, then a sex shop, a hospital next, a home again the following second, and so forth.

3. The status of data is unclear

The definitions used in the current legal framework have an element of indeterminateness. For example, the definition of personal data contains reference to 'identifiable information', which means that data that at this moment in time do not identify anyone, but may do so in the future, will be considered personal data nevertheless when the identification would cost relatively little effort. The other way around, in order to answer the question of whether data should be considered anonymous, an account should be kept of the efforts and investments needed to de-anonymise the data. As the former Working Party 29 explained,

> the assessment of whether the data allow identification of an individual, and whether the information can be considered as anonymous or not depends on the circumstances, and a case-by-case analysis should be carried out with particular reference to the extent that the means are likely reasonably to be used for identification.[22]

Big Data has a number of important consequences for this constellation. First, not only is it possible to change the status of data and datasets within a split second due to the massive computational power and artificial intelligence, undoing these changes is also increasingly easy and cheap. To give an example, in 2010, Paul Ohm conducted a study on anonymisation techniques and discussed three cases in which organisations had made public databases which had been stripped from all identifiers; in each case, third parties, such as academics and journalists, where able to re-identify the people in that database by combining those data with other data. 'Each researcher combined two sets of data – each of which provided partial answers to the question "who does this data describe?" – and discovered that the combined data answered (or nearly answered) the question.'[23] Because of the increased technological powers to harvest indirect identifiable data and to combine existing databases with other open data sources, Ohm was convinced that in order to truly make a dataset anonymous, it has to be stripped from almost all data, hence arriving at the conclusion: 'Data can be either useful or perfectly anonymous but never both.'[24]

Building on this line of argument, Aron Fluitt and colleagues have recently suggested that more attention should be paid to what they call the composition problem of privacy. They explain this problem in basic terms by referring to a classic math puzzle:

> A man opens his door to a census taker, who asks how many people reside at the address and their ages. The man explains that it is just him and his three daughters. Instead of providing his daughters' ages, the man tells the census taker, 'The product of my daughters' ages is 36, and the sum is 13.' He then dismisses the census taker, noting 'I have to get my oldest daughter to her piano lesson.' The census taker thanks the man and accurately records the daughters' ages in his notes. – How was the census taker able to deduce the daughters' ages from the information provided? Each piece of information – the product of the ages, the sum, and the existence of an oldest daughter – narrows down the possible age combinations and ultimately reveals the exact ages. Figure 6.1 illustrates with a dotted circle the possible combinations of the three daughters' ages with a product of 36.

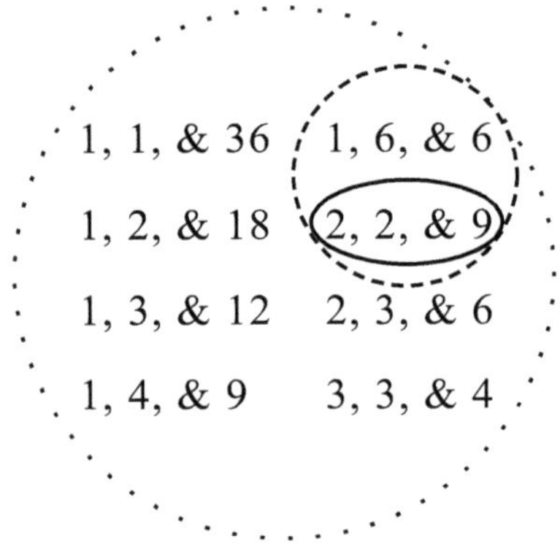

Figure 6.1 Census taker puzzle as an example of composition effects.

> Of those, the dashed circle contains the possible age combinations with a sum of 13. The solid circle contains the only combination that also has an oldest child: 2, 2, and 9. Although the possible age combinations that satisfy each clue independently may seem overwhelmingly vast, together the three clues eliminate all but one set of possible age combinations.[25]

This means that two databases that do not contain personal data by themselves, may when combined. To build on this example: If governmental database A contains information about a small village in which three people lived owning a yellow Ferrari, the school's database B provides that there is one family that always drives their four children to school in a yellow Ferrari, and child protection database C provides that in that village, there is one family with four children, of which there may be signs of domestic violence. Connecting those and other dots may give a very detailed and insightful picture.

> [R]esearchers in 2018 revealed that the underlying confidential data from the 2010 US Decennial Census could be reconstructed using only the statistical tables published by the Census Bureau. They demonstrated a type of attack, called a *database reconstruction attack*, that leveraged the large volumes of data from the published statistical tables in order to narrow down the possible values of individual-level records. The researchers were able to reconstruct the sex, age, race, ethnicity, and fine-grained geographic location (to the block-level) reported by Census respondents *exactly* for 46% of the US population. They also showed that, if they relaxed their conditions and allowed age to vary by up to only one year, these five pieces of information could be reconstructed for 71% of the population. Further, the researchers showed that the reconstructed records could be completely *re-identified* – meaning they were able to assign personally identifiable information to individual records – using commercial databases available at the time. They concluded that, with this attack, they could putatively re-identify 138 million people, and they confirmed that these re-identifications were accurate for 52 million people, or 17% of the US population. These findings are startling. The last time the Census Bureau performed such a simulated re-identification attack on census datasets, the re-identification rate was only 0.0038%. The 2018 test attack demonstrates that previous risk assessments underestimated the re-identification risk by a factor of at least 4,500![26]

With the push to create an open data environment, in which datasets are published and made available for re-use,[27] still other datasets are available upon request or purchase and a high number of born digital data are generated on public websites, discussion fora and social network sites, enriching, merging and combining existing datasets becomes increasingly easy. The fact that technologies are ever more potent and the costs for operating algorithms have dwindled, means that both data and data-driven technologies are democratised.

As explained at the beginning of this section, the status of the data (e.g., non-personal or personal) is determined in part by its to-be nature, which is dependent on the investments likely to be made by parties that have access to the data. Given that in the open data environment, datasets are increasingly made public, shared or made available upon purchase, it will be increasingly difficult to determine who will likely gain access to a dataset and what that party will do with the data.

But two things may be tentatively stipulated. First, given the democratisation of technologies and the minimal investment needed, it is increasingly likely that whenever a database is shared, there will be some party or another that will combine those data with other data, enrich them with data scraped from the Internet or merge them into an existing dataset. Thus, although there is no certainty, it is increasingly likely that if an anonymised dataset is published, there will be some party around the world that will de-anonymise it or combine the data with other data in order to create personal profiles; that when a set of personal data is shared, there will be some party that will use those data to create a dataset with sensitive personal data; etc. Second, there will be other parties that have access to those data but will not engage in those types of activities; parties that will not use the data, use them as they are made available or even de-identify a database containing personal data. Who will do what is unclear beforehand.

Consequently, the legal category the data belong to is no longer a quality of the data itself, but a product of an organisation's efforts and investments. This means that it is unbeknownst beforehand whether an organisation will invest time and energy to harvest a database, and thus what the legal status of the data is. What is known is that it is increasingly easy and affordable to do so and that consequently, the likelihood that non-personal data may become personal data, that personal data may become sensitive personal data, that metadata will be used to create content data and that anonymous data will be re-identified is increasingly high. Applying the current legal categories strictly might mean that indeed almost all data should be seen as personal data and potentially as sensitive personal data, as there will most likely always be parties that will invest enough time, energy and resources to enrich a database. In addition, because data are increasingly available, shared and made public, the same database may have multiple legal statuses at the same time.

To draw from the analogy of the protection of the home again, the difficulty is not only, as described in the previous section, that the status of a building can change in a split second from a home to an office building to a fitness club to a private sex club to a home again. In addition, when determining whether a building should deserve the protection of a home, its future use should be taken into account; and while it is unknown whether the building will be used in the future as a home is unclear, it is increasingly likely that it will, though by whom is uncertain. Furthermore, the same building may have multiple functions for multiple parties at the same time, being a home to some, a restaurant to others, etc.

4. The status of the data is insignificant

The core rationale behind having the various data categories in law is their link to the individual. In general, the more directly data or datasets are linked to an individual and the more sensitive the data are, the higher the level of protection provided. To give an example, one of the first legal instruments to introduce the category of sensitive personal data was the Council of Europe's 1981 Convention. This introduction was elucidated in the explanatory memorandum in the following way:

> While the risk that data processing is harmful to persons generally depends not on the contents of the data but on the context in which they are used, there are exceptional cases where the processing of certain categories of data is as such likely to lead to encroachments on individual rights and interests. Categories of data which in all member States are considered to be especially sensitive are listed in this article.[28]

The previous sections explained why the idea that the sensitivity of data is a quality of the data is increasingly redundant, but they did not question the core rationale underlying the legal categories. They showed that it is increasingly difficult to determine whether a set of information should be considered to contain non-personal, personal or sensitive personal data and that non-personal data may be converted into sensitive data in a split second, meaning that non-personal data should be seen as potential to-be sensitive data. This section will explain why the logic behind the various categories in law is increasingly redundant in the age of Big Data.

To provide an example, metadata can be just as revealing as content data, not just because they can reveal the content[29] – such as when a person visits a website with a xxx domain extension or when a letter is sent to a national cancer institute – but also because they reveal other information that may be even more sensitive than content data. The type of videos a person watches on a pornographic website may reveal one thing; the fact that the person either visits such a site once a year or twice a day may reveal more. What a person says to her mother over the telephone may reveal one thing; the fact that a person either spends two hours a day over the telephone or calls her mother once a year may say more.

The same argument applies to the fact that ordinary personal data may be as or more revealing than sensitive personal data. This is true not only because ordinary data may be used as proxies for sensitive personal data – such as that accurate predictions of someone's sexual preference can be based on her or even her online friends' music taste – but also because personal data may paint a highly personal picture of a person's life. For example, the fact that a person spends about eighteen hours a day on online gaming; the fact that a person stays up until 02.00 binge-watching Netflix series but logs into her work account at 07.00 from work; the fact that a person has founded six successive companies that all went bankrupt within a year; etc. may be more sensitive to many than the fact that they go to church, had a broken leg a year ago or are a member of a certain political party.

Admittedly, these are arguments that apply independently of the Big Data context. In addition, one could argue that what is considered sensitive or not is highly subjective, so that specified categories of sensitive personal data can never cover every aspect that one person or another may find sensitive, or that if in the Big Data era there would be new categories or types of data that should be considered sensitive, these could be included in the definition. Consequently, the previous does not mean per se that the idea of designing a category of sensitive personal data is redundant; it only means that the category of sensitive personal data should be broadened or altered.

Still, Big Data allows organizations to connect metadata trails to gain detailed information about a person's life and allow harvesting of so many non-sensitive data about a person that a very granular picture about a person's life emerges. Not surprisingly, increasingly, companies and governmental organisations rely on gathering metadata rather than content communication, both because processing these types of data is subject to less restrictive rules and regulations and because the analysis of these types of data often yields more valuable results than the analysis of content communication data, among others because fewer datapoints are needed and because the datapoints are less ambiguous. In order to have an algorithm analyse content communication data, the program should be relatively well apt to understand natural languages used within specific contexts. It is far easier to create a heat map of where people go, how long they stay in specific places and who else is there; or which sites they visit, on what items they click, how long they stay on a specific page, etc.

Reference can also be made to the legal categories of aggregated or non-personal data and personal data. Increasingly, data analytics programs operate on anonymised and aggregated data or data that never were personal data. Big Data runs, as the word suggests, on large databases and the general lessons and patterns that are drawn therefrom. The correlations and group profiles may have as relevant determinant personal identifiers but are often based on non-personal datapoints, such as zip codes. Obviously, when such categories are used to the disadvantage of specific individuals, one may argue that data profiles should be considered personal data again. The classic reference here is to *redlining*, in which banks' policy on giving out loans was based on zip code areas, and the policy was disadvantageous to people living in neighbourhoods with a large African-American community. When a specific person is denied a loan on the basis of such a profile, it could be argued that this involves processing personal data.

Still, under such an approach, it is possible to design and make policies that affect groups of people on the basis of general information that were never personal data and may not have an effect on specific individuals but on large groups of society, or everyone living in society. For example, suppose an algorithm produces the result that one of the most effective ways to combat night-time violence in a city is to spray a tangerine scent between 22.00–04.00 in nightlife areas because this makes people less aggressive. No personal data is processed, though such policies may have a high impact on people's lives.

In addition, because data protection regimes rely on the connection of the data to individuals and individual interests, two parts of the Big Data process are left unregulated. The gathering of non-personal or aggregated data is not regulated and the analysis of data, when correlations are found and group profiles are made, is left unregulated because this phase by definition revolves around analysing aggregated data. This holds true for the human rights regime in general. Referring to the example of redlining, the core of the problem is not that a particular black person is disadvantaged by the policy of the bank, but that the algorithm, the data or both are biased so that discriminatory policy emerges. Working with a biased dataset or a biased algorithm is currently not prohibited or sanctioned because analysing biased data or using biased algorithms as such does not harm any specific individual, and analysing that biased dataset with a biased algorithm is not regulated because of the focus on individual interests.

To refer to the metaphor of the home yet again, the reason for giving the home a special status was that within the private sphere, private matters were discussed, intimate actions took place and personal items were stored. If we are moving towards a world in which intimate actions take place irrespective of the physical domain, in which private discussions take place on open fora and in which personal items are stored in the cloud, then the question is whether the rationale behind the distinction between the private and the public domain is still valid. The same holds true for the categories in data protection law. If processing metadata can be just as or even more revealing than processing content data; if non-sensitive personal data can be put together in a way that gives a highly intimate picture of a person's life; if non-personal data can be used in ways that have far greater impact on the lives of ordinary citizens than the processing of sensitive personal data; then the question is whether the underlying rationale for the categorisations should be upheld.

5. Analysis

If these arguments hold true, two conclusions could be drawn. First, basing the level of regulatory protection on the status and nature of data is not the best way forward. Second, given the fact that non-personal data may be changed to sensitive data in a split second and that processing non-personal data can have a bigger impact on persons' lives than the processing of sensitive personal data, as long as the legal regulation *is* based on the status of data, it should provide for a basic framework for the protection of citizens' interests vis-a-vis the processing of non-personal data. This conclusion contrasts sharply with the approach taken by the European Union in 2018, when it adopted a Regulation on the transfer of non-personal data, which only aims at stimulating cross-border data processing, without providing any form of protection to citizens. Article 1 of that Regulation specifies: 'This Regulation aims to ensure the free flow of data other than personal data within the Union by laying down rules relating to data localisation requirements, the availability of data to competent authorities and the porting of data for professional users.'[30] The material provisions of the Regulation do not aim at restricting or laying down conditions for the processing or transfer of non-personal data but in contrast, prohibit any type of restriction or limitation in national laws on the availability, transfer and processing of non-personal data.

Given the previous, the EU might want to amend its approach and also provide protection to the interests of citizens when non-personal data are processed. The principles contained in the General Data Protection Regulation could serve as a source of inspiration. Although its material scope is determined by the identifiability of the data, many of the principles themselves do not so much aim to protect individual interests of specific data subjects but lay down general duties of care and standards for good data governance by data controllers, and can hence be transposed easily to the processing non-personal data.

For example, if an organization collects more non-personal data than it needs for its specified purpose, given that these data may be converted into sensitive personal data and that even the use of non-personal data can have a high impact on the lives of citizens, a data minimization principle could be applied to processing non-personal data all the same. Having a specific purpose for gathering non-personal or aggregated data and limiting the use of the data to that specific purpose seems a basic requirement in the age of Big Data. Given that increasingly, decisions are made on the basis of non-personal data and aggregated datasets are used to design policies, it seems vital to ensure that those aggregated data are correct, complete and up to date. In addition, given the fact that having and processing non-personal and aggregated data potentially provides organizations with just as much power as processing personal data, requirements to ensure transparency seem vital. In addition, as the impact of data processing operations based on non-personal data can be significant, an impact assessment also taking into account broader and societal interests may be regarded as quintessential in the age of Big Data, which also holds true for the requirement to appoint a Data Protection Officer. An obligation to ensure that the non-personal data are processed safely and securely, taking adequate technical and organizational security measures, having a data protection policy and embedding those principles in the technical infrastructure of an organization by design or default could help organizations abide by a regulation that would regulate processing non-personal data. Finally, like the current General Data Protection Regulation does, a Regulation on the processing of non-personal data should contain a rule specifying that transferring non-personal data to other jurisdictions should be prohibited, unless similar rules are applied to the processing of non-personal data.

Such a Regulation could be applicable to metadata and content data, sensitive data and insensitive data, anonymous and statistical data alike to the extent that they are not covered by the GDPR. The introduction of the Regulation on the Processing of Non-Personal Data would ensure that no data processing activity is left unregulated. It would also disallow Big Data organisations to circumvent data protection rules by temporarily aggregating data or stripping a dataset from identifying information.

A proposal for a regulation on the processing of non-personal data

Article 1 Applicability

This regulation applies to any natural or legal person that:

1 Processes non-personal data; and
2 Has an establishment in the European Union

Article 2 Definitions

For the purposes of this Regulation:

1 'non-personal data' means any information not relating to an identified or identifiable natural person;
2 'processing' means any operation or set of operations which is performed on non-personal data or on sets of non-personal data, whether or not by automated means, such as collection, recording, organisation, structuring, storage, adaptation or alteration, retrieval, consultation, use, disclosure by transmission, dissemination or otherwise making available, alignment or combination, restriction, erasure or destruction;
3 'data breach' means a breach of security leading to the accidental or unlawful destruction, loss, alteration, unauthorised disclosure of, or access to, non-personal data transmitted, stored or otherwise processed

Article 3 Principles

Non-personal data shall be:

1 processed lawfully, fairly and in a transparent manner ('lawfulness, fairness and transparency');
2 collected for specified, explicit and legitimate purposes and not further processed in a manner that is incompatible with those purposes ('purpose limitation');
3 adequate, relevant and limited to what is necessary in relation to the purposes for which they are processed ('data minimisation');
4 accurate and, where necessary, kept up to date; every reasonable step must be taken to ensure that non-personal data that are inaccurate, having regard to the purposes for which they are processed, are erased or rectified without delay ('accuracy');

5 kept no longer than is necessary for the purposes for which the personal data are processed ('storage limitation');
6 processed in a manner that ensures appropriate security of the non-personal data, including protection against unauthorised or unlawful processing and against accidental loss, destruction or damage, using appropriate technical or organisational measures ('integrity and confidentiality')

Article 4 Obligations

To the extent reasonable and proportionate, every natural and legal person processing non-personal data has to:

1 adopt a data protection policy that specifies how the rules in this Regulation shall be implemented and respected within its organisation ('data protection policy');
2 implement the policy decisions in its technical infrastructure by design or by default ('data protection by design and default');
3 maintain records specifying the data that are processed, the source of the data, the purpose for processing the data, the period for which the data are stored, the natural and legal persons with whom the data are shared and the technical and organisational measures applied ('records of processing activities');
4 conduct a data protection impact assessment before engaging in specific processing activities, taking into account the likely effects on citizens, groups and society at large and developing strategies for mitigating those effects ('data protection impact assessment');
5 designate a data protection officer, who shall be fully independent, trained and have access to necessary resources to adequately fulfil their tasks; the data protection officer is responsible for ensuring that all relevant principles contained in this Regulation are upheld ('data protection officer'); and
6 process data transparently, meaning that the public is informed through a website of the data that are processed, the source of the data, the purpose for processing the data, the period for which the data are stored, the organisations with whom the data are shared, the technical and organisational measures applied and any data breach having occurred ('transparency')

Article 6 Transfers

The transfer of non-personal data to natural or legal persons outside the European Union is prohibited unless the person or organisation receiving the data signs a legally enforceable agreement in which that natural or legal person commits to upholding all principles contained in this Regulation.

Article 7 Enforcement

The tasks, powers and competences of the national supervisory authority and European Data Protection Board, as specified by the General Data Protection

Regulation, shall also apply to the processing of non-personal data and the respect for the principles contained in this Regulation.

Notes

1 International Bill of Human Rights: A Universal Declaration of Human Rights. <www.un.org/en/ga/search/view_doc.asp?symbol=A/RES/217(III)>.
2 International Covenant on Civil and Political Rights. Adopted and opened for signature, ratification and accession by General Assembly resolution 2200A (XXI) of 16 December 1966. entry into force 23 March 1976, in accordance with Article 49. <www.ohchr.org/en/professionalinterest/pages/ccpr.aspx>.
3 Convention for the Protection of Human Rights and Fundamental Freedoms Rome, 4.XI.1950. <www.echr.coe.int/Documents/Convention_ENG.pdf>.
4 ECmHR, Campion v. France, application no. 25547/94, 06/09/1995. Unofficial Translation: In order to determine in similar cases the extent of the guarantee granted by article 8 (art. 8) against interference by public authorities, the Commission examines whether the taking of photographs constitutes an intrusion into the private sphere of an individual (for example when these were taken at her home), if the photographs refer to private or public events, and if they are intended to be used for a limited purpose or they are likely to fall within the public's knowledge. In the present case, the Commission notes that the photograph for which the applicant complains was taken on the public highway, when he was traveling by car, for the purpose of proof and identification. Nothing indicates that the photograph has been brought to the attention of the public or used for any purpose other than the prosecution of which the applicant has been the subject. Applying the criteria set out earlier, the Commission comes to the conclusion that there has been no interference with the privacy of the applicant.
5 Secretary's Advisory Committee on Automated Personal Data Systems, Records, Computers and the Rights of Citizens (1973).
6 U. Dammann, O. Mallmann & S. Simitis (eds), *Data Protection Legislation: An International Documentation* (Engl) (Frankfurt am Main: Metzner, 1977). F. W. Hondius, *Emerging Data Protection in Europe* (Amsterdam: North-Holland, 1975). H. Burkert, *Freedom of Information and Data Protection* (Bonn: Gesellschaft für Mathematik und Datenverarbeitung, 1983).
7 Council of Europe Committee of Ministers Resolution (73) 22 on the Protection of the Privacy of Individuals Vis-à-vis Electronic Data Banks in the Private Sector (Adopted by the Committee of Ministers on 26 September 1973 at the 224th meeting of the Ministers' Deputies). <https://rm.coe.int/CoERMPublicCommonSearchServices/DisplayDCTMContent?documentId=0900001680502830>. Council of Europe Committee of Ministers Resolution (74) 29 on the Protection of the Privacy of Individuals Vis-à-vis Electronic Data Banks in the Public Sector (Adopted by the Committee of Ministers on 20 September 1974 at the 236th meeting of the Ministers' Deputies). <https://rm.coe.int/16804d1c51>.
8 Charter of Fundamental Rights of the European Union (2000/C 364/01). <www.europarl.europa.eu/charter/pdf/text_en.pdf>.
9 Article 1 Directive 95/46/EC of the European Parliament and of the Council of 24 October 1995 on the protection of individuals with regard to the processing of personal data and on the free movement of such data. <https://eur-lex.europa.eu/legal-content/EN/TXT/?uri=celex%3A31995L0046>.
10 Regulation (EU) 2016/679 of the European Parliament and of the Council of 27 April 2016 on the protection of natural persons with regard to the processing of personal data and on the free movement of such data, and repealing Directive 95/46/EC (General Data Protection Regulation). <https://eur-lex.europa.eu/eli/reg/2016/679/oj>.

11 Article 2 sub a Convention for the Protection of Individuals with regard to Automatic Processing of Personal Data, Strasbourg, 28 January 1981. <https://rm.coe.int/1680078b37>.
12 See for a discussion: B. van der Sloot, *Privacy as Virtue* (Cambridge: Intersentia, 2017).
13 Article 1 Regulation (EU) 2018/1807 of the European Parliament and of the Council of 14 November 2018 on a framework for the free flow of non-personal data in the European Union. <https://eur-lex.europa.eu/legal-content/EN/TXT/?uri=CELEX%3A32018R1807>.
14 Guide on Article 8 of the European Convention on Human Rights Right to respect for private and family life, home and correspondence Updated on 30 April 2019. <www.echr.coe.int/Documents/Guide_Art_8_ENG.pdf>.
15 ECtHR, Big Brother Watch and Others v. The United Kingdom, application nos. 58170/13, 62322/14 and 24960/15, 13 September 2018, § 356.
16 Article 9 GDPR.
17 Article 6 GDPR.
18 Guide on Article 8 of the European Convention on Human Rights Right to respect for private and family life, home and correspondence Updated on 30 April 2019. <www.echr.coe.int/Documents/Guide_Art_8_ENG.pdf>.
19 Another source of inspiration could be the EU's e-Privacy Directive, which differentiates between traffic data, that are defined as any data processed for the purpose of the conveyance of a communication on an electronic communications network or for the billing thereof, location data, meaning any data indicating the geographic position of the terminal equipment of a user of a publicly available electronic communications service, location data other than traffic data, etc. Directive 2002/58/EC of the European Parliament and of the Council of 12 July 2002 concerning the processing of personal data and the protection of privacy in the electronic communications sector (Directive on privacy and electronic communications).
20 Joined cases C-203/15 and C-698/15 Tele2/Watson [2016] ECLI:EU:C:2016:970, para 99. For a full analysis of this CJEU judgment, see Will R. Mbioh, 'Post-och Telestyrelsen and Watson and the Investigatory Powers Act 2016' (2017) 3 (2) *EDPL* 273–282.
21 L. Taylor, L. Floridi & B. van der Sloot (eds), *Group Privacy* (Dordrecht: Springer, 2017), p. 284.
22 Article 29 Data Protection Working Party, Opinion 4/2007 on the concept of personal data, 01248/07/EN WP 136, 20 June 2017. <https://ec.europa.eu/justice/article-29/documentation/opinion-recommendation/files/2007/wp136_en.pdf>. See also: Article 29 Data Protection Working Party, Opinion 05/2014 on Anonymisation Techniques, 0829/14/EN, WP216, 10 April 2014. <https://ec.europa.eu/justice/article-29/documentation/opinion-recommendation/files/2014/wp216_en.pdf>.
23 P. Ohm, 'Broken Promises of Privacy: Responding to the Surprising Failure of Anonymization' (2010) 57 *UCLA Law Review* 1701, p. 1723.
24 Ibid, p. 1704.
25 A. Fluitt et al., 'Data Protection's Composition Problem', (2019) 5 (3) *European Data Protection Law Review*.
26 Ibid.
27 See inter alia: Directive 2003/98/EC of the European Parliament and of the Council of 17 November 2003 on the re-use of public sector information. <https://eur-lex.europa.eu/LexUriServ/LexUriServ.do?uri=OJ:L:2003:345:0090:0096:en:PDF>. <https://eur-lex.europa.eu/legal-content/EN/TXT/PDF/?uri=CELEX:32013L0037&from=FR>.
28 Explanatory Report to the Convention for the Protection of Individuals with regard to Automatic Processing of Personal Data Strasbourg, 28 January 1981. <https://rm.coe.int/CoERMPublicCommonSearchServices/DisplayDCTMContent?documentId=09000016800ca434>.

29 B. Greschbach, 'The Devil is in the Metadata – New Privacy Challenges in Decentralised Online Social Networks'. <www.nada.kth.se/~gkreitz/metadata/sesocMetaPrivacy.pdf>.

30 Article 1 Regulation (EU) 2018/1807 of the European Parliament and of the Council of 14 November 2018 on a framework for the free flow of non-personal data in the European Union. <https://eur-lex.europa.eu/legal-content/EN/TXT/?uri=CELEX%3A32018R1807>.

7 Addressing big data and AI challenges

A taxonomy and why the GDPR cannot provide a one-size-fits-all solution

Maria Tzanou

1. Introduction

Big data analysed through algorithms are considered the oil of the modern online economy. The value of big data is immense, but they also pose significant challenges to individuals and the society as a whole. It is a common assumption that big data, data mining, algorithmic decision-making and Artificial Intelligence (AI) should be considered as data privacy issues[1] that should be addressed by data privacy laws. In this respect, the EU's General Data Protection Regulation (hereinafter the GDPR)[2] is considered as the central legislative measure aimed at addressing big data risks[3] and has been hailed as 'the first piece of legislation for AI' that processes personal data.[4]

This chapter challenges the assumption that data privacy frameworks in general and the GDPR in particular can provide an appropriate regulatory solution for big data.[5] It argues that in order to be able to properly reflect on regulatory approaches that wrestle with big data challenges, closer attention should be paid to these particular challenges. Searching for appropriate regulatory solutions requires a focus on the problems that need to be addressed. While big data challenges have been extensively discussed in the literature, remarkably, there is a lack of systemisation of big data risks that would permit a reflection about potential regulatory responses to these that goes beyond the commonly proposed data privacy frameworks.

In this respect, this chapter makes three distinct contributions to the debate regarding regulatory approaches to big data: First, it develops a taxonomy of big data challenges that allows a comprehensive overview of the issues at stake. Second, it examines the capabilities and limitations of the GDPR to address the risks identified in the proposed taxonomy. Third, it offers some suggestions on the pathways that regulators should be considering when approaching big data and AI.

The chapter is organised as follows: Section 2 proposes a typology of big data and AI challenges. This categorises big data challenges at two levels: *individual* and *societal*. *Individual* level challenges are classified in two further dimensions: those that relate to the *processing* of the data and those that are linked to the *outcomes* of such processing. The taxonomy of big data challenges is necessary if we are to seriously consider regulatory methodologies and analytical prisms to approach these. Rather than relying on the simplistic assumption – which even the GDPR adopts to some extent – that data protection law should catch in its protective net all the issues that big data and AI raise because it applies to the processing of personal data, the proposed taxonomy reveals that big data present challenges – both at the individual and at the societal level – are far from the scope or irrelevant to data protection frameworks due to their complex dynamics, actors, processes and outcomes.

In light of the taxonomy developed, Section 3 examines the role that the GDPR can play to address big data and AI challenges. It finds that this legal instrument can regulate individual big data risks that relate to the *processing* of personal data, despite the scepticisms raised in this respect. The GDPR can also potentially play an indirect role in addressing individual level challenges that occur as *outcomes* of the processing and *societal* level threats but this is very limited and clearly not enough, taking into account the issues arising in the big data age. Section 4 considers the regulatory pathways and methodologies to address big data issues. Section 5 offers brief conclusions.

2. Mapping the challenges of big data: a taxonomy

2.1 Preliminary issues and caveats

Before we proceed with the analysis, a number of caveats and clarifications are required. A first question that arises when attempting to map the challenges of big data is a definitional one. What is meant by big data 'challenges'? Is it the same as speaking of big data 'risks' or 'threats'? Admittedly, the concepts of 'challenges', 'concerns', 'risks' and 'threats' appear semantically similar; nevertheless, this chapter opts to adopt the 'challenges' or 'concerns' terminology to broadly denote the different legal – and to an extent ethical – 'issues' that big data and AI raise.

This is a deliberate choice: I approach big data issues in a neutral way, that steers away from the GDPR's 'risks' terminology. More particularly, it is well-known that the GDPR marks the introduction of a risk-based approach to data protection.[6] This is pursued mainly by data protection impact assessments (DPIAs)[7] that controllers must undertake 'where a type of processing in particular using new technologies, . . . is likely to result in a high risk to the rights and freedoms of natural persons',[8] and *ex post* notifications of data breaches to the supervisory authorities and the data subject[9] when they are 'likely to result in a high risk to the rights and freedoms of natural persons'.[10] Recital 75 explains in this respect that risks 'of varying likelihood and severity may result from personal data processing' and could lead to 'physical, material or non-material damage' and provides an indicative list of these. The 'risk' of processing, therefore, acquires a specific normative significance under the GDPR that triggers several obligations for controllers. It should be clarified from the outset that the taxonomy developed in this chapter understands big data 'issues' and 'challenges' in a way that does not attribute to these any normative value and is not linked to the meaning of 'risks' and 'risk assessments' under the GDPR.

Secondly, big data challenges have been extensively discussed in the academic literature and beyond.[11] The present analysis builds on this literature but aims to move the discussion a step further by providing a classification of these. The classification is proposed as a methodological attempt to systematise these challenges at two *levels* (*individual* and *societal*) and two further *dimensions* at the *individual* level (challenges associated with the *processing* of personal data and challenges associated with the *outcomes* of such processing). The specific challenges falling under each category are depicted in Table 7.1 and are analysed in detail later in the chapter. The taxonomy provides a useful tool to structure the discussion on big data issues and, more importantly, to organise the debate on the appropriateness of regulatory approaches to big data both current (the GDPR) and future. In this respect, this chapter fills an important gap in the literature on regulatory responses to big data.

Thirdly, the chapter uses various examples from big health data, but avoids limiting the discussion only to health data for two main reasons. The first reason concerns the problems around defining health data. As seen in Chapter 1[12] and other chapters in this book, it is very difficult to distinguish sensitive health data from apparently innocuous information (like a supermarket shopping list) that might reveal important details about a person's diet, and therefore their health. Furthermore, big data have numerous lifecycles and different datasets

Table 7.1 A Taxonomy of AI and big data challenges

Individual level challenges	
Issues relating to the processing of the data	*Issues relating to the outcomes of the processing*
Personal data and personally identifiable information	Incorrect or unreliable conclusions
Legal basis for the processing and the problems and limitations of consent	Lack of transparency and foreseeability for the individual affected
Implementation and enforceability of fair and transparent processing	Unfair and discriminatory conclusions and decisions
Big data repurposing	Profiling and the effects of group analysis on individuals
Data security	
Difficulties in identifying special categories of data	
Effective exercise of data subject's rights	
Enforceability and enforcement of (data protection) law	
Societal level challenges	
Surveillance	
Autonomy, equality and human dignity	
The power imbalances of big data	
The lack of accountability of data stakeholders	

are aggregated at different time points, so it is difficult to specify when exactly 'health data' are analysed. Second, the proposed taxonomy applies to big health data analytics – seen here as an application domain of big data analytics – but can be generalised to cover big data issues more broadly. The overall discussion, therefore, adopts a broader scope in this respect.

Finally, this contribution follows the definitions of 'big data', 'AI', 'big data analytics' and 'health data' as provided in Chapter 1 of this book.[13]

2.2 Individual level issues associated with the processing of the data

Big data present a number of challenges at the individual level relating to the processing of the data. These are identified and discussed as follows.

1. Personal data and personally identifiable information

It is normally assumed that the added value of big data is found in its capability to identify novel patterns[14] rather than focus on personal identified information. Indeed, many significant medical trends and conclusions drawn in recent years are based on statistical analysis of huge databases that do not include personal information.[15] Yet, two points should be raised here. Firstly, big data might contain personal information; and secondly, it has been shown[16] that modern data analytics can allow for the reidentification of individuals even if seemingly only anonymised data is processed.

Personal data is defined in the GDPR as 'any information relating to an identified or identifiable natural person'; an identifiable natural person

> is one who can be identified, *directly* or *indirectly*, in particular by reference to an identifier such as a name, an identification number, location data, an online identifier or to one or more factors specific to the physical, physiological, genetic, mental, economic, cultural or social identity of that natural person.[17]

As processing of personal data triggers the application of data protection law, it is very important to establish when big data is composed of or entails personal information, i.e., information that can be linked to a certain individual. In this case, data protection law would apply and govern the processing of the data.

A distinct problem arises when no personal information is contained in the big data, yet there are ways to identify the persons concerned. In such cases, EU data protection legislation is clear. As soon as the data refers to a person who can be identified 'directly' or 'indirectly', this is considered personal data, and therefore data protection law applies. In *Breyer*,[18] the Court of Justice of the European Union (CJEU) adopted a broad interpretation of 'identifiable person', holding that in order to ascertain this, 'account should be taken of all the means likely reasonably to be used either by the controller or by any other person to identify the said person',[19] without requiring that 'all the information enabling the identification of the data subject must be in the hands of one person.'[20] In legal terms, this means that the possibility of reidentification of a person within the context of big data would make data protection safeguards, and in particular the GDPR, applicable.

2. *Legal basis for the processing and the problems and limitations of consent*

The literature has identified different ways in which big data can be generated. The Committee on Civil Liberties, Justice and Home Affairs (LIBE) Report on Big Data and Smart Devices[21] distinguishes three categories of generating data sources: a) volunteered data, that is information volunteered or surrendered by individuals when they 'explicitly share information about themselves or about third parties' (e.g., when someone shares health-related information about herself or other people, such as her children on online social networks, or enters information on a health app that predicts ovulation cycles); b) observed data, that arises by observing the activities of users (e.g., Internet browsing habits, GPS and location data when using mobile phones); and c) inferred data, that arise from the result of the automated analysis of other data (e.g., health insurance premiums calculated on the basis of a number of factors and data volunteered or observed).[22] Based on this classification, it can be argued that the processing of different types of personal data might be based on different legal bases.

Consent is a common legal basis allowing for the processing of volunteered, observed (and inferred) personal data in social media, online apps and wearable devices. The GDPR strengthens consent and requires the informed consent of the data subject[23] in order for processing to take place, but there are several problems regarding consent in the context of big data. Drawing on the existing academic literature,[24] these problems can be summarised in two groups: *data subject-related* problems and *systemic* problems. Data subject-related problems refer to concerns about whether individuals sharing their personal information on social media read privacy policies;[25] whether, even if they read them, they actually understand these in an meaningful way, as well as the consequences of sharing personal data; and whether, even if they read privacy policies and are indeed interested in protecting their privacy online, nevertheless they normally tend to grant their consent almost immediately to proceed receiving the (often free) service/ benefit.[26] While arguably, these concerns apply to consent for the processing of personal data in general, the specific attributes of big data[27] present further *systemic* problems regarding consent.[28] In the context of big data, personal information may be processed multiple times in different 'lifecycles' involving different controllers and processors in each lifecycle.[29] The argument, therefore, goes that even if individuals give their consent for the initial processing of their data, it is impossible to predict – let alone meaningfully consent to – the subsequent virtually limitless possibilities for which these can be processed and aggregated. Furthermore, the information imbalances between data subjects and data controllers such as Facebook and Google in the context of big data may undermine the overall validity of the data subject's consent.[30]

Besides consent, the GDPR provides for other grounds for the processing of personal data[31] and the interpretation of certain grounds, such as processing necessary for the performance of a contract (Article 6 (1) (b) GDPR) and processing necessary for the purposes of the legitimate interests of the controller or a third party, except where such interests are overridden by the interests or fundamental rights and freedoms of the data subject (Article 6 (1) (f) GDPR).

3. Implementation and enforceability of fair and transparent processing

Article 5 GDPR contains a number of data protection principles pertaining to the processing of personal data: lawfulness, fairness and transparency of processing, purpose limitation, data minimisation, accuracy and storage limitation. The Regulation requires that the controller who processes personal data is made 'responsible for' and must be 'able to demonstrate compliance' with these principles.[32] It has been argued that these principles are categorically 'incompatible' with big data practices.[33] Similarly to the case of consent discussed earlier, the alleged challenges or incompatibilities can be grouped in two categories: *systemic* and *actor-related.*

Starting from the principle enshrined in Article 5 (1) (a), 'lawful' processing means that it should be carried out in accordance with the law.[34] Fairness in processing denotes that data controllers must ensure that the collection and further processing of personal data is undertaken in a fair manner in accordance with the reasonable expectations of the data subjects.[35] This also relates to the requirement of transparency of processing that has been explicitly included in the GDPR. The systemic challenges raised in this respect refer to the usage patterns and methods employed to process big data which are considered to be *de facto* at odds with the lawfulness, fairness and transparency principle, as neither the controller collecting the data nor the data subject could have considered or even imagined such methods and patterns at the time of the collection.[36] The actor-related challenges this time refer more to controllers that cannot closely monitor and guarantee transparency in the processing of big data because allegedly they do not know where the information came from, especially in processes of merging different databases and reusing data[37] that would render any transparency requirements costly, difficult or even impossible to deliver.[38]

The principles of data minimisation and storage limitation which require that data are 'adequate, relevant and limited to what is necessary in relation to the purposes for which they are processed'[39] and that they are in principle 'kept in a form which permits identification of data subjects for no longer than is necessary for the purposes for which the personal data are processed'[40] respectively face similar challenges. At a *systemic level*, the 'business model of big data'[41] is perceived to be 'antithetical'[42] to the data minimisation and storage limitation principles.[43] This antithesis is inherent to the nature of big data, which provides controllers with a 'clear incentive to collect and retain as much data as they can for as long as possible'.[44] The argument, therefore, goes that 'diligently enforcing' data minimisation principles would limit the success of big data initiatives and undermine their utility.[45] At the *individual/controller level*, the challenges of big data to the principles of data minimisation and storage limitation are drawn from the same utilitarian argument: Why should controllers collect and store less data, as even more quantities can be easily made available to them? Or to put it differently, even if potential future benefits for collecting more data are uncertain and hypothetical, if the possibility to collect and store as much data as possible[46] exists, why should controllers not take advantage of it? In addition, even if data do not have any known utility currently, why erase them permanently if in the future there might be a potential use, for instance, through aggregation with data that are not even currently available?[47]

Finally, concerns arise regarding the accuracy principle. This requires that personal data must be accurate and, where necessary, kept up to date.[48] It is in the interest of controllers to ensure the accuracy of the data they process, but in the context of big data it might prove difficult to take steps to ensure that inaccurate data are erased or rectified without delays,[49] especially when these have been further merged with other data.[50] Indeed, Article 5 (1) (d) GDPR requires that 'reasonable' steps should be taken in this respect, which raises questions about whether erasing or rectifying the information is a reasonable step that can be taken in the context of big data in order to comply with the principle of accuracy. Indeed, the trend behind big data appears to be 'quantity over quality'.[51]

4. *Big data repurposing*

It has been argued that big datasets are likely to contain 'some intrinsic, hidden, not yet unearthed' treasures and, hence, 'the treasure hunt' race is 'on to discover and capture' all of them.[52] The very idea, therefore, that big data often have 'no fixed purpose'[53] but that their value and potential use will become clear after their hidden treasures are discovered, is arguably at odds with the purpose specification and purpose limitation principle. According to this principle, personal data must be collected for specified, explicit and legitimate purposes and not further processed in a manner that is incompatible with those purposes.[54] The common argument in this respect goes that purpose limitation is incompatible and rendered meaningless by the very nature of big data that cannot specify certain purposes for collecting the data; rather 'data collection and analysis are themselves the purposes' for the data collection.[55] This argument links to the systemic challenges identified previously regarding fair and lawful processing in general and more particularly, the data minimisation problems.

5. *Data security*

In the era of big data and cloud computing, a higher risk of security breaches, including both unauthorised access to the data and accidental loss, will unavoidably emerge.[56] Numerous, troubling security breaches of health data have been recorded over the years.

Safeguarding the security of big data can be a challenging task, taking into account the multiplicity of stakeholders (controllers, processors, data brokers, third parties); the diversity of means through which the data is acquired (the Internet of Things [IoT], mobile phones, wearables, social networks, etc.); and the sheer quantity of data collected, aggregated and stored.[57]

The GDPR includes a general principle that requires data controllers to ensure the appropriate security of personal data (the integrity and confidentiality principle)[58] and introduces new rules regarding the security of processing[59] and data breach notifications.[60]

6. *Difficulties in identifying special categories of data*

The GDPR provides increased protection to special categories of data, such as those revealing racial or ethnic origin, political opinions, religious or philosophical beliefs, trade union membership, genetic data, biometric data for the purpose of uniquely identifying a natural person, data concerning health or data concerning a natural person's sex life or sexual orientation.[61] In fact, the processing of such data is in principle prohibited as a general rule,[62] and only permitted in specific instances.[63]

It is difficult, however, to demarcate what constitutes special and non-special categories of data, and these difficulties are exacerbated in the big data context. Take the example of health data that are considered a special category of data under the GDPR. Health data are found in a variety of sources, such as general practitioners' records and electronic health records (EHRs), prescriptions, laboratory tests, patient hospital monitoring, etc. They are generated by the Internet of Things (IoT) through wearables that monitor everything from physical activity to sleep, stress and pulse rate, smart patches, electronic skins and ingestibles.[64] These are further augmented by the huge amount of health and fitness apps where individuals volunteer information – among others, about their body, sexual activities, mood, smoking habits, women's intimate health (such as menstrual cycles), etc. Health data are also shared on social media, such as Facebook, Twitter and Instagram and specific health networking platforms and online support communities, such as PatientsLikeMe, and are generated by online searches.[65]

These raises fundamental questions as to what type of information will be considered as falling within the sensitive, special category of health data. Even innocuous information, such as supermarket shopping lists, can reveal details about what we eat – and what we do not eat – and therefore, our health condition. Are these also health data protected under Article 9 GDPR? The answer depends ultimately on the particular circumstances, the context and even the purposes for which the data are – or might be – used.[66] This, of course, creates uncertainties as to what types of data should fall under special categories and the relevant grounds of processing applicable in these cases. Such unclear boundaries provide significant discretion to controllers, and concomitantly might result in decreasing the protection of data subjects.

7. *Effective exercise of data subjects' rights*

The GDPR provides a number of rights to data subjects, such as right to information,[67] access,[68] rectification,[69] erasure ('right to be forgotten'),[70] a right to restriction of processing[71] and a right to object[72] and not be subject to a decision based solely on automated processing, including profiling.[73]

The meaningful exercise of these rights in the context of big data is considered 'both unrealistic and deeply paradoxical'.[74] How are individuals expected to monitor all this data deluge every day and have control of how their information is imputed in databases, aggregated and used in order to be able to effectively exercise their access, rectification and erasure rights? Even if they are aware of this information, big data and its multiple lifecycles are notoriously antithetical to the very rationale and ways of exercising these rights. Against which controller should individuals turn, on the basis of which jurisdiction and regulatory framework, when and how? Similar problems arise from the controllers' perspective. In this case, the argument goes that it is not feasible to ask controllers to keep ahead of the big data deluge in order to always be in a position to allow for the effective exercise of data subjects' rights. These *actor-related* challenges for both data subjects and controllers are fed by and explained by the *systemic* issues that arise from the ways big data work. Similar to the case of the various fair information principles, the effective exercise and enforcement of data subjects' rights would allegedly interfere with the successes of big data initiatives.

8. *Enforceability and enforcement of (data protection) law*

Significant concerns regard the temporal and territorial application of data protection law – for instance, the GDPR – to big data as well as the relevant enforcement mechanisms advanced by this. Given that such data are generated via wearables, IoT, mobile and online apps, and virtually the whole world wide web and stored on different clouds that can be located anywhere, it becomes obvious why enforceability issues are exacerbated in this context even if the GDPR has extended its *ratione materiae* and *loci* jurisdictional bite significantly.

In addition to enforceability problems, there are also significant enforcement questions arising in the big data era. The GDPR has been criticised for placing the individual as a data subject at the core of its implementation and enforcement apparatus. By granting individuals the right to 'informational self-determination' or the right to 'have control over their personal information' through various principles and rights, such as the fair information principles and data subjects' rights, it also passes on to individuals the primary responsibility of monitoring the enforcement of such rights.

Enter again the big data systemic issues here. Because of the nature and functions of these, individual data subjects are in most cases virtually unable to maintain effective control of all the pieces of their personal information in this respect. Control over personal information is, therefore, almost meaningless in the big data context. The problems do not stop here. The GDPR has introduced accountability obligations for controllers, but again their effective enforcement in the big data environment appears questionable. Similarly, Data Protection Authorities (DPAs) are already overwhelmed in their supervisory role, and this is going to get worse when they are asked to deal with big data cases.

Overall, enforceability and enforcement problems of legal frameworks in general, and data protection laws such as the GDPR in particular, that might render the written law 'a paper dragon in the age of the "digital tsunami"',[75] pose serious concerns and cannot be ignored in this context. This chapter classifies the practical difficulties concerning the enforceability and enforcement, as an *individual level* challenge of big data concerning the *processing* of the information. Arguably, matters of enforceability and enforcement of legal regulation touch upon the outcomes of the processing of big data and pose societal challenges as well. This demonstrates that there are no clear boundaries between the different risks, as classified in the analytical framework presented in this chapter, but certain risks may fall in more than one category.

2.3 Individual level issues associated to the outcomes of the processing

Big data present complexities and challenges that we have not seen before. Data mining and automated processing using algorithms can create inferences and conclusions that we – as humans – are unable to grasp. This issue is excellently captured by the 'black box' metaphor put forward by Frank Pasquale.[76] Even if we voluntarily grant access to our data to be processed, we are unable to follow how the outcome of this processing was reached. This opacity of the 'black box' makes it impossible to have a clear understanding of the consequences of the processing of our personal data. An infamous example that demonstrates the problem comes from car insurance. People who use pads to protect their furniture are deemed to be more careful drivers, and are therefore granted lower premiums than people who do not use furniture pads. How is the one (careful driving) inferred from the other (use of furniture pads)? The workings of the system are 'mysterious'[77] and they are made even more complicated when the algorithm is a machine-learning one.[78]

The analytical framework of the risks developed in this chapter considers that there are certain risks relating to the black box metaphor that arise at the individual level and can therefore affect the data subjects' fundamental rights. These risks are different from the ones discussed earlier, however, as they refer to the *outcomes* of the processing of big data and not to the *processing* of the data as such. The risks represented on this axis concern the outputs of the data processes and, in particular, the inferences and conclusions that can be drawn following the automated processing of the data using algorithms and the decisions that can be taken as a result. These challenges, in turn, are identified and categorised as follows.

1. Incorrect or unreliable conclusions

Big data analysis is based on correlations. This means that the finding of a mere statistical relationship between two data values is enough to trigger a certain outcome or decision without it being necessary to establish whether there is an actual causal relation that explains this outcome.[79] To take the previously mentioned example, more careful driving is deduced from the fact that people use furniture pads. This is deemed enough to incur lower insurance premiums even if it is clear that a causal relationship between the two cannot be established; the correlation in this regard is spurious (the association might be statistically robust but happens only by chance).[80]

Furthermore, big data come from the aggregation of various datasets and can be often inaccurate or even contain errors. This 'messiness'[81] of the data may lead to unreliable conclusions.[82] Algorithms can, therefore, make incorrect decisions that can have real effects on individuals. In the big data context, this is made possible because there is an abundance of data – often inaccurate and erroneous – and correlations are used to gain valuable insights into them that are fast and cheap,[83] without the need to investigate causality.

2. *Lack of transparency and foreseeability for the individual affected*

As seen earlier, algorithms are 'black boxes', making it impossible for individuals to anticipate their conclusions and to meaningfully comprehend the logic and processes employed to reach these. Algorithms are often protected under intellectual property rights or kept secret for commercial or national security purposes, and are thus inaccessible to individuals.[84] In addition, algorithms are highly complex, often containing many different rules, and it is difficult or impossible to establish which points of entry determined how the resulting outcome was built. This refers to the algorithms' opacity problem; individuals are unable to meaningfully understand how their conclusions came to be. As Pasquale explains, 'we can observe [their] inputs and outputs, but we cannot tell how one becomes the other'.[85] Machine learning is another reason for this opacity; the algorithm can train itself to learn to predict unknown variables and modify its behavioural structure during operation,[86] thus producing outputs untraceable even to programme designers themselves.[87]

3. *Unfair and discriminatory conclusions and decisions*

The processing of big data can lead to biased and discriminatory conclusions. Indeed, it has been argued that big data create 'unimaginable opportunities'[88] for discrimination. 'Employers, financial institutions, marketers, . . . and others can now easily obtain a wealth of bid data about individuals' health status and use it to make adverse decisions relating to data subjects'.[89]

Algorithms are created by humans and unavoidably reflect their authors' values, interests and preconceptions.[90] More often, discriminatory conclusions, rather than being the result of intentional design of the system, reflect 'widespread biases that persist in society at large',[91] replicating 'pre-existing patterns of exclusion and inequality'.[92] For instance, it was found that algorithms that 'could predict skin cancers better than dermatologists turned out to be less accurate when diagnosing dark-skinned people because the system was predominantly trained with data from white people'.[93] Pre-existing biases are particularly problematic, as it is difficult to identify the root of such (unintentional) discriminatory outcomes and effectively challenge them in courts.[94] Biases in the data might also arise for a number of different reasons, including technological errors and failures, inaccuracies in the data that originate from a variety of resources, and other contextual factors present in the context of big data (such as repurposing of the data, different controllers and stakeholders involved in the data lifecycles, etc.).

4. Profiling and the effects of group analysis on individuals

Big data can be used to both uncover (hidden) patterns and correlations and apply these to specific individuals through decisions that affect them directly.[95] Profiling[96] refers to two different phenomena: the creation of a profile and its use in decision-making processes.[97] The creation of profiles requires the identification of general trends, patterns and correlations in the data 'not visible with the naked human eye'[98] through the use of data mining. Such profiles can then be used to categorise and target specific individuals by attributing to them certain characteristics and risks – on the basis of which, decisions that affect them will be made.[99]

Profiling is problematic for several reasons. Big data profiling is predictive and probabilistic. It is based on the analysis of huge amounts of data from past behaviour or known cases to generate predictions about future behaviour and unknown features.[100] Profiles drawn up using data mining are normally non-distributive, meaning that the patterns identified in the data – which make up the specific group profile – do not apply to all members ascribed in the group[101] (as opposed to distributive profiles, where the characteristics of the profile apply to all members of the group).[102] Non-distributive profiles can stereotype and stigmatise people by categorising and treating them according to how their group profile is assumed to behave.[103] Such profiles can also result in unfair conclusions and unjustified discrimination for certain individuals,[104] based on incorrect or unreliable assumptions[105] regarding the categories the latter are inferred to belong to. Outcomes based on social sorting[106] can subject people to financial, social and cultural segregation and exclusion.[107] Finally, profiling touches upon the autonomy of individuals by 'normalising' them in the kind of behaviour the profile predicts' on the basis of their group characteristics.[108]

2.4 Societal level challenges

Big data analytics can affect individuals in several ways, but they have broader consequences on the whole *society* as well. I call these the *societal* (or collective) level risks of big data. A clarification is needed here. As will be seen later in the chapter, the issues that big data raise at the *societal* level can have serious implications on individuals' fundamental rights as well. However, this chapter argues that this separate classification is necessary for two main reasons: First, it is not always clear what the particular harm of big data might be on specific individuals. I will borrow an example from surveillance here. In 2013, Edward Snowden, a Central Intelligence Agency (CIA) contractor, revealed that the United States had been operating a secret mass electronic surveillance programme that granted it access to Internet data, such as email, chat, videos, photos and file transfers held by leading Internet companies, including Facebook, Google, Microsoft, Yahoo, Skype, Apple and YouTube.[109] The revelations caused a public outcry in Europe, but the US side maintained that US intelligence agencies did 'not have the legal authority, the resources, the technical capability or the desire to intercept all of the world's communications. Those agencies are not reading the emails of everyone in the United States, or of everyone in the world'.[110] It is beyond the scope of this chapter to delve into the fallacies of this argument,[111] but if we are to take it on its face value, it is indeed extremely difficult – if not impossible – for individuals to know whether and when they are targeted by surveillance measures, by whom surveillance is undertaken and through which means. Yet, even if harm cannot be particularised on specific individuals, surveillance poses significant risks at the *societal* level. There is a second reason explaining the necessity of drawing a separate category of *societal* level challenges of big data. This is required in order to be able to develop appropriate legal and regulatory solutions. These will be touched upon later in the chapter; for the moment, the analysis focuses on a discussion of the *societal* level challenges.

1. *Surveillance*

Big data analytics have brought forward new concerns of mass surveillance. To be sure, surveillance is not a new phenomenon emerging in the age of big data.[112] Nevertheless, big data have increased exponentially[113] the possibilities for surveillance and have changed to an extent the actors involved in this. Surveillance in the era of big data analytics is ubiquitous, pervasive and goes well beyond the traditional model of state surveillance. Large organisations, like Google and Facebook, hold almost every piece of information about our everyday lives. Surveillance permeates every aspect of our existence, even our most intimate details. From wearables to smart sex toys and 'spying vibrators',[114] data about our bodies and functions are visible to private companies.[115] Indeed, commercial surveillance by Internet giants 'dwarfs the surveillance conducted by national intelligence agencies.'[116]

The problem of widespread surveillance in the context of big data affects individual persons but it is primarily a societal one. While people's lives are rendered transparent, 'organisations engaged in surveillance are increasingly invisible to those whose data are garnered and used.'[117] As a result of surveillance, profiles are built and predictions are made; behaviours are nudged; surveillance then feeds back the individuals to whom these profiles will apply, and so on.

2. *Autonomy, equality and human dignity*

Big data analytics pose challenges to equality, autonomy and human dignity. The issues that arise from data mining, machine learning and profiling were categorised in the taxonomy presented in this chapter as individual level challenges that relate to the *processing* of the data. I argue here that these same issues raise problems that cannot only be captured by their effects on individuals, but we should consider the broader dynamics they create in the society.

Big data analysis leads to predictions that can be consequential, based on past behaviours but also preemptive,[118] aimed to deliberately subvert future choices and equal opportunities.[119] Personal autonomy is stifled if our ordinary, everyday lives are 'determined by algorithms and their continuous variations'.[120] Big data analytics are used to 'seduce, coerce, discipline, regulate and control: to guide and reshape how people, animals and objects interact with and pass through various systems'.[121] Profiling and its group effects can create 'filter bubbles' or 'echo-chambers'[122] undermining other fundamental rights such as freedom of expression and posing threats to democracy. Ultimately, the question that arises for our society is one of human dignity: how will we make sure that individuals are not treated as means to (the big data analytics) end?

3. *The power imbalances of big data*

Big data processing creates significant asymmetries in our society. Personal data have substantial monetary value,[123] and few parties get to reap this. For companies such as Google and Facebook, personal data are their most valuable asset[124] that is not accounted for on their balance sheet.[125] Indeed, such companies trade in personal data by granting 'free' services to users, by harvesting their data and paid services to advertisers and other businesses to use these data. Data brokers mine the web to collect personal information and sell this to interested parties.[126] Significant asymmetries arise as the 'digital dividend'[127] is not shared fairly between users-data subjects and the other stakeholders that trade personal data. As the EDPS observes, successful companies operating personal data services platforms are 'able to discriminate by combining knowledge they extract from data with monopoly power and vertical integration in the markets'.[128]

The asymmetries of big data are not merely about monetary winners and losers; more crucially, they are about imbalances of information – and ultimately, of power – between those who provide the data and those who exploit them. At the micro level, such imbalances might be imperceptible to individuals, yet they have real pernicious effects. For example, the recent revelation that a women's fertility app with which women share the most intimate details about their bodies, including sex and menstruation information, is funded by anti-abortion campaigners[129] shows the disturbing extent of the complexities of the information and power asymmetries in the big data society. At the macro/societal level, the accumulation of such degrees of (market) power by private organisations might have serious social, economic, cultural and political consequences. As Kitchin observes, 'far from being neutral in nature, algorithms construct and implement regimes of power and knowledge and their use has normative implications'.[130]

4. The lack of accountability of data stakeholders[131]

The information and power asymmetries in the big data society exacerbate the 'black box' phenomenon discussed previously. The aggregation of different sets of data through their constantly evolving lifecycles, machine learning, and AI raises questions as to who bears responsibility for the outcomes of big data. Is it the humans that must be held accountable or the algorithms? And to what degree? This lack of accountability is not only frustrating for the innocent individuals who are negatively affected. It seems to be imposing the 'black box' model on the whole society.[132] An unaccountable society undermines the very principles of democracy and the rule of law.

3. Addressing the big data challenges

3.1 The importance of the taxonomy and why the GDPR cannot provide a one-size-fits-all solution

The previous section has presented a conceptual map of the various issues raised by big data, classifying them at the *individual* and the *societal* level. Individual level concerns were furthermore distinguished depending on whether they relate to the *processing* of personal data or they occur as *outcomes* of the processing. The taxonomy attempts to capture the more important issues raised by big data, pulling them together in broader themes, but these might entail further unknown risks. At the same time, several of the issues identified are not clear-cut; they often overlap and recur – albeit in slightly different forms – at the individual and the societal levels. Moreover, similar challenges can be framed in different lights and examined through different lenses, often in such ways that it becomes difficult to properly define the problem and distinguish its effects (is it commercial surveillance or 'surveillance capitalism' understood as a 'privately administered compliance regime of rewards and punishments aimed at modifying and commoditising behaviour for profit'?[133]) Nevertheless, this mapping is not of a merely theoretical, academic value. On the contrary, the taxonomy is crucial in order to be able to reflect on the ways that the risks of big data can be properly addressed.

Taking the conceptual map as a starting point, I would like to advance two main arguments: First, regulatory approaches to big data risks cannot be all-encompassing one-size-fits-all measures. Solutions to big data problems should be searched at the particular level – individual or societal – where the issue arises and may vary depending on the specific type of problem. On the one hand, individual level regulatory measures should be aimed at preventing harm to individuals and at safeguarding their basic rights and interests. On the other hand, approaches that aim to deal with the societal risks of big data should address the dynamics and the types of power that big data analytics bring forward.

Against this backdrop, I come now to the main question of this chapter: What is the role of data protection laws in general and the GDPR in particular in regulating big data? The short answer is limited. The GDPR has been at the same time both hailed as the first piece of legislation that deals with big data and AI,[134] and accused of failing to cope[135] or being entirely incompatible[136] with big data developments. Despite being diametrically antithetical – the one praises the GDPR's capabilities, the other condemns them as insufficient – these two views share an interesting common point. They both seem to assume that data protection regulation, and in particular the GDPR, represent the main legal methodological solution attempting to grapple with big data. This assumption is not completely unfounded; indeed, the GDPR seems to make the same self-assertion.[137] Yet, this individualistic methodology is not appropriate to deal with the power configurations and the dynamics that concern us here.[138] Big data certainly entails personal data processing, but not all problems this raises are necessarily data privacy problems that should be dealt with by the GDPR just because they fall *rationae materiae* within its scope of application.[139] Such an assumption overlooks mechanisms and outcomes that are often completely irrelevant to data protection frameworks. Big data are less about identifying individuals – although they do have these capabilities – and more about 'algorithmic forms of constantly evolving, impersonal categorisations of risks and opportunities'[140] and generalistic, predictive and even preemptive profiles. The data itself has a 'relational' value: 'it is the (cor)relations between data that makes them valuable and useful',[141] sensitive or less so.

This explains why the typology of the big data challenges presented in this chapter is of crucial importance. By ignoring the two levels or conflating big data challenges at the individual and the societal level,[142] we end up trying to understand why data protection legislative measures such as the GDPR are not fit for purpose for big data contexts. The challenge facing us, therefore, is not as has been — erroneously – suggested, 'how to take account, in *personal data protection instruments*, of the relational, and therefore also collective, nature of what, *through data*, merits protection?'[143] In my view, the challenge is how to construct a regulatory framework of what merits protection in the age of big data by going beyond short-sighted visions that everything can be fitted in *personal data protection instruments* just because *personal data* is at stake.

3.2 The limited but important role of the GDPR

Where does all this leave the GDPR? I argue that its role is limited but important. The GDPR is an instrument that regulates personal data processing through its fair information and accountability principles and the rights it grants to data subjects. It cannot be denied, therefore, that by regulating personal data – the raw material of the big data society – it plays an instrumental role in dealing with the risks that big data analytics might incur. This instrumentality of the

GDPR, however, in preventing big data risks is only of indirect and probable value. It is possible that some big data risks could be indirectly mitigated if the GDPR principles are properly applied. Considering the seriousness of big data challenges, it is clear that this is not good enough. To put it differently, we should not be expecting the GDPR to address all the big data issues.

That being said, the GDPR has a role to play besides its indirect instrumental value. Going back to the taxonomy of big data challenges proposed earlier, I argue that the GDPR is able to deal with *individual level* challenges that relate to the *processing* of personal data. These are various, and are discussed in detail in Section 2 but can be summarised as follows: some are data-subject- or data controller- related (I call these *actor-related*); some are *systemic*; and all of them are modelled on and concern specific data protection rules.

Data subject-related issues describe the difficulties of data subjects to take advantage of rights granted to them under the GDPR. For instance, it is alleged that data subjects do not properly exercise their right to inform themselves as they do not read privacy policies, and even when they do it is not certain that they understand them. *Data controller-related* problems concern the difficulties controllers face to comply with their GDPR obligations. For example, it is difficult and costly for controllers to closely monitor and guarantee transparency in the processing of big data because allegedly they do not know where the information came from, due to the aggregation and repurposing of the data. *Systemic* challenges refer to the perceived inherent antithesis of big data with data protection principles. In this regard, the argument goes that big data are *de facto* incompatible with GDPR principles, such as data minimisation and storage limitation, as their utility is linked to the amount of data collected (the more, the better) and the length of periods retained (the longest, the best).

Despite the particular problems – *actor-related* or *systemic* – all the big data issues analysed previously concern specific GDPR provisions (personal data and personally identified information, problems and limitations of consent, implementation of fair and transparent processing, big data repurposing, data security, etc.) and are addressed by this instrument. In this respect, *actor-related* concerns either from the data subject's or the controller's side assume the non-enforceability of GDPR rights and rules just because it might be difficult to enforce them. These difficulties are not unique to big data, but arguably they augment within this context. Nevertheless, it is wrong to assume that the GDPR does not apply to big data just because it is difficult to enforce its principles. This argument is based on circular reasoning, and it ends up denying legal protection for no good reason.

The *systemic* challenges raised against the GDPR look more serious, but they are not insurmountable. The argument this time seems to be deontological (rather than ontological) in nature: the GDPR principles should not apply because they undermine the utility of big data. This implies a somewhat fake dilemma.[144] The GDPR does not contain abstract rules aimed to be antithetical to the big data business model. On the contrary, it has two equally important objectives: to ensure that personal data move freely while the rights and freedoms of natural persons with regard to the processing of personal data are protected.[145] The GDPR aims to act as an 'enabler of big data services in Europe'[146] by providing for context-specific rules[147] that could open up 'some concrete doors for big data to flourish'[148] while safeguarding at the same time the rights of data subjects. The *systemic* challenges argument is also based on the assumption that big data should remain an unregulated space because any regulation limiting these risks might undermine their utility. As Zuboff has astutely put it, this somehow implies 'the attribution of agency to "technology." "Big data" is cast as the inevitable consequence of a technological juggernaut with a life of its own entirely outside the social. We are but bystanders.'[149] This cannot be accepted. Big data should be able to produce their potential while respecting relevant regulatory frameworks applicable to them.

To sum up, the GDPR has a role to play when individual-level issues relating to the *processing* of personal data in the age of big data are at stake. This is because the GDPR sets out a comprehensive legal framework and contains a variety of mechanisms to address these. These are flexible and allow for context-specific solutions. They include legal rules (and their exemptions and exceptions thereof) stipulating the conditions under which processing is lawful and the obligations of data controllers. They also entail technological solutions; data protection by design and by default[150] aim at developing systems, programmes and applications that incorporate data protection principles such as data anonymisation, pseudonymisation, transparency and enhanced security into the design of the system.[151] Finally, alongside mandatory requirements, the GDPR allows for 'soft law' tools such as codes of conduct and certification mechanisms that can take account 'of the specific characteristics of the processing carried out in certain sectors and the specific needs of micro, small and medium enterprises'.[152]

Whether specific solutions enshrined in the GDPR are fit for purpose and effective in practice in the age of big data remains an open issue, allowing for the possible re-working of certain models and approaches in the future. For example, the concept of consent and its seemingly enhanced emphasis under the GDPR is an issue that should be revisited in the future.[153] This, however, does not negate the fact that the GDPR is a legislative instrument well placed to deal with the individual-level challenges relating to the *processing* of personal data identified earlier.

4. Addressing issues that relate to the *outcomes* of the processing and *societal* level challenges of big data

As mentioned previously, the GDPR has only an indirect instrumental role to play when issues relating to the *outcomes* of the processing and *societal* challenges of big data are at stake; by regulating personal data, it could potentially minimise or prevent some of the risks analysed earlier. Yet, the GDPR itself aims at a much higher objective: it purports 'to address the risks arising from profiling and automated decision-making, notably, but not limited to, privacy'.[154] For instance, Article 22 GDPR 'establishes a general prohibition for decision-making based solely on automated processing'[155] that produces legal effects concerning the data subject or significantly affects her.[156] The GDPR also grants data subjects rights to access[157] and be informed[158] about the existence of automated decision-making, including profiling, and to receive meaningful information about the logic involved, as well as the significance and the envisaged consequences of such processing and the right to contest the decision.[159]

Admittedly, automated decision-making involving personal data constitutes processing within the meaning of the GDPR[160] but it is not the application of the *general* data protection principles and data subject rights to this that is contested.[161] What is problematic is the *specific* rules on automated decision-making and profiling seen earlier. Leaving aside questions regarding the effectiveness of such provisions in the age of big data, there is another fundamental problem that arises here. This is about regulatory overreach and, perhaps more crucially, what Brownsword termed 'normative disconnection'[162]: the GDPR essentially attempts to control the outcomes of algorithmic processing and grant due-process rights to the persons affected by this. But even if AI risks arise at the individual level, they are hardly issues that concern the data subject. They concern decision-making processes, dynamics and outcomes that should not be confounded with data-processing issues. Therefore, the problem is not that these GDPR provisions are not fit for purpose; the problem is that they are not appropriate at all to deal with outputs irrelevant to the GDPR's scope.[163]

The individual-level challenges that occur as *outcomes* of the processing and the *societal* challenges of big data require regulatory methodologies that go beyond the atomistic, data subject-centred GDPR approach. What would these look like? The answer to this could be the subject of a whole monograph, but four preliminary points could be advanced here.

First, regulatory responses should correspond directly to the level and the types of risks we are facing. It is for this reason that the taxonomy of challenges presented in the first part of this chapter becomes relevant. For instance, the problems raised by profiling at the individual level should be addressed by '*sui generis*'[164] (and often sector-specific) measures that mandate the audit of algorithms and grant interested groups – and wherever possible, individuals – specific profiling due-process rights[165] that are independent to whether the personal data of a certain data subject were processed at a certain time point by unknown controllers.

Second, AI and big data challenges require a combination of different approaches rather than a single legislative measure. In this respect, the methodological approach of the EDPS of viewing big data as posing data protection, competition and consumer law problems and therefore requiring a holistic inter-sectorial methodology is certainly a step in the right direction.

Third, solutions require innovative thinking that includes both a transformational evolution of current ways of regulating ever-existing problems, such as discrimination, as well as the adoption of completely new rules addressing specific AI and big data challenges. For example, in the US context, Sharona Hoffmann proposes that in the era of big health data, the Americans with Disabilities Act (ADA) (the federal law that prohibits public and private bodies from discriminating against individuals because of their disabilities) should be amended to expand its anti-discrimination scope to include a prohibition of 'future' physical or mental impairments.[166] Given that predictive medicine profiling has been a reality for several years now,[167] legislators should proactively reflect on how to protect people from predictive, inferential discriminatory decisions as well.

Fourth, separate, specific rules might be needed for different stakeholders in the big data society, such as data brokers,[168] platforms,[169] the insurance sector, etc. These should ensure the accountability of these actors and account for the societal responsibilities of big data players.

5. Conclusion

Big data and AI raise a number of different challenges that legislators are still trying to grasp. In this respect, the GDPR is often presented as an example of a legislative solution aimed at addressing big data risks such as automated decision-making and profiling. This chapter has made three distinct contributions to the debate regarding regulatory approaches to big data: 1) it has provided a taxonomy of big data challenges; 2) it has examined the capabilities and limitations of the GDPR to address the risks identified; and 3) it has offered some suggestions on the pathways that the regulators should be considering.

Big data challenges are mapped in three categories: individual issues that relate to the *processing* of personal data; individual level issues relating to the *outcomes* of the processing; and *societal* level challenges. It is argued that the GDPR is well placed to deal with individual issues relating to the *processing* of personal data, but its atomistic, 'privacy self-management',[170] data-subject-focused approach is completely inappropriate to address risks that occur as the result of processing and *societal* level challenges. These require innovative ways of thinking that approach the players and complex dynamics of the big data and AI society in a holistic way, while presenting targeted solutions to the specific risks identified at each level.

Notes

1 For instance, Yeung notes: 'The right most clearly implicated by Big Data driven hypernudging is the right to informational privacy, given the continuous monitoring of individuals and the collection and algorithmic processing of personal digital data'. Karen Yeung, '"Hypernudge": Big Data as a Mode of Regulation by Design' (2017) 20 (1) *Information, Communication & Society*, 118, 124.

2 Regulation (EU) 2016/679 of the European Parliament and of the Council of 27 April 2016 on the protection of natural persons with regard to the processing of personal data and on the free movement of such data, and repealing Directive 95/46/EC (General Data Protection Regulation), Official Journal of the European Union, L 119/1, 4 May 2016.

3 EDPS, Opinion 7/2015 *Meeting the Challenges of Big Data: A Call for Transparency, User Control, Data Protection by Design and Accountability*.

4 Paul Nemitz, 'Constitutional Democracy and Technology in the Age of Artificial Intelligence' (2018) *Philosophical Transactions. R. Soc.* 1. The European Commission notes that 'the rules laid down in the [General Data Protection] Regulation provide a general framework and contain specific obligations and rights that are particularly relevant for the processing of personal data in AI'. See Commission, Communication from the Commission to the European Parliament and the Council, Data Protection Rules as a Trust-enabler in the EU and Beyond – Taking Stock, Brussels, 24.7.2019, COM(2019) 374 final.

5 For instance, the EDPS states: 'The question is not whether to apply data protection law to big data, but rather how to apply it innovatively in new environments.' EDPS, Opinion 7/2015, n 3, 4.

6 See Maria Eduarda Gonçalves, 'The EU Data Protection Reform and the Challenges of Big Data: Remaining Uncertainties and Ways Forward' (2017) 26 (2) *Information & Communications Technology Law*, 90, 99.

7 Articles 35, 36 GDPR and Recital 76. For an ethical and social impact assessment see Alessandro Mantelero, 'AI and Big Data: A Blueprint for a Human Rights, Social and Ethical Impact Assessment' (2018) 34 *Computer Law & Security Review*, 754.

8 Article 35 (1) GDPR.

9 Articles 33 and 34 GDPR.

10 Article 34 (1) GDPR.

11 EDPS, Opinion 7/2015, n 3.

12 See Maria Tzanou, 'The GDPR and (Big) Health Data: Assessing the EU Legislator's Choices'.

13 Ibid.

14 Viktor Mayer-Schonberger and Yann Padova, 'Regime Change? Enabling Big Data Through Europe's New Data Protection Regulation' (2016) *Colum. Sci. & Tech. L. Rev*, 315, 319.

15 See Tal Zarsky, 'Incompatible: The GDPR in the Age of Big Data' (2017) 47 *Seton Hall Law Review* 995, 1000.

16 See Ira Rubinstein and Woodrow Hartzog, 'Anonymization and Risk' (2016) 91 *Washington Law Review* 703, 710–711.

17 Article 4 (1) GDPR.

18 Case C-582/14, *Patrick Breyer v. Bundesrepublik Deutschland* [2016] ECLI:EU:C:2016:779. For case-note see Frederik Zuiderveen Borgesius, 'Breyer Case of the Court of Justice of the European Union: IP Addresses and the Personal Data Definition' (2017) 3 (1) *European Data Protection Law Review*, 130.

19 Ibid, para 42.

20 Ibid, para 43.

21 Gloria González Fuster and Amandine Scherrer, 'Big Data and Smart Devices and their Impact on Privacy' (2015) *Study for the LIBE Committee.*

22 Ibid, 21. Schneier has developed a taxonomy of personal data, on the basis of social media that includes six categories: service data, which is provided to open an account (e.g., name, address, credit card information, etc.); disclosed data, which is entered voluntarily by the user; entrusted data, for example the comments made on other people's entries; incidental data, which refers to a specific user but is uploaded by someone else; behavioural data, which contains information about the actions users are undertaking when using the site and may be used for targeted advertising; and inferred data, which is information deduced from someone's disclosed data, profile or activities.

23 GDPR, Art. 7.

24 See Solove, 'Introduction: Privacy Self-Management and the Consent Dilemma' (2013) 126 *Harvard Law Review* 1880.

25 Aleecia Mcdonald and Lorrie Cranor, 'The Cost of Reading Privacy Policies' (2008) 4 (3) *I/S: A Journal of Law and Policy for the Information Society*, 543.

26 See José van Dijck, 'Datafication, Dataism and Dataveillance: Big Data Between Scientific Paradigm and Ideology' (2014) 12 (2) *Surveillance & Society*, 199; Nina Gerber, Paul Gerber and Melanie Volkamer, 'Explaining the Privacy Paradox: A Systematic Review of Literature Investigating Privacy Attitude and Behavior' (2018) 77 *Computers and Security* 226.
27 See Tal Zarsky, 'The Trouble with Algorithmic Decisions: An Analytic Road Map to Examine Efficiency and Fairness in Automated and Opaque Decision Making' (2016) 41 (1) *Science, Technology, & Human Values* 118.
28 Art. 7 (4) GDPR provides 'when assessing whether consent is freely given, utmost account shall be taken of whether, *inter alia*, the performance of a contract, including the provision of a service, is conditional on consent to the processing of personal data that is not necessary for the performance of that contract.'
29 See Tzanou, 'Introduction', n 12.
30 See Orla Lynskey, *The Foundations of EU Data Protection Law* (Oxford: Oxford University Press, 2015), 189 and references therein.
31 GDPR, Article 6.
32 GDPR, Art. 5 (2).
33 Zarsky (n 15), 1020.
34 See Maria Tzanou, *The Fundamental Right to Data Protection: Normative Value in the Context of Counter-Terrorism Surveillance* (Oxford: Hart Publishing, 2017), 26.
35 Ibid.
36 Zarsky (n 15), 1006.
37 Bart van der Sloot and Sascha van Schendel, 'Ten Questions for Future Regulation of Big Data: A Comparative and Empirical Legal Study' (2016) *JIPITEC* 1, 10.
38 Ibid, 1006.
39 GDPR, Art. 5 (1) (c).
40 GDPR, Art. 5 (1) (e).
41 See Colin Bennett and Robin Bayley, 'Privacy Protection in the Era of "Big Data": Regulatory Challenges and Social Assessments', in Bart van der Sloot et al. (eds.), *Exploring the Boundaries of Big Data* (Amsterdam: Amsterdam University Press, 2016), 205, 210.
42 Ibid.
43 As put by the Dutch DPA in an empirical study 'Big Data is all about collecting as much information as possible.' See van der Sloot and van Schendel (n 37), 9.
44 Zarsky (n 15), 1011.
45 Ibid.
46 See van der Sloot and van Schendel (n 37), 9.
47 As eloquently put by van der Sloot and van Schendel 'Data can always be given a second life.' Ibid.
48 GDPR, Art. 5 (1) (d).
49 Ibid.
50 See relevant comments by Slovenian DPA as reported by van der Sloot and van Schendel (n 37), 9–10.
51 Ibid, 10.
52 Victor Mayer-Schoenberger and Kenneth Cukier, *Big Data: A Revolution that Will Transform How We Live, Work and Think* (London: John Murray, 2013), 15.
53 Van der Sloot and van Schendel (n 37), 9.
54 Article 5 (1) (b) GDPR.
55 Lokke Moerel and Corien Prins, 'Privacy for the Homo Digitalis, Proposal for a New Regulatory Framework for Data Protection in the Light of Big Data and the Internet of Things' <https://papers.ssrn.com/sol3/papers.cfm?abstract_id=2784123>, 2.
56 See Ernesto Damiani et al., 'Big Data Threat Landscape and Good Practice Guide', *ENISA*, January 2016. <www.enisa.europa.eu/publications/bigdata-threat-landscape>

and Rossen Naydenov et al., 'Big Data Security. Good Practices and Recommendations on the Security of Big Data Systems', *ENISA*, December 2015. <www.enisa.europa.eu/publications/big-data-security>.

57 See Antoinette Rouvroy, '"Of Data and Men" Fundamental Rights and Freedoms in a World of Big Data', Bureau of the Consultative Committee of the Convention for the Protection of Individuals with regard to Automatic Processing of Personal Data [ETS 108], 29.

58 Article 5 (1) (f) GDPR.

59 Article 32 GDPR.

60 Articles 33 and 34 GDPR.

61 Article 9 GDPR.

62 Article 9 (1) GDPR.

63 Article 9 (2) GDPR.

64 See Nathan Cortez, 'The Internet of Things (IoT) and Health Big Data: Introduction', in Glenn Cohen et al. (eds.), *Big Data, Health Law, and Bioethics* (Cambridge: Cambridge University Press, 2018), 125.

65 For details on health data sources see Introductory chapter. See also, Urs Grasser, 'Shifting Paradigms – Big Data's Impact on Health law and Bioethics: Introduction', in G. Cohen et al. (eds.), *Big Data, Health Law, and Bioethics* (Cambridge: Cambridge University Press, 2018), 15.

66 Moerel and Prins, n 55, 2.

67 Article 13 GDPR.

68 Article 15 GDPR.

69 Article 16 GDPR.

70 Article 17 GDPR. See also Maria Tzanou, 'The Unexpected Consequences of the EU Right to Be Forgotten: Internet Search Engines as Fundamental Rights Adjudicators', in M. Tzanou (ed.), *Personal Data Protection and Legal Developments in the European Union* (IGI Global, 2020) <https://papers.ssrn.com/sol3/papers.cfm?abstract_id=3277348>.

71 Article 18 GDPR.

72 See Article 21 GDPR.

73 Article 22 GDPR.

74 Rouvroy, n 57, p. 34.

75 Mireille Hildebrandt and Bert-Jaap Koops, 'The Challenges of Ambient Law and Legal Protection in the Profiling Era' (2010) *Modern Law Review*, 428, 440.

76 Frank Pasquale, *The Black Box Society: The Secret Algorithms That Control Money and Information* (Cambridge, MA: Harvard University Press, 2016).

77 Ibid, 3.

78 See Tzanou, 'Introduction', n 12.

79 Mayer-Schoenberger and Cukier, n 52, 52.

80 González Fuster and Scherrer, n 21.

81 Mayer- Schoenberger and Cukier, n 52, 32.

82 'Garbage in, garbage out' refers to this problem. See Brent Daniel Mittelstadt et al., 'The Ethics of Algorithms: Mapping the Debate' (2016) *Big Data & Society*, 1, 15.

83 Mayer-Schoenberger and Cukier, n 52, 66.

84 Mittelstadt et al., n 82, 6.

85 Pasquale, n 76, 3.

86 Mittelstadt et al., n 82, 6.

87 Jenna Burrell, 'How the Machine "Thinks:" Understanding Opacity in Machine Learning Algorithms' (2016) 3 *Big Data and Society*, 1.

88 Sharona Hoffman, 'Big Data's New Discrimination Threats: Amending the Americans with Disabilities Act to Cover Discrimination Based on Data-Driven Predictions of Future Disease in Big Data', in Glenn Cohen et al. (eds.), *Big Data, Health Law, and Bioethics* (Cambridge: Cambridge University Press, 2018), 85, 85.

89 Ibid.

90 Mittelstadt et al., n 82, 6.
91 Solon Barocas and Andrew D. Selbst, 'Big Data's Disparate Impact' (2016) 104 *California Law Review*, 671.
92 Ibid.
93 Allison Gardner, 'Medical AI Can Now Predict Survival Rates – But It's Not Ready to Unleash on Patients', *The Conversation*, 21 November 2019 <https://theconversation.com/medical-ai-can-now-predict-survival-rates-but-its-not-ready-to-unleash-on-patients-127039> and references therein; Angela Lashbrook, 'AI-Driven Dermatology Could Leave Dark-Skinned Patients Behind', *The Atlantic*, 16 August 2018 <www.theatlantic.com/health/archive/2018/08/machine-learning-dermatology-skin-color/567619/>.
94 Ibid.
95 Zarsky, n 15, 1000.
96 Art 4 (4) GDPR defines profiling as 'any form of automated processing of personal data consisting of the use of personal data to evaluate certain personal aspects relating to a natural person, in particular to analyse or predict aspects concerning that natural person's performance at work, economic situation, health, personal preferences, interests, reliability, behaviour, location or movements'.
97 Paul De Hert and Hans Lammerant, 'Predictive Profiling and Its Legal Limits: Effectiveness Gone Forever?', in Bart van der Sloot, Dennis Broeders and Erik Schrijvers (eds.), *Exploring the Boundaries of Big Data* (Amsterdam: Amsterdam University Press, 2016), 145, 147. The Art 29 WP identifies four stages of the profiling process: 1) collecting data; 2) analysing data; 3) building a profile for an individual; 4) applying a profile to make a decision affecting the individual. See Art 29WP, Guidelines on Automated individual decision-making and Profiling.
for the purposes of Regulation 2016/679, Adopted on 3 October 2017, 12.
98 Hildebrandt and Koops, n 75, 440.
99 De Hert and Lammerant, n 97, 147.
100 Ibid.
101 Ibid.
102 Ibid.
103 Article 29WP, Guidelines on Automated individual decision-making n 97, 5.
104 See previously described discrimination.
105 See previously discussed incorrect and unreliable conclusions.
106 See David Lyon, 'Surveillance, Snowden, and Big Data: Capacities, Consequences, Critique' (2014) *Big Data & Society* 1, 10.
107 European Data Protection Supervisor (EDPS), EDPS Opinion 4/2015 *Towards a New Digital Ethics: Data, Dignity and Technology*, 11 September 2015, 13.
108 Hildebrandt and Koops, n 75, 434.
109 See Maria Tzanou, 'European Union Regulation of Transatlantic Data Transfers and Online Surveillance' (2017) 17 (3) *Human Rights Law Review* 545–556.
110 Annex VI, Commission Implementing Decision of 12 July 2016 pursuant to Directive 95/46/EC of the European Parliament and of the Council on the adequacy of the protection provided by the EU – US Privacy Shield, Brussels, 12 July 2016, COM (2016) 4176 final, 93.
111 See Tzanou, n 109.
112 Lyon, n 106.
113 Ibid.
114 Janet Burns, 'We-Vibe Settles For $3.7M In "Spying Vibrator" Data Suit', *Forbes*, 15 March 2017 <www.forbes.com/sites/janetwburns/2017/03/15/we-vibe-settles-for-3-7m-in-spying-vibrator-data-lawsuit/#3ee371316021>.
115 Janet Burns, 'The "Spying Vibrator" Suit Is Over, But Sex Toys Are Still Talking Data', *Forbes*, 14 December 2016 <www.forbes.com/sites/janetwburns/2016/12/14/the-spying-vibrator-suit-is-over-but-sex-toys-are-still-talking-data/#692879384417>.
116 Yeung, n 1, 123.

117 Lyon, n 106, 4.
118 Ibid.
119 For example, see Samuel Gibbs, 'Women Less Likely to be Shown Ads for High-Paid Jobs on Google, Study Shows', *The Guardian*, 8 July 2015 <www.theguardian.com/technology/2015/jul/08/women-less-likely-ads-high-paid-jobs-google-study>.
120 EDPS, Opinion 4/2015, n 107, 13.
121 Rob Kitchin, 'Thinking Critically about and Researching Algorithms' (2017) 20 (1) *Information, Communication & Society*, 14, 19.
122 EDPS, Opinion 4/2015, n 107, 13.
123 See OECD, 'Exploring the Economics of Personal Data: A Survey of Methodologies for Measuring Monetary Value' (2013) OECD Digital Economy Papers, No. 220, OECD Publishing <http://dx.doi.org/10.1787/5k486qtxldmq-en>.
124 Ibid.
125 EDPS, Opinion 8/2016, Opinion on coherent enforcement of fundamental rights in the age of big data, 23 September 2016, 13.
126 Federal Trade Commission (FTC), *Data Brokers: A Call for Transparency and Accountability*, May 2014.
127 EDPS, Opinion 8/2016, n 125, 13.
128 Ibid.
129 Jessica Glenza, 'Revealed: Women's Fertility App is Funded by Anti-Abortion Campaigners', *The Guardian*, 30 May 2019 <www.theguardian.com/world/2019/may/30/revealed-womens-fertility-app-is-funded-by-anti-abortion-campaigners> and Eva Wiseman, 'Beware the Fertility App that Wants to Share Your Data with Anti-Abortion Campaigners', *The Guardian*, 9 June 2019 <www.theguardian.com/lifeandstyle/2019/jun/09/app-creep-and-the-dark-side-of-sharing-private-date-on-our-phones>.
130 Kitchin, n 121, 19.
131 Accountability is understood differently here from the 'accountability principle' under Article 5 (2) GDPR.
132 Pasquale, n 76, 217.
133 Shoshana Zuboff, 'Big Other: Surveillance Capitalism and the Prospects of an Information Civilization' (2015) 30 *Journal of Information Technology*, 75, 83 and 85.
134 See earlier.
135 Gonçalves, n 6, 114.
136 Zarsky, n 15.
137 Art 29 WP notes 'The GDPR introduces new provisions to address the risks arising from profiling and automated decision-making, notably, but not limited to, privacy.' Article 29WP, Guidelines on Automated individual decision-making n 97, 6.
138 Rouvroy, n 57, 22. See also Bart van der Sloot, 'The Individual in the Big Data Era: Moving towards an Agent-based Privacy Paradigm', in Bart van der Sloot et al. (eds.), *Exploring the Boundaries of Big Data* (Amsterdam: Amsterdam University Press, 2016), 177.
139 See also Purtova, who argues that 'the material scope of . . . the GDPR, is growing so broad that the good intentions to provide the most complete protection possible are likely to backfire in a very near future, resulting in system overload.' Nadezhda Purtova, 'The Law of Everything. Broad Concept of Personal Data and Future of EU Data Protection Law' (2018) 10 (1) *Law, Innovation and Technology*, 40, 41.
140 Rouvroy, n 57, 22.
141 Ibid.
142 The indicative list of risks that can arise from the processing of personal data provided in Recital 75 GDPR demonstrates this conflation and confusion of issues. More particularly, Recital 75 states that risks of processing of personal data include 'discrimination, identity theft or fraud, financial loss, damage to the reputation, loss of confidentiality of personal data protected by professional secrecy, unauthorised reversal of pseudonymisation, or any other significant economic or social disadvantage; where data subjects might be deprived of their rights and freedoms or prevented from exercising control over their

personal data; where personal data are processed which reveal racial or ethnic origin, political opinions, religion or philosophical beliefs, trade union membership, and the processing of genetic data, data concerning health or data concerning sex life or criminal convictions and offences or related security measures; where personal aspects are evaluated, in particular analysing or predicting aspects concerning performance at work, economic situation, health, personal preferences or interests, reliability or behaviour, location or movements, in order to create or use personal profiles; where personal data of vulnerable natural persons, in particular of children, are processed; or where processing involves a large amount of personal data and affects a large number of data subjects.' With the necessary caveats that 'risks' under the GDPR have a slightly different meaning from 'challenges' and 'issues' as discussed in this chapter and they do not concern big data in particular but any type of processing of personal data, Recital 75 contains a mixture of different types of risks (some concern the *processing* of personal data, some the *outcomes* of processing, some are *societal*) put together without any differentiation. This is also problematic for controllers, who are required to decide when processing is of 'high risk' or which data breaches entail such 'risks'.

143 Rouvroy, n 57, 22. Emphasis added.

144 The ICO notes 'It's not a case of big data *or* data protection, it's big data *and* data protection; the benefits of both can be delivered alongside each other.' Information Commissioner's Office, *Big Data, Artificial Intelligence, Machine Learning and Data Protection*, 20170904 Version: 2.2, para 28.

145 Art. 1 GDPR.

146 Commission, 'The EU Data Protection Reform and Big Data, Factsheet' March 2016. See also Gonçalves n 6, 114 who argues that the GDPR demonstrates 'the EU's deliberate, actually explicit intent to simplify rules for companies in the digital age' and 'caught between its twofold objective of strengthening the rights of the data subjects, and facilitating business, the EU legislator ended up favouring the latter to the detriment of the former.'

147 See Art. 5 (1).

148 Mayer-Schonberger and Padova, n 14, 318.

149 Zuboff, n 133, 75.

150 Art 25 GDPR and Recital 78.

151 As the EDPS correctly recommends 'Designers and manufacturers should apply the same level of creativity and dynamicity they usually display in introducing attractive devices and apps to also provide individuals with effective and user-friendly privacy notices and setting options. As a result, individuals should be able to set options relevant to their privacy and data protection with the awareness that this is an important element of the devices and apps' use, in their own personal interest, and not a boring formality or a useless burden.' EDPS, Opinion 1/2015 Mobile Health: Reconciling Technological Innovation with Data Protection, 13. See also EDPS, Opinion 7/2015 (n 3), 14.

152 Recital 98 GDPR. See also Art 40 GDPR.

153 The Centre for Information Policy Leadership (CIPL) observes that 'Despite the fact that there are six legal basis contained in the GDPR, none of which are privileged over the other, there is a general feeling among data protection practitioners, lawyers and DPOs that DPAs, lawmakers and policymakers in the EU place strong emphasis on consent as a more important legal basis . . . For the GDPR to serve as a modern privacy law, its consent requirements cannot be emphasised as the principal legal ground for processing, nor should the other legal bases be continuously construed narrowly.' Centre for Information Policy Leadership, 'GDPR One Year In: Practitioners Take Stock of the Benefits and Challenges', 31 May 2019 <www.informationpolicycentre.com/uploads/5/7/1/0/57104281/cipl_report_on_gdpr_one_year_in_-_practitioners_take_stock_of_the_benefits_and_challenges.pdf>, 8.

154 Art 29 WP Guidelines on Automated individual decision-making and Profiling for the purposes of Regulation 2016/679, 6.

155 Ibid, 19.
156 See also Recital 71.
157 Article 15 (1) (h) GDPR.
158 Articles 13 (2) (f) and 14 (2) (g) GDPR.
159 Article 22 (3) GDPR.
160 Article 4 (2) GDPR.
161 See Article 29WP, Guidelines on Automated individual decision-making n 97, 9–19.
162 Roger Brownsword, *Rights, Regulation, and the Technological Revolution* (Oxford: Oxford University Press, 2008), 166.
163 As Koops observes 'This . . . requires stretching the concept of personal data (sometimes to the point of breaking, or perhaps rather of becoming void of meaning), or stretching the regulatory problem so that it becomes a problem of processing personal data.' Bert-Jaap Koops, 'The Trouble with European Data Protection Law' (2014) 4 (4) *International Data Privacy Law*, 250, 258.
164 Ibid, 260.
165 See Danielle Keats Citron and Frank Pasquale, 'The Scored Society: Due Process for Automated Predictions', University of Maryland Francis King Carey School of Law Legal Studies Research Paper No. 2014–8; Crawford and Schultz propose 'procedural data due process' for big data that 'rather than attempt regulation of personal data collection, use, or disclosure ex ante, procedural data due process would regulate the fairness of Big Data's analytical processes with regard to how they use personal data (or metadata derived from or associated with personal data) in any adjudicative process, including processes whereby Big Data is being used to determine attributes or categories for an individual.' Kate Crawford and Jason Schultz, 'Big Data and Due Process: Toward a Framework to Redress Predictive Privacy Harms' (2014) 55 *B.C.L. Rev.*, 93, 109.
166 Hoffman, n 88, 85.
167 EDPS, Opinion 1/2015 *Mobile Health: Reconciling Technological Innovation with Data Protection*, 21 May 2015, 10.
168 Data brokers should comply with data protection legislation, but specific legislative measures could also be applicable to them. See Privacy International, 'Why We've Filed Complaints Against Companies that Most People Have Never Heard Of – And What Needs to Happen Next', 8 November 2018 <https://privacyinternational.org/advocacy/2434/why-weve-filed-complaints-against-companies-most-people-have-never-heard-and-what>; Amit Katwala, 'Forget Facebook, Mysterious Data Brokers are Facing GDPR Trouble', *Wired*, 8 November 2018 <www.wired.co.uk/article/gdpr-acxiom-experian-privacy-international-data-brokers>.
169 See Christian Sandvig et al., 'An Algorithm Audit', in Seeta Peña Gangadharan (eds.), *Data and Discrimination: Collected Essays* (Washington, DC: New America Foundation, 2014). <http://www-personal.umich.edu/~csandvig/research/An%20Algorithm%20Audit.pdf>. The authors propose audits for online platforms that 'will ascertain whether algorithms result in harmful discrimination by class, race, gender, geography, or other important attributes.'
170 Solove, n 24, 1880.

8 The GDPR, AI and the NHS Code of Conduct for Data-Driven Health and Care Technology

Joseph Savirimuthu

I. Introduction

The potential of artificial intelligence (AI) and machine learning to revolutionise the delivery of healthcare in the UK National Health Service (NHS) has brought the General Data Protection Regulation 2016 (GDPR) into mainstream information governance debates.[1] As part of its strategy for harnessing the "potential of cutting-edge technologies to support preventative, predictive and personalised care" solutions, the UK Government has called for a reassessment of the type of governance mechanisms that will help bring to fruition the political goals set out in the *Next Steps on the NHS Five Year Forward View*.[2] It is particularly striking to note that a crucial plank to ushering the transition to a "radical new [governance] approach to technology" involves the reorientation of existing data protection rules governing the collection, use and sharing of personal information in the age of AI systems and big data analytics.[3] The Code of Conduct for Data-Driven Health and Care Technology (Code of Conduct) is presented as the mechanism through which the regulatory discourse targets those "pain points" that create barriers to innovation.[4] In light of this logic, one may be led to assume that the immediate outcome of the principles-based approach would be to enable the NHS to draw on the knowledge and expertise of clinicians, designers of digital health infrastructure providers and healthcare professionals to help clarify and develop common understandings of data protection rules, adapt these where appropriate and implement and monitor their application in diverse healthcare settings.[5] Arguably, codes of conduct are preferable as an information governance mechanism, when compared with the time-consuming and costly task of enacting a comprehensive set of statutory rules governing the integration of AI into the healthcare environment.[6] Enacting another set of rules would also create additional challenges for compliance, given the existence of a dense framework of regulations and bodies monitoring compliance of healthcare professionals and utilization of digital devices and innovative solutions for diagnosis and treatment of patients.[7] There is also unlikely to be much disagreement that a centralised 'command and control' regulatory framework will lack the agility in grappling with the dynamic and transformative reach of AI and complex data-driven processes. The need for a responsive framework managing disruptions ushered in by new and innovative technologies, it should be said, is not a new one and clearly is not unique to healthcare.[8] The aim of this chapter is to engage with two specific problems with assumptions made about the role and significance of the Code of Conduct's principles-based approach as critical to the Government's vision for modernising healthcare. First, it questions the implication that data protection law, unlike the Code of Conduct, is a monolithic centralised framework of rigid rules which constrain the ability of relevant parties to tailor regulations to the novel use of technologies and data-driven processes in discharging their responsibilities towards patients.[9] Second, a close examination of the Code of Conduct suggests that the GDPR already provides a legal infrastructure aimed at promoting a bottom-up approach of spontaneous 'regulatory conversations' with a view to speeding up access to personal information and minimise obstacles to collection, pave the way towards harnessing insights from the use of big data analytical systems and provide assurances of data quality and trustworthiness.[10] It will be argued that many of the principles in the Code of Conduct which are perceived as being responsive to the challenges that clinicians face in dynamic settings originate in the law's reflexive and flexible framework that is polycentric, and which provides mechanisms for steering actors processing health data at multiple levels with the aim of ensuring that collective understandings of norms and practices being developed and operationalised are consistent with the GDPR.[11] The chapter is structured as follows. Section 2 sets the context by outlining how the integration of AI systems into healthcare holds the prospect for radically transforming the means and ways through which decisions are made. The discussion then turns to data protection law's response to the transformations being ushered in by AI – specifically, the collection, manipulation and use of personal data. Two questions form the focus of the discussion. First, how data protection law enables actors in the dynamic healthcare environment to apply their knowledge, expertise and skills when using novel data-driven processes for prediction, treatment and diagnosis; and second, what significance is to be attached to the Code of Conduct. Section 3 considers the first question and Section 4 the second.

2. AI and healthcare

In order to understand and grapple with the data protection issues that arise in the data-driven healthcare environment, a brief account of AI, machine learning processes and big data analytics and its application to the healthcare context, will be provided.

Artificial intelligence: a working definition

Artificial intelligence can be described as a computational process that enables machines to "to perceive, reason, and act".[12] The significance of the speed with which machines can process vast amounts of data and undertake tasks commonly associated with human knowledge and reasoning does not of itself make them a disruptive technology. AI systems are not simply data processing tools, but rather they can be regarded as "agents that can form representations of the world, use a process of inference to derive new representations about the world, and use these new representations to deduce what to do".[13]

With the rise of ubiquitous computing, cheap processing and increased storage capacities, sensors can now capture raw data created by individuals and the environment to produce results that can be measured. AI systems have decision-making and self-learning capabilities that enable them to operate as analytical models, classify outputs, detect hidden patterns and reach decisions without human input.[14]

AI and healthcare

Knowledge discovery from mining data from databases has long been used in healthcare – from detecting fraud to precision targeting of public health strategies and differential diagnosis of chronic health conditions. Automated data mining processes and AI solutions are integrated into all aspects of medical practice. Data captured by sensors can be now be used to inform diagnosis and predict onset of health or related problems.[15] For example, mobile phone applications can now be used to capture and transmit information to clinicians so that they can analyse the health condition of patients with kidney disease and detect the onset of kidney failure.[16] Opportunities for enhancing health outcomes are not limited to patients suffering with chronic kidney disease. AI technologies and systems are being used to offer personalised treatments such as screening for breast cancer[17] and eye diseases,[18] as well as augmenting the skills and expertise of clinicians.[19] In addition, AI systems are being used for preventative health purposes in non-communicable diseases, such as offering recommendations based on the analysis of patterns detected from behavioural data.[20] AI neural networks have been used to identify skin lesions to help optimise clinical decision making and facilitate the exchange of ideas and information to advance medical treatments[21] and medications.[22] Standardised assessments of AI-based health solutions are being developed to support medical diagnostics.[23] Increasingly, AI-based health solutions are being used in clinical settings to enhance the quality of decision making through the analysis of information from diverse databases which include images, text and patient data.[24] Innovations in digital health infrastructures have also enabled clinicians and those engaged in primary care to track and monitor patients' health conditions, with real-time medical diagnosing and treatments taking place.[25] Recent developments in blockchain technologies and applications have seen systems developed with technological management of the delivery and information stewardship processes.[26] With advances in AI-based health solutions taking place with such pace, for organizations like the NHS, new opportunities for data-driven innovations are integrating the entire health and social care sector.[27]

Conclusion: AI and dynamic healthcare environment

Data-driven innovation as a public health strategy offers considerable value for individuals, the NHS and society.[28] Growing expectation of the benefits to be derived from rapid deployment of AI and machine learning systems into the NHS has renewed the Government's interest in developing a governance mechanism that enables actors from both the public and commercial sectors to help realise the strategic and public health goals.[29] Trustworthiness, management of consent and data stewardship are critical to the development, design and implementation of a "digital architecture of the health and care system".[30] The distributed nature of decision-making processes, the range of actors involved in the provision of AI systems, sensitivities surrounding consent to the use of personal information and allocating responsibility raise important questions for the design of an information governance framework that maintains trust in a data-driven healthcare environment. It comes as no surprise that the strategy for a data-driven innovation in healthcare requires translating questions such as what is personal data, who can access the data and how and when it can be used in the context of AI-based health systems and solutions into clinical settings.[31] With data-driven innovation being tied up with continued access to vast amounts of personal sensitive data and the ease with which such data can be distributed across disparate healthcare platforms, and the lifecycle of personal data being extended through AI-based optimisation tools, maintaining trust will require coordination amongst those with direct expertise and knowledge to assess the suitability of data-driven processes, and to manage privacy risks and develop mechanisms necessary to subject human behaviour and practices to the governance of rules.[32] Before we turn to a consideration of the likely significance of the Code of Conduct, it may be useful to describe and explain how data protection law plays a critical role in mobilising relevant parties using novel data-driven processes for prediction, treatment and diagnosis in a way that helps them manage compliance risks.[33]

3. Data protection law and the evolving complexion of regulatory conversations

A conventional way of understanding the interaction between information governance in healthcare and data protection law would be through a description of the rights, interests and obligations of relevant parties, coupled with an account of authoritative opinions and judicial interpretations.[34] However, given the significance attached to the Code of Conduct as establishing the ground rules[35] for providers and users of data-driven processes and innovation[36] or that it subjects the use of AI in a way that is safe and responsible,[37] it is important that we take into account the GDPR – not just because its rules regulate the type of processing activity with which we are concerned but also because it provides a framework where parties can organise their behaviours and practices when "thinking about the risks to data subjects and how to mitigate" privacy, personal data and security concerns.[38] As the European Data Protection Board recently observed, the GDPR provides a "rulebook for controllers and processors who design and implement GDPR compliant data processing activities which give operational meaning to the principles of data protection set out in European and National law".[39]

Two points need to be emphasised here with regard to the standard-setting role of data protection law in managing societies' transition into an increasingly data-driven environment. First, because data-driven decision in the healthcare setting involves multilayered technological infrastructures and involvement of various actors, data protection manages these interactions by embedding questions that inevitably arise with regard to legitimacy, accountability and fairness to the governance of rules. Additionally, guidance can be obtained from a diverse range of sources, such as data protection authorities and sector-specific organisations and regulatory authorities, when novel forms of data processing are undertaken through the use of innovative solutions and technological infrastructures being integrated into the healthcare environment data. Second, the data protection framework is cognizant of the reality that shaping privacy-respecting behaviours not only requires clarity and flexibility but also that weight be attached to the judgment and expertise of providers of data processing systems, and those utilising these when operationalising the law. Even though the GDPR does not provide specific standardized methodology, processing decisions must be capable of being justified and reconciled with existing rules, duties and principles. Black views these decision-making and rule-compliance practices as "regulatory conversations" which involve "continual interpretation, adjustment, and discussion".[40] There are three crucial ways the GDPR helps empower relevant actors in the healthcare environment, including those responsible for designing healthcare infrastructures to embed data protection standards and mitigate the uncertainties that may arise when using AI systems and novel processes for collection and decision making: i) framing the subjects and objects of regulation; ii) providing mechanisms for determining transparency, accountability and legitimacy; and iii) enhancing the ideals of responsiveness through processes for managing risks from the use of digital health solutions.[41]

Framing subjects and objects of regulation

In framing the objects and subjects of regulation, the law provides guidance to two questions encountered when personal information is processed: Who is responsible for the processing activities, and what data becomes subject to the obligations? Under the "accountability principle", data controllers are required to demarcate the specific responsibilities of those engaged in the processing of personal data, which include providers of digital health platforms, providers of mobile health applications, programmers and other operators.[42] Data controllers are vested with a number of obligations.[43] These include their responsibility for all data processing activity, demonstrating proactive implementation of and compliance with the rules, identifying all controllers and operations so that responsibilities can be correctly allocated, undertaking data protection impact assessments and ensuring security and trustworthiness of systems.[44] The accountability principle is closely aligned with the requirement that data controllers adopt appropriate organizational and technical measures to mitigate privacy and data protection risks.

Data-driven health technologies such as AI, machine learning, the Internet of Things (IoT) and big data analytics require access to personal information to facilitate medical treatment and diagnosis. Sharing of personal information is also critical to advancing knowledge and promoting innovations in healthcare.[45] Processing involves the collection, storage, sharing and manipulation of personal data. The accountability of data controllers and the risk management measures to be adopted depend on the type of personal data and risks associated with the type of processing involved. Data protection rules aim to balance opportunities for exchange of knowledge and ideas on the one hand, and respect for the fundamental right to the protection of personal data on the other hand.[46] It is true that the boundaries between personal and non-personal data are becoming blurred with the growing use of AI systems to generate insights from vast amounts of data stored in large datasets.[47] Article 4(1) of the GDPR defines personal data as "any information relating to an identified or identifiable natural person" and further specifies that

> an identifiable natural person is one who can be identified, directly or indirectly, in particular by reference to an identifier such as name, an identification number, location data, an online identifier or to one or more factors specific to the physical, physiological, genetic, mental, economic, cultural or social identity of that natural person.

The GDPR provides a broad, non-exhaustive definition of personal data, which expands the scope of protection to ensure that the risks to patient safety and privacy are not undermined by the ease with which large volumes of data can be collected and repurposed, and new knowledge generated by data mining tools and analytics.[48] Any digital health device, AI system or image captured by an smartphone will be brought within the law's remit.[49] Article 4(15) states explicitly that the definition of health data will extend to any "personal data related to the physical or mental health of a natural person, including the provision of health care services, which reveal information about his or her health status".[50] Where the information is sufficiently anonymised and the data subject is not identifiable, the GDPR is not applicable.[51] However, pseudonymous data is treated as personal data because the risks of re-identification are present if additional information is used.[52] Identifiability is a key feature in the concept of personal data and will include pseudonymous data.[53] Recital 26 also makes clear that where data analytics can be used to single out or re-identify individuals from otherwise pseudonymised or anonymised information, the data will be treated as personal.[54] Article 9 of the GDPR is intended to make clear to data controllers the expectation that compliance with its high standards for processing sensitive personal data, such as medical health data, is mandatory.[55]

Mechanisms for accountability, fairness and lawfulness

The seamless way that AI systems continue to be integrated into the healthcare environment pose important questions about accountability, fairness and lawfulness of the data-driven innovations as the lifecycle of health data continues to be extended through computational processes which generate new or inferred information from manipulating volunteered information or through use of machine learning and probabilistic analytical tools.[56] The GDPR provides a standardised governance framework that enables data controllers to identify how their data-related and process-related tasks can be structured in a way that helps better manage complexity and uncertainty.[57] The governance framework mirrors the foundational values that already define the therapeutic relationship between physicians and patients on the one hand, and balancing the public interest in harnessing the benefits of personal health information with respect for patients' dignity and privacy on the other.[58] The GDPR sets down six principles that enable data controllers and those utilising data-driven devices and technologies to exercise their discretion when calibrating processing practices with the principle of accountability: lawfulness, fairness and transparency; purpose limitation; data minimisation; accuracy; storage limitation; and integrity and confidentiality.[59] There are two aspects to the 'light touch' data governance featured in Article 5.[60] The first provides a governance framework within which normative and practice issues arising from the collection and processing of personal information can be undertaken. Second, the fair processing principles reflect an ideological belief that for the law to keep pace with rapid technological changes and avoid being overly prescriptive, physicians should be afforded the space to determine what types of data are necessary to the treatment and diagnosis while fulfilling their specific obligations to data subjects.[61] For example, it is right that clinicians' expertise and judgment should be relied upon, in accordance with the guidance provided by the professional body when determining the legitimacy, proportionality, necessity of gaining access to the information and compatibility in light of the purpose for which it was obtained. As the Court of Justice of the European Union (CJEU) noted in *Digital Ireland*, that exercise of discretion is subject to judicial oversight:[62]

> Article 52(1) of the Charter provides that any limitation on the exercise of the rights and freedoms laid down by the Charter must be provided for by law, respect their essence and, subject to the principle of proportionality, limitations may be made to those rights and freedoms only if they are necessary and genuinely meet objectives of general interest recognised by the Union or the need to protect the rights and freedoms of others.

Another point worth highlighting in this regard is that cases where personal data is to be used for purposes other than immediate diagnosis or treatment (secondary purposes), data controllers have the obligation to demonstrate that any subsequent use is commensurate with the reasonable expectations of the data subject, the type of personal data involved, the likely impact and that steps have been taken to ensure that appropriate safeguards have been put in place.[63] To ensure that risks to data subjects are minimised, data controllers are required to design systems that are secure, and implement an organizational framework ensuring that the information being used is accurate and updated and that data used for processing are no more than needed for the task and not stored for a period longer than necessary.[64] In summary, the data quality, compatibility and necessity principles seek to ensure that data controllers can implement measures and processes that can be audited, justified and evaluated continuously. Within this context, data controllers have the obligation to ensure that the personal data being processed is accurate and to take appropriate steps if a request has been made to erase or rectify the information.[65]

The GDPR not only provides a framework drawing on the input of relevant parties to demonstrate that their use of AI systems and big data analytics is compliant with its principles for fair and lawful processing; it also stipulates that a legal basis is a pre-condition to the processing of personal data.[66] Article 6(1) requires that data controllers establish at the outset which of the six lawful grounds being relied upon. In addition to satisfying Article 6(1), there is the additional requirement for data controllers to comply with additional safeguards provided for the processing of sensitive health data in Article 9.[67] The requirement for a legal basis needs to be considered in light of the dual objectives of data protection law, which is to balance public interest in accessing personal information with that of a data subject's right to withhold consent.[68] Sensitive personal data can, for example, be lawfully processed if it is necessary to "protect the vital interests of the data subject or of another natural person where the data subject is physically or legally incapable of giving consent."[69] Another legal basis is the processing of sensitive personal data for the purposes of medical diagnosis, treatment or the management of health or social care treatment and systems.[70] Processing of such data would also be lawful where it is necessary for reasons of public interest in the area of public health or where it is necessary for scientific research.[71]

A major area of considerable discussion with regard to the processing of personal sensitive information concerns the requirement for explicit consent.[72] Article 9(2)(a) provides that sensitive personal data may be processed if "the data subject has given explicit consent to the processing of those personal data for one or more specified purposes . . ." EU Member States, it should be noted, are permitted to enact laws which restrict the circumstances when explicit consent is required or introduce conditions limiting its scope.[73] As a number of scholars have observed, judicial rulings, guidance on the application of legal rules and principles provided by data protection supervisory authorities and evolution of stewardship-type obligations have played an important role to help ensure that careful balances are struck to minimise the adverse impacts of technology on society.[74]

Within the healthcare context, the requirement for a legal basis enables personal information to be processed, even in the absence of explicit consent, where it is vital to provide life-saving treatment. The availability of a wide range of legal basis for processing personal information provides data controllers with grounds that may be suited to particular contexts and objectives. Viewed together, the provisions in Articles 5, 6 and 9 enable relevant parties to determine for which purposes the personal data is being used; the reasonable and appropriate situations where information can be shared, and with whom; and provide data subjects with opportunities to express their agreement or refusal.

Responsive mechanisms for managing risks and impact

Regulatory conversations about data controllers' obligations regarding the protection of patients' privacy and personal data protection also involve the broader challenge of identifying, assessing and managing in a "proactive and responsible manner".[75] The mechanisms for managing risks associated with the processing of personal information need to be seen alongside the way the principle of accountability interacts with the rights provided to data subjects.[76] For example, data controllers undertake to provide data subjects with relevant information about their processing activity so that the information rights can be exercised in a meaningful way.[77] These rights include access to personal data which have been directly or indirectly obtained,[78] the purposes for which the information has been proposed and the way it has been classified,[79] rectification,[80] erasure when the purpose for which information has been obtained has ceased to be relevant or consent withdrawn,[81] objection when there are no legitimate grounds for processing[82] and the right to have automated decision making, which give rise to significant legal effects subjected to review.[83] These rights lead to the focus being directed towards addressing concerns expressed with the role of the law framing the issues to be addressed and the justifications needed for continued processing of personal information. The exercise of the rights enjoyed by data subjects can be seen as a way of structuring conversations that take into account the specific circumstances and help reconcile any conflicts in expectations with regard to the processing operation.

There is another category of governance challenges that should be discussed. This relates to a digital health infrastructure predicated by AI-based health solutions that automates decision making and creates profiles of individuals from processing sensitive personal data to a high level of specificity.[84] As an example, consider the problems of transparency, accountability and legitimacy that may arise when algorithms are programmed to capture, process, analyse and share raw data captured from mobile sensors, applications and information about a group of patients suffering chronic health conditions.[85] Data points from the sensitive personal data can be generated from volunteered personal data, which may include blood samples, scans, medical history and prescriptions – all of which, when combined, will provide the raw data for the AI system. Machine learning tools can be utilized, for example, to synthesise data in combination with other structured or unstructured data to measure, predict and create risk models revealing life expectancies, diagnosis and treatment options; generate hidden patterns; and develop new insights.[86] Natural language processes enable AI systems to analyse complex datasets and draw inferences, and modelling new approaches to the use of statistical modelling has provided the impetus for a paradigm shift in the way processes for drawing correlations and generating new health, behavioural, lifestyle and mental insights with a sufficient degree of specificity have become important drivers of data-driven innovation.[87] These problem-solving and predictive capabilities also introduce an epistemological aspect into the regulatory conversation – as the boundaries between AI system and clinician decision making become blurred, how will risks be conceptualised, justified and managed?[88] Uncertainties about AI decision-making processes, risks of values and biases being introduced into the system, the range and quality of training and unstructured data, verification standards and adverse implications for patients from misdiagnosis by machine learning processes require careful assessment of risks and benefits.[89] It is also worth noting that risks to patients' safety, dignity and privacy can also arise even where processing is lawful.[90] The example provided suggests that the management of the dynamics of risk will not be straightforward. It is not surprising that questions have arisen with regard to risks of bias, discrimination and problems with understanding the way decisions are reached by AI systems.[91] However, irrespective of the debates being generated, the important point to be highlighted here is that even though novel use is made of AI processes, data protection law focuses on how issues arising in clinical settings can be addressed by those subject to its regulation. Floridi's view of governance as a collaborative process through which parties develop common understandings of standards, practices and compliance corresponds very much with the ongoing role of data protection law in providing *ex ante* mechanisms which structure the way decisions are made about managing the type of risks with which we are concerned.[92] As the European Data Protection Supervisor recently observed, data protection law aims to provide the

> assurance that controllers (here represented by you as a person responsible on behalf of the controller/business owner) adequately address privacy and data protection risks of "risky" processing operations. By providing a structured way of thinking about the risks to data subjects and how to mitigate them, DPIAs help organisations to comply with the requirement of "data protection by design" where it is needed the most, i.e. for "risky" processing operations.[93]

The data protection impact assessment and privacy by design provisions in the GDPR are particularly relevant here.[94] Both sets of provisions seek to provide "assurance" through authoritative interpretations, as well as increasing incentives for parties to comply with the law by providing a "structured way of thinking" about risks. Regulated parties and organizations can, as a result, also draw on their knowledge and expertise to identify the specific "risks to data subjects" encountered in the clinic setting and take steps to "mitigate them" against the background of data protection rules. The framework provided serve as a template requiring data controllers and operators to contextualise, prioritize and target privacy and safety concerns.[95]

There is more to the data protection risk governance model. Article 35, for example, prescribes the context and processes involved even where new technologies are not used in the processing of personal information.[96] For example, data controllers are required to clearly stipulate the nature, scope, context and purposes of the processing. By focusing on the context, the law aims to ensure that data controllers identify and assess the likelihood of "high risk to the rights and freedoms of natural persons" and then proceed to undertake an "assessment of the impact of the envisaged processing operations on the protection of personal data". Data controllers are required to provide a justification by explaining "the necessity and proportionality of the processing operations", the measures taken to "address the risks, including safeguards, security measures and mechanisms", that they have taken into "the rights and legitimate interests of data subjects and other persons concerned" and can demonstrate compliance.[97] An impact assessment audit must comprise "a systematic and extensive evaluation of personal aspects relating to natural persons" where processing is automated, profiles generated and which results in decisions "that produce legal effects concerning the natural person or similarly significantly affect the natural person".[98]

The effect of requiring data controllers to contextualise, prioritize and assess the likely risks and impact on specific privacy concerns highlights the role of law in constructing understandings of what type of *ex ante* behaviours and organizational processes need to be put in place.[99] Processing activities that will be regarded as "high risk" involve those concerning the evaluation or scoring, including profiling and predicting; automated decision making that will give rise to significant legal or similar effects or outcomes; large-scale systematic surveillance and monitoring; the integration of personal sensitive information; manipulation or combination of datasets; personal data of data subjects categorised as being vulnerable; or mosaic operations involving combination of facial, text, biological processes and technologies.[100] The references to the rights and interests of data subjects and the importance of consultation also relates the obligations owed by data controllers in ensuring that risks to the processing of personal data are mitigated and that fair processing principles are complied with.[101] Admittedly, Article 35 is not free of arguments arising from the discretion being devolved to data controllers, and reconciling data controllers' interests and data subjects' reasonable expectations, and interpretation difficulties, will be an ongoing governance challenge.[102]

Another *ex ante* feature of the risk-based governance framework can be seen in the role of the law in mandating the use of organizational and engineering solutions.[103] Even though the data protection by design and by default principle has been a well-discussed area, it is striking to note that the analysis often revolves around the privacy risks faced by data subjects in an environment of ubiquitous computing and AI processes.[104] Article 25 requires data controllers to implement appropriate technical and organisational measures, such as pseudonymisation, which are designed to implement data-protection principles, such as data minimisation, in an effective manner and to integrate the necessary safeguards into the processing in order to meet the requirements of this Regulation and protect the rights of data subjects.

The strategy of allocating data controllers with the responsibility of considering the level and type of processing activity that complies with fair processing and accountability principles mirrors the approach taken in Article 35. From a regulatory perspective, Article 25 can be seen as an *ex ante* governance mechanism requiring data controllers to view compliance as an ongoing process.[105] Given that sensitive personal data can be easily captured, distributed and manipulated in ways without consent being obtained or that its subsequent use can result in unintended consequences, data controllers are expected to be proactive in the design of systems in a way that demonstrates adherence to standards of fairness, security and transparency. A recurring privacy concern relates to the exchange and processing of information from multiple databases involving a number of actors, and multiple purposes. Article 25 requires the data controller to articulate the rationale of the processing activity and compatibility of the operation with the reasonable expectations of data subjects.

Both provisions underline the responsive nature of the risk governance model for anticipating, designing and mobilising clinicians, organizations and providers of AI health-based solutions.[106] Data protection law provides a framework through which human operators are allocated with responsibility for designing digital health infrastructures and tools through which data is classified, selected and ordered.[107] It also requires processing decisions and choices made in the type of data being collected to be evaluated against the background of its rules on fairness, transparency and safeguards needed in the context of sensitive personal data.[108] Finally, where decisions and risk scores are automated, the responsibility for managing risks to data subjects' fundamental rights is vested with data controllers to ensure that robust data protection by default governance processes are in place.[109]

4. Code of conduct: principles and commentary

The Code of Conduct operates within an institutional framework governed by the NHS constitution:

> The ultimate ambition is that the code is complementary to the health research, medical device regulations and the CE mark process as well as other regulatory approvals. When used as part of an overarching strategy it will help to create a trusted environment that supports innovation of data-driven technologies while being: (i) the safest in the world, (ii) appropriately responsive to progress in innovation, (iii) ethical, legal, transparent and accountable, (iv) evidence-based, (v) competitive and collaborative, (v) in alignment with the NHS Constitution[110]

The drafting and ultimate release of the Code of Conduct was not the result of a public consultation exercise but seems to have evolved organically, building on best practices and interactions with key stakeholders within the context of healthcare. The Code of Conduct can be seen as being consistent with the strategic and public health ambitions set out in the previous extract, as well as realising the political goals of the UK Government. The Personalised Health and Care 2020, it will be recalled, reinforces the commitment to revolutionise healthcare as set out in the NHS England's *Five Year Forward View*.[111] The Code of Conduct produced by the Department of Health and Social Care mirrors this commitment. Its principles specify the type of practices and conduct to be engaged in by NHS healthcare professionals and services providers from the public and commercial sector when using AI systems and data-driven innovations.[112] The range of governance issues that AI-enhanced devices generate in healthcare has also seen a widening of the regulatory discourse. The 'state of the nation' report can be seen as part of the dialogue to create a normative and contextual basis for information governance and problem solving through the provision of a "national set of 'rules of engagement' for any NHS organisation entering into a partnership with an AI developer."[113]

Some general observations can be provided with regard to the 10 foundational principles in the Code of Conduct:

Principle 1: Understand users, their needs and the context

As the integration of data-driven innovation into the health and care environment marks an important paradigm, this principle describes the importance of situational awareness, engaging end users and managing expectations in order to promote trust in the use of AI processes and innovative health solutions.

Principle 2: Define the outcome and how the technology will contribute to it

Confidence in the adoption and uptake of AI-based health solutions and devices are unlikely to be enhanced if the benefits to be derived cannot be demonstrated. The benefits in terms of enhanced care and health outcomes can include early detection of diseases, identifying positive health outcomes and improvements to patient experience.

Principle 3: Use data that is in line with appropriate guidelines for the purpose for which it is being used

Where data is used in clinical settings, there should be processes in place that document compliance with data protection regulations or sector-specific standards such as the Data Ethics Framework.[114] Compliance with these standards should be clearly communicated to the patient so that concerns can be identified at the outset and addressed with regard to the collection and processing of personal sensitive information. For example, when data is collected, steps must be taken to communicate to the patient the lawfulness of the collection, and that it is both proportionate and necessary. Where data is collected for secondary purposes other than primary care, such as healthcare research or testing digital health solutions, this information should be clearly communicated.[115]

Principle 4: Be fair, transparent and accountable about what data is being used

This standard overlaps with existing data protection rules (such as fair processing, data protection impact assessment and data protection by design and by default) and aims to ensure consistency in the standards for collection, processing and use of personal sensitive information. The NHS provides an online self-assessment tool that enables data controllers and organisations to determine if their processing operations comply with data protection rules and the National Data Guardian's 10 data security standards.[116]

Principle 5: Make use of open standards

The emphasis on open standards is consistent with the government's policy to enable suppliers with equal access to government contracts, ensure effective data sharing across NHS systems, facilitate interoperability across AI-based systems and maintain information security, clinical safety and data processing standards throughout the digital health infrastructure.[117]

Principle 6: Be transparent about the limitations of the data used

This principle is designed to improve the quality and precision of data-driven decision-making capabilities of AI-based health systems. Precision and growing use of large-scale data mining operations will place demands for clinicians and consultants as they seek to use AI processes for decision making and development of risk models. Increased precision and utilization of AI systems for diagnosis, treatment and prediction also require risks associated with opacity of computational decision making to be fully understood and managed.

Principle 7: Show what type of algorithm is being developed or deployed, the ethical examination of how the data is used, how its performance will be validated and how it will be integrated into health and care provision

Increased automation in the delivery of health and care services has an epistemological dimension (see previous discussion).

Principle 8: Generate evidence of effectiveness for the intended use and value for money

This principle serves as a reminder of the ever-present financial pressures and the strategic value of harnessing innovation opportunities. The National Institute for Health and Care Excellence has recently developed an evidence standards framework for digital health technologies. It is beyond the scope of this chapter to assess this standard-setting framework.

Principle 9: Make security integral to the design

See previous discussion and comments in Principle 5.

Principle 10: Define the commercial strategy

See comment on Principle 8.

The 10 principles are presented as a framework guiding clinicians and digital health solutions service providers tasked with the responsibility of developing and using them with a framework for problem solving and decision making.[118] Given the speed of advances in medicine and technological innovation, the expectation is that the principles will create a process and focum for participation and deliberation.[119] The obligation to focus on the need to define "the outcome and how the technology will contribute to it" does more than entail consultation with a checklist but permits its use only after an impact assessment is undertaken.[120] Principle 3 serves as a reminder that clinicians will play an important role in interpreting and implementing data use practices that are relevant and appropriate to the particular context.[121] Given the diverse situations and increased use of patient data in the delivery of healthcare, principle 4 proposes the use of data protection by design principles that create an audit trail, complemented by statements that all aspects of data protection law have been considered. The mirroring of data protection standards such as security, data quality, principles of proportionality, necessity and fairness and management of risks through impact assessment and technical processes are reinforced by principles 6, 7 and 9.[122]

5. Conclusion

The Code of Conduct has been presented as a critical framework that will provide the momentum for a radical period of innovation and improvement of healthcare in the United Kingdom. It is particularly striking in this debate that the Code of Conduct's strategic value is premised on its ability to mobilise and guide key stakeholders in the provision of healthcare. Situating data protection rules as a reflexive and flexible framework within the governance debates revolving around the integration of AI into the healthcare environment serves three purposes. First, it allows us to better understand its pivotal role as a standard-setting instrument with inbuilt mechanisms that are responsive to the challenges that clinicians and providers of AI-enhanced devices and services encounter in polycentric settings; its governance mechanisms prescribe the objects of regulation, identify the rights, interests and duties of relevant parties and techniques through which decisions regarding the use of personal information and risks are to be identified and managed. Second, because dynamic healthcare settings involve end users (patients), clinicians and consultants, corporate actors (providers of AI systems and technological infrastructures) and organizations monitoring their implementation and adaptation (UK Caldicott Guardian Council, National Institute for Health and Care Excellence, Care Quality Commission) have different expectations and roles, the model of information governance enables these actors to identify specific privacy and data protection challenges the utilization of AI-enhanced devices generates. Third, that data protection values rather than its prescriptions will continue to provide the foundation for practical problem solving. Lon Fuller famously observed that law is the "enterprise of subjecting human conduct to the governance of rules". To this we can add that data protection law serves as a reminder that as big data, AI and machine learning introduce complexity and uncertainty into dynamic settings such as the healthcare environment, its regulatory project remains the same – which is to enable people and organizations, when responding to the privacy challenges, to subject their practices to the governance of rules.

Notes

1 Department of Health & Social Care, 'The Future of Healthcare: Our Vision for Digital, Data and Technology in Health and Care' (2018) <www.gov.uk/government/publications/the-future-of-healthcare-our- vision-for-digital-data-and-technology-in-health-and-care/the-future-of-healthcare-our-vision-for- digital-data-and-technology-in-health-and-care>, Future Advocacy and Wellcome, 'Ethical, Social and Political Challenges of Artificial Intelligence in Health' (2018) <https://wellcome.ac.uk/sites/default/files/ai-in-health-ethical-social-political-challenges.pdf>, House of Commons Science and Technology Committee, 'Algorithms in Decision-making' (HC 351, 2018) and <https://publications.parliament.uk/pa/cm201719/cmselect/cmsctech/351/351.pdf>, National Advisory Group on Health Information Technology in England, 'Making IT Work: Harnessing the Power of Health Information Technology to Improve Care in England' (2018) <www.gov.uk/government/publications/using-information-technology-to-improve-the-nhs>.

2 Department of Health and Social Care (n 1). See for example National Data Guardian, 'National Data Guardian for Health and Care 2017 Report: Impact and Influence for Patients and Service Users' (2017) <www.gov.uk/government/publications/national-data-guardian-2017-report>.

3 Department of Health and Social Care (n 1).

4 NHSx, 'Artificial Intelligence: How to Get It Right: Putting Policy into Practice for Safe Data-driven Innovation in Health and Care' (2019) <www.nhsx.nhs.uk/assets/NHSX_AI_report.pdf>, 37–39.

5 Ibid 27.

6 Luciano Floridi, 'Soft Ethics, the Governance of the Digital and the General Data Protection Regulation' (2018) 376 *Philosophical Transactions of the Royal Society A:*

Mathematical, Physical and Engineering Sciences 20180081, Alan F.T. Winfield and Marina Jirotka, 'Ethical Governance Is Essential to Building Trust in Robotics and Artificial Intelligence Systems' (2018) 376 *Philosophical Transactions of the Royal Society A: Mathematical, Physical and Engineering Sciences* 20180085.

7 The principal bodies engaged with developing information governance policies include the Care Quality Commission, the Information Commissioner's Office, the General Medical Council, the Health Research Authority and the Medicines and Healthcare products Regulatory Agency. In addition to these organizations is another set of bodies which provide governance oversight: National Data Guardians, NHS Digital, NHS England & Improvement and the National Institute for Health and Care Excellence.

8 René von Schomberg and Europäisches Parlament (eds), *Towards Responsible Research and Innovation in the Information and Communication Technologies and Security Technologies Fields: Presentations Made at a Workshop Hosted by the Scientific and Technological Assessment Unit of the European Parliament in November 2010* (Public Office of the European Union, 2011), British Academy & Royal Society, 'Data Management and Use: Governance in the 21st Century' (2017) <https://royalsociety.org/~/media/policy/projects/data-governance/data-management-governance.pdf>, Academy of Medical Sciences & Royal Academy of Engineering, 'Health Apps: Regulation and Quality Control' (2015) <https://acmedsci.ac.uk/file-download/37073-552cc937dcfb4.pdf>, National Data Guardian for Health and Care, 'Review of Data Security, Consent and Opt-Outs' (2016) <www.gov.uk/government/publications/review-of-data-security-consent-and-opt-outs>, House of Lords Select Committee on Artificial Intelligence, 'AI in the UK: Ready, Willing and Able?' (HL Paper 100, 2018), ch 1–6 and Nuffield Council on Bioethics, 'Bioethics Briefing Note: Artificial Intelligence (AI) in Healthcare and Research' (2018) <http://nuffieldbioethics.org/wp-content/uploads/Artificial-Intelligence-AI-in- healthcare-and-research.pdf>.

9 It should be noted that Article 40 GDPR permits the design and use of "codes of conduct, or amend or extend such codes, for the purpose of specifying the application of this Regulation . . . " but for specified purposes. See also Robert Baldwin, Martin Cave and Martin Lodge, *Understanding Regulation: Theory, Strategy, and Practice* (Oxford University Press, 2011), chapters 2–3.

10 See for example European Data Protection Supervisor (EDPS), 'Opinion 8/2016, Coherent Enforcement of Fundamental Rights in the Age of Big Data', 23 September 2016, 'Opinion 4/2015, Towards a New Digital Ethics: Data, Dignity and Technology', September 2015 and Julia Black, 'Talking about Regulation' [1998] *Public Law* 77, 78.

11 See Recital 13 and Article 5 (2) of the General Data Protection Regulation 2016 (GDPR). Also consider Articles 24 (3), 28 (5) and 32 (3) GDPR. It should be noted that Article 40 GDPR permits the design and use of "codes of conduct, or amend or extend such codes, for the purpose of specifying the application of this Regulation . . . " but for specified purposes. See EDPS, 'Preliminary Opinion, Privacy and competitiveness in the age of big data: The interplay between data protection, competition law and consumer protection in the Digital Economy', March 2014 and 'Opinion, on the Communication from the Commission on 'eHealth Action Plan 2012–2020 – Innovative healthcare for the 21st century, 27 March 2013. See also European Commission, eHealth Action Plan 2012–2020 – Innovative healthcare for the 21st century COM (2012) 736 final.

12 Patrick Henry Winston, *Artificial Intelligence* (3rd ed, Addison-Wesley Pub Co, 1992), 5.

13 Stuart J. Russell and Peter Norvig, *Artificial Intelligence: A Modern Approach* (2nd ed., Prentice Hall, 2003), 194.

14 Organisation for Economic Cooperation and Development, *Recommendation of the Council on Artificial Intelligence, OECD/LEGAL/0449* (2019).

15 Fei Jiang and others, 'Artificial Intelligence in Healthcare: Past, Present and Future' (2017) 2 *Stroke and Vascular Neurology* 230.

16 Julia Schnatz, 'NHS England's Smartphone App for Identifying Acute Kidney Injury' (2016) <www.centreforpublicimpact.org/case-study/nhs-englands-smartphone-app-identifying-acute-kidney-injury-2016-2018/> accessed 11 January 2020.

17 Scott Mayer McKinney and others, 'International Evaluation of an AI System for Breast Cancer Screening' (2020) 577 *Nature* 89, Anabik Pal and others, 'Psoriasis Skin Biopsy Image Segmentation Using Deep Convolutional Neural Network' (2018) 159 *Computer Methods and Programs in Biomedicine* 59 and Stacy M. Carter and others, 'The Ethical, Legal and Social Implications of Using Artificial Intelligence Systems in Breast Cancer Care' (2020) 49 *The Breast* 25.

18 Daniel Shu Wei Ting and others, 'Artificial Intelligence and Deep Learning in Ophthalmology' (2019) 103 *British Journal of Ophthalmology* 167.

19 Kun-Hsing Yu, Andrew L, Beam and Isaac S, Kohane, 'Artificial Intelligence in Healthcare' (2018) 2 *Nature Biomedical Engineering* 719.

20 Orlando Simpson and Sergio G. Camorlinga, 'A Framework to Study the Emergence of Non-Communicable Diseases' (2017) 114 *Procedia Computer Science* 116, Abrar Alturkistani and others, 'Health Information Technology Uses for Primary Prevention in Preventive Medicine: A Scoping Review Protocol' (2018) 8 *BMJ Open* e023428 and François Bastardot and David Gachoud, 'Visual Diagnosis: Between Medical Education and Advances in Artificial Intelligence' (2019) 15 *Revue Medicale Suisse* 2145. <www.sciencedirect.com/science/article/pii/S1877050917318203> accessed 11 January 2020. See also Department of Health and Social Care, 'Prevention is better than cure' (2018) <https://assets.publishing.service.gov.uk/government/uploads/system/uploads/attachment_data/file/753688/Prevention_is_better_than_cure_5-11.pdf> 12–13.

21 Andre Esteva and others, 'Dermatologist-Level Classification of Skin Cancer with Deep Neural Networks' (2017) 542 *Nature* 115.

22 Abrar Alturkistani and others, 'Health Information Technology Uses for Primary Prevention in Preventive Medicine: A Scoping Review Protocol' (n 20) and François Bastardot and David Gachoud, 'Visual Diagnosis: Between Medical Education and Advances in Artificial Intelligence' (n 20).

23 Geraldine M. Clarke and others, 'Evaluating the Impact of Healthcare Interventions Using Routine Data' (2019) 365 *BMJ*.

24 Gary Marcus and Ernest Davis, *Rebooting AI: Building Artificial Intelligence We Can Trust* (First edition, Pantheon Books, 2019), 5–10. Royal Society, 'Digital Healthcare: The Impact of Information and Communication Technologies on Health and Healthcare' (2006), Ch 4.

25 D. Warner, J. Sale and E. Viirre, 'Distributed Medical Intelligence. A Systems Approach for Developing and Integrative Health Care Information Distribution Infrastructure' (1996) 29 *Studies in Health Technology and Informatics* 80.

26 Tim K. Mackey and others, '"Fit-for-Purpose?" – Challenges and Opportunities for Applications of Blockchain Technology in the Future of Healthcare' (2019) 17 *BMC Medicine* 68, Gary Leeming, James Cunningham and John Ainsworth, 'A Ledger of Me: Personalizing Healthcare Using Blockchain Technology' (2019) 6 *Frontiers in Medicine* 171 and Dee Luo and others, 'Mobile Apps for Individuals With Rheumatoid Arthritis: A Systematic Review' (2019) 25 *Journal of Clinical Rheumatology: Practical Reports on Rheumatic & Musculoskeletal Diseases* 133.

27 Naomi J. Fulop and Angus I.G. Ramsay, 'How Organisations Contribute to Improving the Quality of Healthcare' (2019) 365 *BMJ*.

28 David J. Duffy, 'Problems, Challenges and Promises: Perspectives on Precision Medicine' (2016) 17 *Briefings in Bioinformatics* 494 and Aisling McMahon, Alena Buyx and Barbara Prainsack, 'Big Data Governance Needs More Collective Responsibility: The Role of Harm Mitigation in the Governance of Data Use in Medicine and Beyond' [2019] *Medical Law Review* 1, 2–5.

29 Cameron Holley, Neil Gunningham and Clifford D. Shearing, *The New Environmental Governance* (Earthscan, 2012), 4–7.

30 Department of Health and Social Care, *The Future of Healthcare: Our Vision for Digital, Data and Technology in Health and Care* (n 1).
31 EDPS, 'A Preliminary Opinion on Data Protection and Scientific Research', 6 January 2020.
32 See Lon Fuller, *The Morality of Law* (Yale University Press; Revised edition, 1977), 106. See also EDPS, 'Opinion 5/2018 Preliminary Opinion on Privacy by Design', 31 May 2018, 10 and EDPS 'Opinion 7/2015, Meeting the Challenges of Big Data: A Call for Transparency, User Control, Data Protection by Design and Accountability', 19 November 2015, 16–17.
33 EDPS, 'Accountability on the Ground Part II: Data Protection Impact Assessments & Prior Consultation' (v1.9 July 2019), 5.
34 Orla Lynskey, *The Foundations of EU Data Protection Law* (OUP, 2015), Ch 3 and Gloria González Fuster, *The Emergence of Personal Data Protection as a Fundamental Right of the EU* (Springer, 2014), Ch 2.
35 Claudia Martínez Imogen Farhan, 'Making the Right Choices: Using Data-driven Technology to Transform Mental Healthcare' (2018) <https://reform.co.uk/index.php/research/data-driven-healthcare-regulation-regulators>, 31–39.
36 Academy of Royal Medical Colleges, 'Artificial Intelligence in Healthcare' (2019) 23.
37 NHSx, 'Artificial Intelligence: How to Get It Right Putting Policy into Practice for Safe Data-driven Innovation in Health and Care' (n 4) 28–36.
38 EDPS, 'Accountability on the Ground Part II: Data Protection Impact Assessments & Prior Consultation' (n 33) 5.
39 European Data Protection Board, 'Guidelines 1/2019 on Codes of Conduct and Monitoring Bodies under Regulation 2016/679, adopted 12 February 2019, para 7.
40 Julia Black, 'Talking about Regulation' (1998) *Public Law* 77, 77.
41 Tony Prosser, *The Regulatory Enterprise: Government, Regulation, and Legitimacy* (OUP, 2010), 2–3.
42 See for example ECtHR, I v Finland, No. 20511/03, 17 July 2008, paragraph 38 and ECHR 25 November 2008, 2010] ECHR 2229, 36919/02, paragraph 40.
43 See, for example, EDPS Opinion on the Commission proposals for a Regulation on medical devices, and amending Directive 2001/83/EC, Regulation (EC) No 178/2002 and Regulation (EC) No 1223/2009 and a Regulation on in vitro diagnostic medical devices, 8 February 2013, para 4–13. Also see Article 29 Working Party, 'Opinion on Apps on Smart Devices', adopted 27 February 2013 (WP 202).
44 See Article 29 Working Party, 'Opinion 1/2010 on the Concepts of "Controller" and "Processor", adopted on 16 February 2010 (WP 169).
45 Menno Mostert et al., 'From Privacy to Data Protection in the EU: Implications for Big Data Health Research' (2017) 25 (1) *European Journal of Health Law* 43, 44.
46 It is beyond the scope of this chapter to assess if the appropriate balance has been struck.
47 See EDPS, 'Comments of the EDPS on a Proposal for a Regulation of the European Parliament and of the Council on a Framework for the Free-Flow of Non-Personal Data in the European Union', 8 June 2018 <https://edps.europa.eu/data-protection/our-work/publications/comments/edps-comments-framework-free-flow-non-personal-data_en>, 2–6. Also Nadezhda Purtova, 'The Law of Everything. Broad Concept of Personal Data and Future of EU Data Protection Law' (2018) *Law, Innovation and Technology* 10 (1) 40–81 Tal Zarsky, 'Incompatible: The GDPR in the Age of Big Data' (2016) *Seton Hall L. Rev* 47 and Raphaël Gellert, 'Understanding the Notion of Risk in the General Data Protection Regulation' (2018) 34 (2) *Computer Law & Security Review* 279–288.
48 Boston Consulting Group, 'The Value of our Digital Identity' (2012) <www.libertyglobal.com/PDF/public-policy/The-Value-of-Our-Digital-Identity.pdf>.
49 Michael Phillips and others, 'Assessment of Accuracy of an Artificial Intelligence Algorithm to Detect Melanoma in Images of Skin Lesions' (2019) 2 *JAMA Network Open* e1913436.

50 See also Recital 35 GDPR.
51 Recital 26 GDPR.
52 Article 4 (5) and Recital 26 GDPR. Miranda Mourby and others, 'Are "Pseudonymised" Data Always Personal Data? Implications of the GDPR for Administrative Data Research in the UK' (2018) 34 *Computer Law & Security Review* 222.
53 Nadezhda Purtova, 'Property Rights in Personal Data: Learning from the American Discourse' (2009) 25 (6) *Computer Law & Security Review* 507–521.
54 For identifiability and dynamic IP addresses, see CJEU, C-582/14, Patrick Breyer v. Bundesrepublik Deutschland, 19 October 2016. Also observations in CJEU, C-70/10, Scarlet Extended SA v. Société belge des auteurs, compositeurs et éditeurs SCRL (SABAM), 24 November 2011 para 51.
55 ECtHR, Szuluk v the United Kingdom, No. 36936/05, 2 June 2009 and 'Letter from Chair of Article 29 Working Party on New Draft Code of Conduct', 11 April 2018 <https://ec.europa.eu/newsroom/article29/item-detail.cfm?item_id=625391>.
56 Giovanni Comandè and Giulia Schneider, 'Regulatory Challenges of Data Mining Practices: The Case of the Never-Ending Lifecycles of "Health Data"' (2018) 25 *European Journal of Health Law* 284 and OECD, 'Data-Driven Innovation: Big Data for Growth and Well-Being' (2015) <www.oecd-ilibrary.org/science-and-technology/data-driven-innovation_9789264229358-en>.
57 See Jaap-Henk Hoepman, 'Privacy Design Strategies (The Little Blue Book)' (2019) <www.cs.ru.nl/~jhh/publications/pds-booklet.pdf>.
58 European Commission, Communication on enabling the digital transformation of health and care in the Digital Single Market; empowering citizens and building a healthier society, COM (2018) 233. See Simon Woods, 'Big Data Governance: Solidarity and the Patient Voice' in Brent Daniel Mittelstadt and Luciano Floridi (eds), *The Ethics of Biomedical Big Data* (Springer, 2016), 221–238 and Annemarie Mol, *The Logic of Care. Health and the Problem of Patient Choice* (Routledge, 2008) who argues how regulations frame choices and create the impression of autonomy and freedom.
59 See CJEU, Joined cases C-92/09 and C-93/09, Volker und Markus Schecke GbR and Hartmut Eifert v Land Hessen [GC], 9 November 2010, para 48 and Alvin Liu, 'Smartphone-Based, Artificial Intelligence – Enabled Diabetic Retinopathy Screening' (2019) 137 *JAMA Ophthalmology* 1188.
60 See EDPS, 'Guidelines on Assessing the Proportionality of Measures that Limit the Fundamental Rights to Privacy and to the Protection of Personal Data' 19 December 2019, 6–12.
61 Lee A. Bygrave, *Data Protection Law: Approaching Its Rationale, Logic and Limits* (The Hague, Kluwer Law International, 2002), 50–52. See also CJEU, C-543/09, Deutsche Telekom AG v. Bundesrepublik Deutschland, 5 May 2011, para 51–52 on the balancing requirements.
62 CJEU, Joined Cases C-293/12 and C-594/12, Digital Rights Ireland Ltd v. Minister for Communications, Marine and Natural Resources and Others and Kärntner Landesregierung and Others [GC], 8 April 2014, para. 38.
63 CJEU, C-73/07, Tietosuojavaltuutettu v. Satakunnan Markkinapörssi Oy and Satamedia Oy [GC], 16 December 2008, para 54–56. Article 29 Working Party, 'Opinion 03/2013 on Purpose Limitation', adopted on 2 April 2013 (WP 203) para 45–47 and 'Opinion 06/2014 on the Notion of Legitimate Interests of the Data Controller under Article 7 of Directive 95/46/EC', adopted on 9 April 2014 (WP 217) para 9–11.
64 Article 29 Working Party, 'Guidelines on Automated Individual Decision-making and Profiling for the Purposes of Regulation 2016/679', 3 October 2017 (WP 251) 4.
65 CJEU, C-131/12, Google Spain SL, Google Inc. v. Agencia Española de Protección de Datos (AEPD), Mario Costeja González [GC], 13 May 2014, para 88 and Article 29 Working Party, 'Guidelines on the implementation of the CJEU judgment on "Google Spain and Inc v. Agencia Española de Protección de Datos (AEPD) and Mario Costeja González" C-131/12, (WP 225).

66 Maria Tzanou, *The Fundamental Right to Data Protection: Normative Value in the Context of Counter-Terrorism Surveillance* (Hart Publishing, 2017).

67 See Article 29 Working Party, 'Statement on the Role of a Risk-based Approach in Data Protection Legal Frameworks', adopted 30 May 2014 3–4 and EDPB-EDPS, 'Joint Opinion 1/2019 on the Processing of Patients' Data and the Role of the European Commission within the eHealth Digital Service Infrastructure (eHDSI)' (2019) <https://edpb.europa.eu/our-work-tools/our-documents/edpbedps-joint-opinion/edpb-edps-joint-opinion-12019-processing_en>.

68 The satisfaction of the legal basis requirement does not absolve data controllers from fulfilling other obligations, such as those set out in Article 5: See Article 29 Working Party, 'Opinion 03/2013 on Purpose Limitation' (WP203), 15–16.

69 Article 9 (2)(c) GDPR.

70 Article 9 (2) (h) GDPR.

71 Article 9 (2)(i) GDPR. However see Mary Donnelly and Maeve McDonagh, 'Health Research, Consent and the GDPR Exemption' (2019) 26 *European Journal of Health Law* 97 does not take sufficient account of the contextual nature of problem solving and the risk-based approach which underpins data protection law.

72 It is important to reiterate that under the GDPR, explicit consent is only one lawful basis for processing. Additionally, Recital 26 for anonymous data.

73 As an example, see the information standard DCB3058 Compliance with National Data Opt-outs in light of section 250 of the Health and Social Care Act 2012.

74 Charlotte Bagger Tranberg, 'Proportionality and Data Protection in the Case Law of the European Court of Justice' (2011) 1 (4) *International Data Privacy Law* 239–248, Federico Ferretti, 'Data Protection and the Legitimate Interest of Data Controllers: Much Ado about Nothing or the Winter of Rights? (2014) *Common Law Market Review* 51, 843–868, Christopher Docksey, 'Four Fundamental Rights: Finding the Balance' (2016) 6 International Data Privacy Law 2, Irene Kamara and Paul De Hert, 'Understanding the Balancing Act behind the Legitimate Interest of the Controller Ground. A Pragmatic Approach', in Evan Selinger, Jules Polonetsky and Omer Tene (eds), *The Cambridge Handbook of Consumer Privacy* (CUP, 2018) and Michael Veale and Lilian Edwards, 'Clarity, Surprises, and Further Questions in the Article 29 Working Party Draft Guidance on Automated Decision-making and Profiling' (2018) 34 (2) *Comp Law Sec Rev* 398, See Joined cases C-468/10 and C-469/10, ASNEF, ECLI:EU:C:2011:777, paras. 28–29, Joined Cases C-465/00, C-138/01 and C-139/01, Österreichischer Rundfunk, ECLI:EU:C:2003:294, paras. 17–21, C-275/06, Promusicae, ECLI:EU:C:2008:54, paras. 29–33. C-73/07, Satamedia, ECLI:EU:C:2008:727, paras. 25–26. Joined Cases C-92/09 and C-93/09, Schecke, ECLI:EU:C:2010:662, paras. 26–29. Joined Cases C-293/12 and C-594/12, Digital Rights Ireland, ECLI:EU:C:2014:238, paras. 17 and 20. Also EDPS, 'Developing a Toolkit for Assessing the Necessity of Measures that Interfere with Fundamental Rights', 11 April 2017 <https://edps.europa.eu/sites/ edp/files/publication/16–06–16_necessity_paper_for_consultation_en.pdf>, 4–6.

75 EDPS, 'Opinion 1/2015 Mobile Health Reconciling Technological Innovation with Data Protection', 21 May 2015 para 57.

76 ibid. para 55–63.

77 Article 12 (1) GDPR.

78 Articles 13 and 14 GDPR.

79 Article 15 GDPR.

80 Article 16 GDPR.

81 Article 17 GDPR.

82 Article 21 GDPR.

83 Article 22 GDPR.

84 OECD, 'Recommendation of the Council on Health Data Governance', OECD/LEGAL/0433, Pratik Shah and others, 'Artificial Intelligence and Machine Learning in

Clinical Development: A Translational Perspective' (2019) 2 *Digital Medicine* 1 <www.nature.com/articles/s41746-019-0148-3> accessed 11 January 2020.

85 Trishan Panch and others, 'Artificial Intelligence: Opportunities and Risks for Public Health' (2019) 1 *The Lancet Digital Health* e13 <www.thelancet.com/journals/landig/article/PIIS2589-7500(19)30002-0/abstract> accessed 11 January 2020. Viet-Thi Tran, Carolina Riveros and Philippe Ravaud, 'Patients' Views of Wearable Devices and AI in Healthcare: Findings from the ComPaRe e-Cohort' (2019) 2 *Digital Medicine* 1 <www.nature.com/articles/s41746-019-0132-y> accessed 11 January 2020.

86 NHSx, 'Artificial Intelligence: How to Get it Right: Putting Policy into Practice for Safe Data-driven Innovation in Health and Care' (n 4) 17 and Ryan Poplin and others, 'Prediction of Cardiovascular Risk Factors from Retinal Fundus Photographs via Deep Learning' (2018) 2 *Nature Biomedical Engineering* 158–164.

87 EDPS, Meeting the Challenges of big data, Opinion 7/2015 (n 32) and European Data Protection Supervisor (2016), Coherent enforcement of fundamental rights in the age of Big Data, Opinion 8/2016 (n 10) and Kun-Hsing Yu, Andrew L. Beam and Isaac S. Kohane, 'Artificial Intelligence in Healthcare' (2018) *Nature Biomedical Engineering* 2, 719–731.

88 Michael V. Hayes, 'On the Epistemology of Risk: Language, Logic and Social Science' (1992) 35 *Social Science & Medicine* 401, Michael Snyder and Wenyu Zhou, 'Big Data and Health' (2019) 1 *The Lancet Digital Health* e252, Jessica Morley, Mariarosaria Taddeo and Luciano Floridi, 'Google Health and the NHS: Overcoming the Trust Deficit' (2019) 1 *The Lancet Digital Health* e389 and Mariarosaria Taddeo, 'Modelling Trust in Artificial Agents, A First Step Toward the Analysis of e-Trust' (2010) 20 *Minds and Machines* 243 <http://link.springer.com/10.1007/s11023-010-9201-3>.

89 Saskia Hendriks and others, 'Ethical Challenges of Risk, Informed Consent, and Post-trial Responsibilities in Human Research With Neural Devices: A Review' (2019) 76 *JAMA Neurology* 1506.

90 Aisling McMahon, Alena Buyx and Barbara Prainsack, 'Big Data Governance Needs More Collective Responsibility: The Role of Harm Mitigation in the Governance of Data Use in Medicine and Beyond' (n 28) 8 and Filippo Pesapane and others, 'Artificial Intelligence as a Medical Device in Radiology: Ethical and Regulatory Issues in Europe and the United States' (2018) 9 *Insights into Imaging* 745.

91 Raphaël Gellert, 'Data Protection: A Risk Regulation? Between the Risk Management of Everything and the Precautionary Alternative' (2015) 5 *International Data Privacy Law* 3.

92 Luciano Floridi, 'Soft Ethics, the Governance of the Digital and the General Data Protection Regulation' (2018) 376 *Philosophical Transactions of the Royal Society A: Mathematical, Physical and Engineering Sciences* 20180081, Claudia Quelle, 'Enhancing Compliance under the General Data Protection Regulation: The Risky Upshot of the Accountability- and Risk-Based Approach' (2018) 9 *European Journal of Risk Regulation* 502 and Michael Snyder and Wenyu Zhou, 'Big Data and Health' (2019) 1 *The Lancet Digital Health* e252. See also European Parliament and the Council of the European Union, Regulation (EU) 2017/745 of the European Parliament and of the Council on medical devices, amending directive 2001/83/EC, regulation (EC) No 178/2002 and regulation (EC) No 1223/2009 and repealing Council directives 90/385/EEC and 93/42/EEC, Official Journal of the European Communities (2017) and European Parliament and the Council of the European Union Regulation (EU) 2017/746 of the European parliament and of the Council on in vitro diagnostic medical devices and repealing directive 98/79/EC and commission decision 2010/227/EU, Official Journal of the European Communities (2017).

93 European Data Protection Supervisor (2019), 'Accountability on the Ground Part II: Data Protection Impact Assessments & Prior Consultation' (n 33).

94 Lee A. Bygrave, *Data Protection Law – Approaching Its Rationale, Logic, and Its Limits* (Kluwer, 2002), 3–15, Raphaël Gellert, 'Data Protection: A Risk Regulation? Between

the Risk Management of Everything and the Precautionary Alternative' (2015) 5 *International Data Privacy Law* 3.

95 Ibid.

96 European Data Protection Board, 'Opinion 22/2018 on the draft list of the competent supervisory authority of the United Kingdom Regarding the processing operations subject to the requirement of a data protection impact assessment (Article 35.4 GDPR)', 25 September 2018). It endorses Article 29 Working Party, 'Guidelines on Data Protection Impact Assessment (DPIA) and determining whether processing is "likely to result in a high risk" for the purposes of Regulation 2016/679' (WP 248). See also Christopher Hood, Henry Rothstein and Robert Baldwin, *The Government of Risk – Understanding Risk Regulation Regimes* (Oxford University Press, 2001), 3. They suggest that governance involves three interacting elements: standard-setting, information-gathering and behaviour-modification.

97 Article 35 (7) GDPR.

98 Article 35 (3) (a) (b) GDPR.

99 Roger Clarke, 'An Evaluation of Privacy Impact Assessment Guidance Documents' (2011) 1 *International Data Privacy Law* 111.

100 European Data Protection Board endorses Article 29 Working Party, Guidelines on Data Protection Impact Assessment (DPIA) 9–11.

101 See Article 36 GDPR.

102 Article 29 Working Party, 'Guidelines on Data Protection Impact Assessment (DPIA) and determining whether processing is "likely to result in high risk" for the purposes of Regulation 2016/679' (n 95). See critique Reuben Binns, 'Data Protection Impact Assessments: A Meta-Regulatory Approach' (2017) 7 *International Data Privacy Law* 22.

103 Athena Bourka and others, 'Recommendations on Shaping Technology According to GDPR Provisions: Exploring the Notion of Data Protection by Default' (2018) <http://dx.publications.europa.eu/10.2824/518496> accessed 9 January 2020. Henry Rothstein and others, 'The Risks of Risk-Based Regulation: Insights from the Environmental Policy Domain' (2006) 32 *Environment International* 1056, 1057. The Royal Society, *Protecting Privacy in Practice: The Current Use, Development and Limits of Privacy Enhancing Technologies in Data Analysis* (The Royal Society, 2019), 1, Lee Bygrave, 'Data Protection by Design and by Default: Deciphering the EU's Legislative Requirements' (2017) 4 (2) *Oslo Law Review* 105–120.

104 Dag Wiese Schartum, 'Making Privacy by Design Operative' (2016) 24 *International Journal of Law and Information Technology* 151, Michael Veale, Reuben Binns and Jef Ausloos, 'When Data Protection by Design and Data Subject Rights Clash' (2018) 8 *International Data Privacy Law* 105, Mélanie Bourassa Forcier and others, 'Integrating Artificial Intelligence into Health Care through Data Access: Can the GDPR Act as a Beacon for Policymakers?' (2019) 6 *Journal of Law and the Biosciences* 317.

105 Royal Society Working Group, 'Machine Learning: The Power and Promise of Computers that Learn by Example' (2017) <https://royalsociety.org/-/media/policy/projects/machine-learning/publications/machine-learning-report.pdf> and Sicco Verwer and Toon Calders, 'Introducing Positive Discrimination in Predictive Models', in Bart Custers, Toon Calders, Bart Schermer and Tal Zarsky (eds), *Discrimination and Privacy in the Information Society: Data Mining and Profiling in Large Databases* (Springer, 2013), 255–270.

106 Isak Mendoza and Lee Bygrave, 'The Right Not to be Subject to Automated Decisions based on Profiling', in Tatiani Synodinou, Philippe Jougleux, Christiana Markou and Thalia Prastitou (eds), *EU Internet Law: Regulation and Enforcement* (Springer, 2017), 77–98 and Sandra Wachter and Mittelstadt Brent, 'A Right to Reasonable Inferences: Re-Thinking Data Protection Law in the Age of Big Data and AI' (2019) *Columbia Business Law Review*, 495.

107 Nicholas Diakopoulos and others, 'Principles for Accountable Algorithms and a Social Impact Statement for Algorithms' (nd) <www.fatml.org/resources/principles-for- accountable-algorithms>.

108 Dillon Reisman, Jason Schultz, Kate Crawford and Meredith Whittaker, 'Algorithmic Impact Assessments: A Practical Framework for Public Agency Accountability' (2018) <https://ainowinstitute.org /aiareport2018.pdf>.

109 Sharon Vallor, 'An Ethical Toolkit for Engineering/Design Practice' (2018) <www.scu.edu/ethics-in-technology-practice/ethical-toolkit/>.

110 Department of Health and Social Care, 'NHS Constitution for England' (2015) <www.gov.uk/government/publications/the-nhs-constitution-for-england>.

111 See National Information Board, 'Framework for Action' Entitled Personalised Health and Care 2020: Using Data and Technology to Transform Outcomes for Patients and Citizens' (2014) <www.gov.uk/government/publications/personalised-health-and-care-2020>.

112 See for example, Department for Business, Innovation and Skills, 'Better Regulation Delivery Office, Regulators' Code' (2014) <www.gov.uk/government/publications/regulators-code> and sections 21 and s22 of the Legislative and Regulatory Reform Act 2006.

113 AHSN Network, 'Accelerating Artificial Intelligence in Health and Care: Results from a State of the Nation Survey' (2018) <www.ahsnnetwork.com/> 7.

114 Department for Digital, Culture, Media & Sport, 'Data Ethics Framework' (2018) <www.gov.uk/government/publications/data-ethics-framework/data-ethics-framework>.

115 See for example, Health Research Authority and the UK Health Departments, 'UK Policy Framework for Health and Social Care Research' (2017) </planning-and-improving-research/policies-standards-legislation/uk-policy-framework-health-social-care-research/>. Where identifiable sensitive personal data is used data protection rules on lawful basis must be complied with. Additionally, the provisions under section 251 of the NHS Act 2006 and Health Service (Control of Patient Information) Regulations 2002 must be complied with. For AI based medical devices, the Medical Devices (Amendment etc.) (EU Exit) Regulations 2019 should be complied with in addition to fulfilling the guidance provided by the Medicines and Healthcare products Regulatory Agency.

116 NHS Digital, 'Data Security and Protection Toolkit' (2018) <https://digital.nhs.uk/data-and-information/looking-after-information/data-security-and-information-governance/data-security-and-protection-toolkit>.

117 See Section 250 Health and Social Care Act 2012 definition of standards and DCB0160: Clinical Risk Management: its Application in the Deployment and Use of Health IT Systems. The UK Caldicott Guardian Council provides regulatory oversight with regard to the protection and use of sensitive personal information of individuals when providing health and care services.

118 Julia Black, 'Paradoxes and Failures: "New Governance" Techniques and the Financial Crisis' (2012) 75 *The Modern Law Review* 1037.

119 Principle 1 Code of Conduct.

120 Principle 2 Code of Conduct.

121 Graeme Laurie and Nayha Sethi, 'Towards Principles – Based Approaches to Governance of Health – Related Research Using Personal Data' (2013) 4 *European Journal of Risk Regulation* 43.

122 Principle 9 Code of Conduct.

Contributors

Isabel de la Torre-Díez is Professor in the Department of Signal Theory and Communications and Telematics Engineering at the University of Valladolid, Spain and the leader of the GTe Research Group.

Jos Dumortier is Honorary Professor at KU Leuven Faculty of Law and Partner at Timelex Lawyers, Brussels.

Susel Góngora-Alonso is a telecommunications researcher at the University of Valladolid, Spain. She is completing a PhD in Telecommunications Engineering. Her research interests include development and evaluation of telemedicine applications.

Yordanka Ivanova is a joint PhD candidate in the Law Faculty of Sofia University 'St. Kliment Ohridski' (Bulgaria) and Vrije Universiteit Brussel (Belgium), writing a thesis on the EU General Data Protection Regulation (GDPR) and its interaction with Big Data and Artificial Intelligence. She is also working as a legal and policy officer in the European Commission, Directorate-General for Communications Networks, Content and Technology. Yordanka holds an LLM in EU Law from Leiden University (the Netherlands) and has worked as an attorney-at-law in Bulgaria.

Rosemary Jay is Senior Consultant Attorney at Hunton, Andrews Kurth. She has been a privacy lawyer for 33 years. She is currently ranked as a Senior Statesperson for data protection in Chambers and has been ranked Band 1 or above since Chambers introduced the practice area. She has worked both for regulators and in private practice. She is the author of *Data Protection Law & Practice* (5th edition due for publication 2020).

Miguel López-Coronado is Professor of Telecommunications at the University of Valladolid, Spain. Since 1991, he has been devoted to the promotion of the Information Society in the Castille and Leon region.

Mahault Piéchaud Boura is a legal consultant at Timelex Lawyers, Brussels.

Beatriz Sainz-de-Abajo is Associate Professor in Telecommunications Engineering at the University of Valladolid, Spain. Her research focuses on the development and evaluation of eHealth and mHealth systems, medicine 2.0 and cloud computing.

Joseph Savirimuthu is Senior Lecturer in Law at the School of Law and Social Justice, University of Liverpool (UK). His research interests revolve around the regulatory and governance challenges raised by new and emerging technologies, with particular focus on privacy and data protection and related ethical/moral anxieties.

Maria Tzanou is Senior Lecturer in Law at Keele University. Her research focuses on European constitutional and human rights law, privacy, data protection, Big Data and the Internet of Things, counterterrorism surveillance and transatlantic data privacy cooperation. She is the author of *The Fundamental Right to Data Protection*.

Bart van der Sloot specializes in questions revolving around privacy and Big Data. He also publishes regularly on topics such as the liability of Internet providers, data protection and Internet regulation. He works as a senior researcher at the Tilburg Institute for Law, Technology, and Society, Tilburg University, and is the General Editor of the *European Data Protection Law Review* and the director of the Privacy and Identity Lab.

Index

Page numbers in *italic* indicate a figure and page numbers in **bold** indicate a table on the corresponding page.

5G networks 71
2010 US Decennial Census 95

accountability 10, 120, 137, 139
accuracy 10, 19n83, 139
advertisers 75, 81n54
AEGLE project 56–57
African-American community 98
aggregated data 90
algorithmic decision making 106
algorithms 4, 116; analysis 5, 7; Code of Conduct 146; machine-learning 115
Allen, Anita 3
Americans with Disabilities Act (ADA) 124
analysing 92
analysis 99–103; algorithms 5, 7; Big Data 8; group 117; non-personal data 99–101
anonymous data 90, 93
anti-discrimination 125
Apple 118
apps 8; *see also* mHealth
Article 1 GDPR 86, 88
Article 4 (15) GDPR 138
Article 4 (1) GDPR 19n73, 30, 138
Article 4 (4) GDPR 20n109
Article 4 (7) GDPR 24
Article 4 (8) GDPR 27
Article 5 (1) 19n80, 19n81, 19n82, 19n83, 19n84, 19n85
Article 5 (1) (a) 111
Article 5.1(b) 62
Article 5.1(e) 65
Article 5 GDPR 40, 111
Article 5 (1) (d) GDPR 112
Article 6 (1) 140
Article 6 (1) (f) 39, 49
Article 6 GDPR 60
Article 8 39
Article 8 (1) 40, 51
Article 8 ECHR 85, 89, 91, 93
Article 9 (2) (a) 140
Article 9 GDPR 30, 59
Article 9 (2) GDPR 20n117, 32
Article 9 (2) (g) GDPR 21n124
Article 9 (2) (h) GDPR 21n125
Article 9 (2) (i) GDPR 21n130
Article 12 GDPR 39
Article 17 (1) GDPR 40
Article 17 (1) (b) GDPR 52
Article 17 (1) (f) GDPR 51
Article 17.3 (d) GDPR 65
Article 17 GDPR 20n90, 30
Article 22 GDPR 123
Article 23 (2) GDPR 21n135
Article 25 143–144
Article 26 GDPR 23, 26
Article 28 (3) 27
Article 28 GDPR 27
Article 29 WP 37, 45, 52, 57, 61
Article 35, EUCFR 12
Article 40 (2) (g) GDPR 40
Article 49 (1) (d) GDPR 21n139
Article 52 (1) GDPR 139
Article 57 (1) (b) GDPR 40
Article 85 GDPR 30
Article 89.1 GDPR 65–66
Article 89.2 GDPR 65
Article 179 (1) GDPR 57
Articles 35 GDPR 20n97
Articles 36 GDPR 20n97
artificial intelligence (AI) 4; big data 4; challenges 106–125; data-driven health

technologies as 138; defined 134–135; developer 145; dynamic healthcare environment 136; health-based solutions 144; healthcare and 134–136; learning 5; potential of 133; technologies 32; *see also* big data; machine learning
Automatic Processing of Personal Data 87
autonomy 4, 52, 117, 119
availability 75

BBC Editorial Guidelines 49
big data 7; analysing 92; analysis and distribution 8; analytics 4–5, 7, 14, 56–58, 109, 117, 118–119, 121, 133, 138, 140; artificial intelligence (AI) 4; challenges 106–125; characteristic of 4; collection/access 8; five Vs 4; gathering 91–92; outcomes of the processing 123–125; power imbalances of 119–120; processes 92–93; profiling 117; repurposing 112; risks 106; societal level challenges **108**, 123–125; storage and aggregation 8; technologies 32; usages 8, 92; *see also* artificial intelligence (AI); machine learning
big health data 109, 124; analytics under the GDPR 56–68; described 5–8; European-wide platform 56–68; sources of 8–9; terminology 8
biometric data 12
black/white approach, GDPR 14
Bluetooth sensors 75
Bodil Lindqvist judgment 30
Breyer 109
Bring Your Own Device (BYOD) 72–73
broad consent 61
Buivids case 30
Bulgarian DPA 29

Census Bureau 95
census taker puzzle *94*
Central Intelligence Agency (CIA) 118
challenges: artificial intelligence (AI) 106–125; Big Data 106–125; individual level **108**, 109–117; preliminary issues and caveats 107–109; safeguarding 113; societal level **108**, 117–120
children: data of 37, 42; DPA 2018 41–42; under the GDPR 39; health data 43–44
Children's Online Privacy Protection Act (COPPA) 74
chips 31
chronic lymphocytic leukaemia (CLL) patients 56
Civil Liberties Committee (LIBE) 58, 110
claim inadmissible 85–86
Clinical Trial Regulation 29, 35n45
clinical trials 28–29
Code of Conduct 133–136, 144–147; accountable 146; algorithm 146; be fair 146; commercial strategy 147; data usages 145–146; generate evidence 147; make security integral 147; open standards 146; outcome 145; principles and commentary 144–147; technology 145; transparent 146; understand users 145
Committee on Civil Liberties 110
compliances: as an ongoing process 144; challenges for 133; with data processing principles 24; with data protection law 23, 24; demonstrate 24, 111, 143; with the GDPR 23, 24, 28; of healthcare professionals 133; with the internal procedures 28; with a legal obligation 53; of the personal data processing 68, 138; privately administered 120; risks 136; with the rules 137; with the sponsor's guidelines 28; with the trial protocol 28, 29
composition effects *94*
computer programs 4
confidentiality 72, 75, 139
confidential medical data 76–77
conflict 74
consent 28, 29, 35n59, 43, 49–51, 58–60; age of digital 52; of data subject 110; data subject's autonomy 52, 63; explicit 11, 13, 32, 51, 74, 140; legal basis 60–62, 110–112; legally valid 32; parental 39, 50–52
consumer information 76
content data 91, 97
Contract Research Organisation (CRO) 29
controllers 9–10, 75; independent 25, 31; joint 26–27, 31; personal data 25; safeguards implemented by 65–66; *see also* data controllers
Council of Europe 86, 87, 97
Council of Ministers 59
Court of Justice of the European Union (CJEU) 23, 24–25, 31, 46, 109, 139
COVID-19 14, 21n145; adequate protection to 13; as an unprecedented health emergency 3; datastore 22n148; Government Response Tracker 15n3; overview of 15n3; personal health data 13; social distancing rules 3
cybercriminals 77

data: biometric 12; breaches 10; concerning health 6, 7, 57; content 91; controller-related problems 122; heterogeneous 75
database reconstruction attack 95
data controllers 23, 110; data processor 27–28; defined 24–27; independent controller(s) 25, 31; joint controllers 26–27, 31; obligations of 40
data-driven health technologies 138
data minimisation 10, 19n82, 139
data privacy: issues 106; law 9, 74, 106, 153n74; regulatory 3
data processing actor, capacity 24–28
data processing principles 10, 24
data processors 23, 27–28
Data Protection Authorities (DPA) 72, 115; *see also* National Data Protection Authorities (DPA)
data protection by design 87
Data Protection Impact Assessments (DPIA) 10, 73, 87, 107
data protection law: enforceability and enforcement of 114–115; regulatory conversations 136–144
Data Protection Law Enforcement Directive (DPLED) 38
Data Protection Officer (DPO) 11, 75, 87, 100
data protection policy 87
data protection regimes 86
data security 76, 112–113
data stakeholders 120
data subjects 9–10, 39, 63–64; autonomy 52; consent of 110; related issues 122; related problems 110; rights of 11, 30, 64, 114
Decision 2008/977 38
decision-making processes 117
decisions 116–117
Declaration of Helsinki 59
Deer v Oxford University 46
de minimis rule 85
digital content 61
Digital Ireland 139
digital revolution 4
digital services 61
Directive 95/46/EC 17n43, 23, 37, 44, 53
Directive 2011/24/EU 6, 17n45
Directive (EU) 2016/680 37–38
Directive 2019/770 61
Directive (EU) 2019/770 70n19
discrimination 116, 117, 124, 142
discriminatory conclusions 116–117
DPA 2018 41–42, 44, 48–50; *see also* National Data Protection Authorities (DPA)
dynamic consent 61
dynamic healthcare environment, AI 136

Editors' Code of Practice 49
electronic health care (eHealth) 75
Electronic Health Registers (EHR) 75, 113
elektronische Gesundheitsakte (ELGA) 68
enforceability and enforcement of data protection law 114–115
England 50
equality 119
EU Charter of Fundamental Rights (EUCFR) 12, 39, 54n9
Europe 123
European and National law 137
European Charter 49
European citizens value 4
European Clinical Trial Regulation 59
European Commission 4, 56
European Commission of Human Rights (ECmHR) 85
European Convention on Human Rights (ECHR) 85, 91
European Court 44–45
European Court of Human Rights (ECtHR) 85, 89
European Data Protection Board (EDPB) 37, 102, 136–137
European Data Protection Regulation 74
European Data Protection Supervisor (EPDS) 8, 27, 35n39
European Parliament Committee 59
European Research Area 57
European Union (EU) 38, 57, 86
Evaluating Mhealth Adoption Barriers 75
everyday activities 3
explicit consent 11, 13, 32, 74, 140

Facebook 9, 29, 31, 110, 113, 118
Facebook fan page judgment 25
fair and transparent processing 111–112
fairness 10, 19n80
Fashion ID judgment 25, 31–32
Federal Trade Commission Act 74, 76
Figg, William Douglas 76, 82n64
fitness trackers 31
Five Year Forward View 145
Fluitt, Aron 94
foreseeability for the individual affected 116
framing subjects and objects of regulation 137–138
freedom of expression 30, 48–50

gathering 91–92
General Data Protection Regulation (GDPR) 37–38, 72, 87; amendment 41; big data and 3–15; black/white approach 14; capacity under 50–51; challenges 37–53; children and 39; Data Protection Impact Assessments 73; data protection regimes 86; European-wide big health data analytics 56–68; exceptions 11–12; exemptions 11–12; health and 9–14; health data under the 10–11, 113; health-related legislative choices 13–14; impact of 48; important role of 121–123; individual rights *vs.* research needs 57–59; lays down rules 74; omnibus regulation 9; overview 9–10; personal and household exclusion 44–48; principles-based regulation 10; provisions relevant to children 39–40; public health 12–13; responsibility 23–33; rights of 10; risk-based approach 10; safeguards and rights 43; social media site 51–53
genetic data 6, 12, 59, 67, 90, 113
geolocation 42
Germany 68
global platforms, health data 29–31
Góngora-Alonso, Susel 71
Google 29–30, 53, 110, 118
Google Spain judgment 30
Government Response Tracker 15n3
Greece 56
group analysis 117

health: data concerning 6; insurance 6; monitoring 75; public 6; purposes 6; security 6; status 6, 42
healthcare: delivery 71; management 71; time and location 71
health data 74, 109, 113; about children in social media 37–53; clinical trials 28–29; defined 6, 42, 57, 138; exemptions 11–12; explicit consent 74; under the GDPR 10–11, 42; genetic data 6; within the global platforms 29–31; intrinsic nature 7; legal basis 60–62; levels of protection 10–11; lifecycle of 139; medical 138; processing 11–12, 23, 28–33, 59; provisions for children 43–44; public health 12; research purposes 59–62; for scientific research 62–63; secondary use 62–63; surveillance 4; wearables at the workplace 31–33; widespread 4; wireless body area network (WBAN) 71; *see also* big data
Health Insurance Portability and Accountability Act (HIPAA) 74
heterogeneous data 75
Hoboken, J. 26, 34n33
Horizon 2020 programme 56
household activity 30, 44
household exception 30
household exemption 30
human dignity 108, 119
human rights instruments 86
Human Services of the United States of America 72

IBM 72
identifiable information 93
identifiable natural person 109, 138
identifiable person 87
identifying and anonymous data 90
identifying special categories of data 113
incorrect or unreliable conclusions 115–116
independent controller(s) 25, 31
individual data 90
individual level challenges **108**, 122
individual level issues 108, 109–117
individual rights 57–59
informational privacy 85
information and communications technology (ICT) 32
Information Commissioner's Office (ICO) 31, 48–49, 50, 52
information technology (IT) 71
insignificant status of the data 97–99
Instagram 9, 113
integrity 75, 139
integrity and confidentiality 10, 19n85
intensive care unit (ICU) 56
Inter alia 87
international Covenant on Civil and Political Human Rights 85
Internet of Things (IoT) 4, 113, 138
Internet user 30–31
intrinsic nature 7
Italy 56
Ittihadieh v 5–11 Cheyne Gardens & Ors. 46–47
Ivanova, Yordanka 23

Jay, Rosemary 37
joint controllers 23–24, 26–27, 31

Kam, Hwee Joo 76, 82n64
Kidron, Baroness 41
Kumar, Sunil 75

lack of accountability of data stakeholders 120
lack of transparency 116

lawfulness 10, 19n80, 139
Law Society v Kordowski 46
legal basis, consent 60–62, 110–112
legal paradigm 88
Lindqvist case 44–45, 54n25
Liu, Ling 77, 82n71
lockdowns 3
López-Coronado, Miguel 71
Lupton, D. 8, 17n32, 17n36, 19n69

machine learning 4, 115, 116, 119, 120, 133, 134, 136, 138, 139, 141–142, 148; algorithm 115; data-driven health technologies as 138; *see also* artificial intelligence (AI); big data
Mahieu, R. 26, 34n33
McCarthy, M. 76, 82n62
mechanisms: for accountability 139–141; for fairness 139–141; for lawfulness 139–141; for managing risks and impact 141–144; responsive 141–144
medical center 29
medical identity theft 76
Medical Research Involving Human Subjects 59
Member State law 65
metadata 88, 89, 96, 97, 98–100; content data and 91; defined 93
mHealth 8–9, 11; defined 71; privacy issues in 71–77
Microsoft 118
mobile app 71–77
mobile broadband (MBB) 71
mobile phone data 3
mobile phones 71

National Committee on Vital and Health Statistics (NCVHS) 72
National Data Protection Authorities (DPA) 10, 23, 28, 33, 44, 72, 115, 137
National Health Service (NHS) 68, 144–147; *see also* Code of Conduct
National Institute for Health and Care Excellence 147
NHS England 145
non-discrimination *see* anti-discrimination
nonessential 27
non-personal data 85–103; analysis 99–101; applicability 101; defined 101; enforcement 102–103; insignificant status of data 97–99; obligations 102; overview 85–89; personal data and 88, 90; principles 101–102; processing or transfer of 88; proposal for a regulation 101–103; transfers of 102; unclear status of data 93–96; unstable status of data 89–93
normative disconnection 124
Northern Ireland 50
novel patterns 109

Ofcom Broadcasting Code 49
Ohm, Paul 94
omnibus regulation, GDPR 9
online mHealth 76
Open Web Application Security Project (OWASP) 75, 77
operating system (OS) 77
Organisation for Economic Co-operation and Development (OECD) 8, 18n59

paramount 75
parental consent 39
Pasquale, Frank 115
passwords 75
PatientsLikeMe 5, 9, 113
persistent fragmentation 66–68
personal data 4, 97; about child's health 39; controller 25; defined 6, 30, 87, 93, 109; European citizens 4; free movement of 9; non-personal data and 88, 90; personally identifiable information and 109–110; processing of 9–10, 26; sensitive personal data and 90–91; special categories of 10
personalised medicine 5
personally identifiable information 109–110
pluralistic control 26
Ponemon Institute 72
power imbalances of big data 119–120
preliminary issues and caveats 107–109
principles-based regulation, GDPR 10
privacy 72; challenges 75–77; by default guarantees 74; by design 87; impact assessment 87; officer 87; policy 87; protection 73
privacy issues: in eHealth 71–77; in mHealth 71–77
privacy laws: in Europe 73–75; in United States 73–75
Privacy Rights Clearinghouse 76
probabilistic analytical tools 139
processor 27, 75; *see also* controllers; data controllers; data processors
professional/commercial activity 24
profiling 8, 18n58, 117
pseudonymisation 66, 72
public events 3
public health 3, 6; ambitions 145; COVID-19 pandemic 14; data repositories 68; exceptions and restrictions 12–13; GDPR

12–13; goals 136; health data 12; as a health-related reasons or areas 43; practice 71; restrictions 14; strategies 135–136
public interest 12–13
public security 9
public transport 3
purpose limitation 10, 19n81, 111–112, 139

Quantified-Self 5
quarantines 3

Recital (35) GDPR 42
Recital 18 GDPR 30, 44, 45
Recital 26 GDPR 58
Recital 32 GDPR 60
Recital 33 GDPR 61
Recital 38 GDPR 39, 40
Recital 46 GDPR 13
Recital 50 GDPR 63
Recital 53 GDPR 14, 20n102
Recital 58 GDPR 39
Recital 65 GDPR 40
Recital 71 GDPR 18n58, 40
Recital 75 GDPR 10, 40, 103n142–131n142, 107
Recital 76 GDPR 20n97
Recital 157 GDPR 57
Recital 159 GDPR 57
Recital 162 GDPR 58
Regulation (EU) 2016/679 34n2, 37
Regulation (EU) No 536/2014 69n14
Regulation (EC) No 1338/2008 21n127
regulatory conversations 136–144
remote monitoring 71
research needs 57–59
research purposes: health data 59–62; scientific 13, 57–58, 61–63, 65–67
Rights of the Child 49
right to data protection 87, 89
right to privacy 85–87
Rynes v Urad pro ochranuosobnichudaju 46

safeguarding 65–66, 113
Sainz-de-Abajo, Beatriz 71
Savirimuthu, Joseph 133
schools 3
scientific research 57, 62–63
scientific research purposes 13, 57–58, 61–63, 65–67
security 72, 75–77; *see also* privacy
Security Module Layer (SML) 77
self-isolation 3
self-knowledge through numbers 5
sensitive personal data 90–91, 93, 97
Serjejs Buivids v Datu valsts inspekcija 45
sexual orientation 113
sharenting 37, 38–39
Skype 118
Sloot, Bart van der 85
small data 7
Smart Devices 110
smartphone 71
smartwatches 31
Snowden, Edward 118
social distancing rules 3
social media 8–9, 11–12, 15, 126n22; complaints about individual postings 48; data shared on 113; healthcare data about children in 37–53; overuse of 38; personal data in 110; protective provisions 43–44; site 51–53; users and providers of 44
societal level challenges **108**, 117–120, 123–125
special categories of personal data 10, 14, 59
stakeholders 8
status of data: insignificant 97–99; unclear 93–96; unstable 89–93
storage limitation 10, 19n84, 139
substantial public interest 12, 21n124
sunbathing 3
surveillance 4, 118
surveillance capitalism 8
Sweden 56
Swedish legislation 44
systemic challenges 122–123
systemic problems 110
System Interface Layer (SIL) 77

taxonomy, importance of 120–121
technological reality 88
telecommunications 71
Torre-Díez, Isabel de la 71
transparency 10, 19n80, 139
Treaty on the Functioning of the European Union (TFEU) 57
trial autonomously 28
trial protocol 28
Twitter 9, 29, 31, 113
Tzanou, Maria 3, 106

UK Center of Data Ethics and Innovation 32
UK Data Protection Act (UK Act) 38
UK Government Office for Science 4
UK National Health Service (NHS) 133
UK Samaritans charity organization 31
unclear status of data 93–96
unfair conclusions 116–117

unimaginable opportunities 116
Union or Member State law 24
United Kingdom 56
United Nations (UN) Convention 49, 50
United States 86
Universal Declaration of Human Rights 85
Unpopular Privacy (Allen) 3, 15n1
US Children's Online Privacy Protection Act of 1998 39

vagina fitbits 5
value 4
variety 4
velocity 4
veracity 4, 16n18
volume 4

Wales 50
Wall Street Journal 38
wearable devices 31–33
weather data 7, 18n50
wellness packages 32
widespread: biases 116; health data surveillance 3; medical conditions 57; of personal data 47; surveillance 118
Wikipedia 38
wireless body area network (WBAN) 71
wireless system 72
Working Party Article 29 (WP29) 23, 24–26, 27–32, 93
workplaces 3
World Health Organization (WHO) 71
World Medical Association 59
World Privacy Forum 76
World War II 85

Yahoo 118
Yehovah's witnesses case 25, 29
YouTube 29, 45–46, 118

Zhang, Rui 77, 82n71
Zuboff, S. 7, 18n52, 19n68, 123, 130n133

Taylor & Francis Group
an informa business

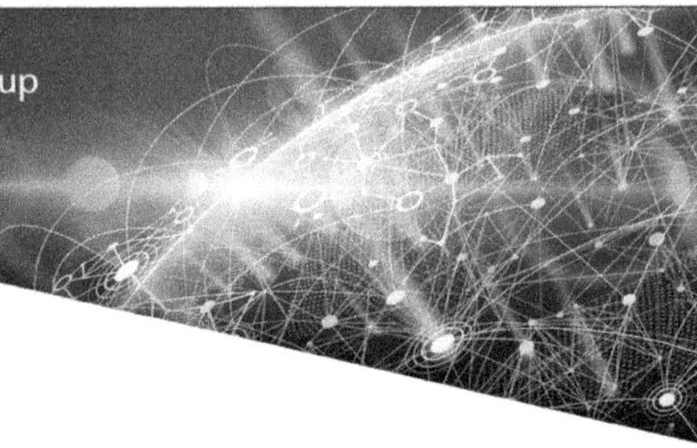

Taylor & Francis eBooks

www.taylorfrancis.com

A single destination for eBooks from Taylor & Francis with increased functionality and an improved user experience to meet the needs of our customers.

90,000+ eBooks of award-winning academic content in Humanities, Social Science, Science, Technology, Engineering, and Medical written by a global network of editors and authors.

TAYLOR & FRANCIS EBOOKS OFFERS:

- A streamlined experience for our library customers
- A single point of discovery for all of our eBook content
- Improved search and discovery of content at both book and chapter level

REQUEST A FREE TRIAL

support@taylorfrancis.com

Routledge
Taylor & Francis Group

CRC Press
Taylor & Francis Group

For Product Safety Concerns and Information please contact our EU
representative GPSR@taylorandfrancis.com
Taylor & Francis Verlag GmbH, Kaufingerstraße 24, 80331 München, Germany

www.ingramcontent.com/pod-product-compliance
Ingram Content Group UK Ltd.
Pitfield, Milton Keynes, MK11 3LW, UK
UKHW020002200926
475702UK00015B/2435
9780367632601